BUILDING THE NEW MANAGERIALIST STATE

Building the New Managerialist State

Consultants and the Politics of Public Sector Reform in Comparative Perspective

Denis Saint-Martin

OXFORD
UNIVERSITY PRESS

OXFORD
UNIVERSITY PRESS

Great Clarendon Street, Oxford OX2 6DP

Oxford University Press is a department of the University of Oxford.
It furthers the University's objective of excellence in research, scholarship,
and education by publishing worldwide in

Oxford New York

Athens Auckland Bangkok Bogotá Buenos Aires Calcutta
Cape Town Chennai Dar es Salaam Delhi Florence Hong Kong Istanbul
Karachi Kuala Lumpur Madrid Melbourne Mexico City Mumbai
Nairobi Paris São Paulo Shanghai Singapore Taipei Tokyo Toronto Warsaw

and associated companies in Berlin Ibadan

Oxford is a registered trade mark of Oxford University Press
in the UK and certain other countries

Published in the United States
by Oxford University Press Inc., New York

British Library Cataloguing in Publication Data

Data available

Library of Congress Cataloging in Publication Data

Data available

ISBN 0-19-924037-X

1 3 5 7 9 10 8 6 4 2

Typeset by Graphicraft Limited, Hong Kong
Printed in Great Britain
on acid-free paper by
Biddles Ltd., Guildford and King's Lynn

To Dominique, who gives meaning to my life and inspiration to my work. And to Jérémie and Romane, who always remind me of the most important things in life

Acknowledgements

In the course of writing this book I have benefited from the intellectual support and material assistance offered by a variety of organizations, colleagues, and friends. One of the rewards of completing this book is to finally be able to thank them.

This book has its origins in my Ph.D. thesis at Carleton University in Ottawa. I owe a special debt to the members of my dissertation committee, Leslie Pal and Jane Jenson; they both provided a rare blend of intellectual guidance and personal support as I worked on the dissertation, and they have continued to offer encouragement and advice.

My intense and frequent interactions with each of them over past years have contributed significantly to my knowledge and understanding of the interrelations between ideas, institutions, and interests. They have been very generous and patient with the unusual writing style of someone who thinks in French but writes in English. Their guidance and good cheer have been central to my intellectual development.

As a post-doctoral fellow at the Harvard Center for European Studies, I was immersed in a stimulating intellectual and cultural environment that shaped the approach taken in this book. Much of my thinking about politics and ideas was influenced by Peter A. Hall. I benefited immensely from his generosity while I was at the CES. He gave me invaluable advice on earlier versions of the manuscript. At the Center, my work also greatly benefited from the sage advice on key issues related to the French case offered by Professor Pierre Grémion of the Centre de sociologie des organisations. I received help at various stages of my research from a host of colleagues, some whom I know personally, others only virtually, through e-mail communications: Herman Bakvis, my good friend Alexandra Dobrowolsky, James Iain Gow, Martin Thunert, Jean-Claude Thoenig, Justin Vaisse, and the late Vincent Wright. All deserve my thanks.

I also wish to thank the senior civil servants and management consultants in large firms in London, Ottawa, and Paris who spent time answering my questions. Their insights and knowledge of government operations and consultancy were extremely helpful. I owe special thanks to the librarian of the Cabinet Office in London who efficiently helped me to locate key documents. Mr Will White of the Management Consultancies Association, Mrs Sarah Foster-Hogg of the Institute of Management Consultants, and Ms Brigitte David-Gardon of Syntec Management in Paris, all provided helpful assistance and access to valuable information.

Financial assistance came from a variety of sources. I am grateful to the Social and Humanities Research Council of Canada and to the Quebec

Government's Fonds pour la Formation des chercheurs et l'aide à la recherche. A pre-dissertation fellowship from the Council of European Studies at Columbia University in New York proved crucial at the outset, when this work first began as a doctoral dissertation proposal.

Finally, I thank my family. My aunt Madeleine and my father-in-law Marc for their constant support. Vivi, Koutsy, Paul, and 'the gang' for their warm hospitality while I was doing research in Paris and London. Dominique Launay enriched my existence in several ways. Without her inimitable support and her editing skills this book could not have been completed.

The illustration which is reproduced as Figure 1.1 is taken from HM Treasury, *Seeking help from Management Consultants*, London, 1990. Every effort has been made to trace the copyright holder. If the legal copyright holder wishes to contact the publisher, the correct acknowledgement will appear in any future edition of this work.

Contents

List of Figures

List of Tables

List of Abbreviations

ACME	Association of Consulting Management Engineers [USA]
AIC	Associated Industrial Consultants [UK]
C&AG	Comptroller and Auditor General [UK]
CAMC	Canadian Association of Management Consultants [Canada]
CDR	Centre de responsabilité [France]
CES	Canadian Evaluation Society [Canada]
CGT	Confedération Générale du Travail [France]
CMC	Certified Management Consultant [Canada and UK]
CNCC	Compagnie Nationale des Commissaires aux Comptes [France]
CPRS	Central Policy Review Staff [UK]
CSD	Civil Service Department [UK]
DEA	Department of Economic Affairs [UK]
DTI	Department of Trade and Industry [UK]
EIP	Executive Interchange Program [Canada]
ENA	École Nationale d'Administration [France]
FEACO	[European Federation of Management Consulting Associations]
FMCS	Financial Management Control Study [Canada]
FMI	Financial Management Initiative [UK]
FRAC	Fond régionaux d'Aide au Conseil [France]
GSD	Government Services Division
HÉC	École des Hautes Etudes Commerciales [France]
ICMCC	Institute of Certified Management Consultants Canada [Canada]
ILO	International Labour Organization
IMC	Institute of Management Consultants [UK]
MCA	Management Consultancies Association [UK]
MFPRA	Ministère de la Fonction publique et de la Réforme administrative [France]
MINIS	Management Information System for ministers [UK]
MIS	Management information systems
MPO	Management and Personnel Office [in UK Cabinet Office]
NAO	National Audit Office [UK]
OAG	Office of the Auditor General [Canada]
OCG	Office of the Comptroller General [Canada]
OECCA	Ordre des Experts-Comptables et des Comptables Agréés [France]
OECD	Organization for Economic Cooperation and Development

OPQCM	Office Professionnel de Qualification des Conseils en Management [France]
PAR	Programme Analysis and Review [UK]
PCO	Privy Council Office [Canada]
PPBS	Planning, Programming and Budgeting System
PS 2000	Public Service 2000 [Canada]
PSC	Public Service Commission [Canada]
PSRU	Public Sector Research Unit [UK Conservative Party]
PUMA	Public Management Committee of the OECD
RCB	Rationalisation des Choix Budgétaires [France]
SME	Small and medium-sized enterprises
SOA	Special Operating Agencies [Canada]
SOE	State Owned Enterprises
SPICE	Study on Procedures in Cost Effectiveness [Canada]
TBS	Treasury Board Secretariat [Canada]
TQM	Total Quality Management
VFM	Value for money

I

Variations on a managerialist theme

The 1980s and 1990s witnessed a renewed emphasis on reforming the bureaucracies of most Western states. Bureaucratic reform 'came of age in the 1980s' as the winds of change drove political leaders to make radical alterations in the conduct of public administration (Caiden, 1991). The rigid, centralized, hierarchical, or pyramidal form of public bureaucracy is reported to be changing into a more flexible, responsive, market-based, and client-oriented form of public management (OECD, 1990a). This is not simply a matter of minor transformation in management style. This is a political change to governance itself and to the relationship between state and citizenry, as the state tries to become more responsive by opening up its functions to competition in order to make it easier for citizens, redefined as 'clients', to express their preferences and make choices in a market-like fashion. This change represents, according to some, a 'paradigm shift' from the traditional Weberian model of public administration, dominant for most of the century, to the 'new managerialism' (Barzelay, 1992; Zifcak, 1994). The new managerialism is a loose term used as a shorthand name for the set of broadly similar management ideas imported from business administration that has dominated the bureaucratic reform agenda of many OECD states since the 1980s (Hood, 1990). The new managerialism is treated variously as an ideology, a philosophy, a culture, or a set of techniques and practices (Considine, 1990; Nethercote, 1989; Sinclair, 1989). Its essence lies in the belief that there is something called 'management' which is a generic, purely instrumental activity, embodying a set of principles that can be applied to both the public and private sectors (Boston, 1991: 9). The main guiding principles of the new managerialism are the pursuit of efficiency, effectiveness, and value for money (Enteman, 1993).

The new managerialism encompasses a number of terms which are used more or less interchangeably such as 'new public management' (Hood, 1991), 'market-based administration' (Lan and Rosenbloom, 1992) or 'entrepreneurial government' (Osborne and Gaebler, 1992). These various names reflect differing views of what is occurring, but they all refer to the process by which states transform their bureaucratic arm by internalizing core values and management practices identified with the private sector (Hughes, 1994; Farnham and Horton, 1993).

In responding to the pressures and challenges of citizens' demands for more democratic participation, technological change, fiscal pressures, globalization, and international competitiveness, governments in most Western countries have all tried to make significant changes in the management of the state. But to deal with these similar problems, various nations have chosen different policy paths and some have more consciously modelled their reforms on management practices imported from the private sector than others. The new managerialism during the 1980s was enthusiastically embraced by British decision makers, but new managerialist ideas and policies, often directly imported from London by Canadian and French officials, did not receive strong support from the federal government in Ottawa and have not yet penetrated very deeply into the French administrative system.

Accordingly, this is a book about policy change: it seeks to understand why the changes produced by the new managerialism on public administration have been more radical and profound in some countries than in others. It asks why Britain, Canada, and France embraced managerialist ideas differently in the process of reforming their bureaucracies. This is a crucial question because, while important new work has shown that the degree of acceptance and implementation of management paradigms in private industry historically varied across nations (Guillén, 1994), no similar attempts have been made in public administration to understand why managerialism has had more influence in some places and periods, yet not as much in others. It is certainly not false to argue, as many have done, that the bureaucratic reform initiatives implemented since the late 1980s by states such as Britain, Canada, and France have all been influenced by new managerialist ideas. The three countries have all incorporated in their reform policies key aspects of the new managerialist paradigm, including: an emphasis on the delegation of authority; a shift from process to results in controls and accountability mechanisms, particularly through the development of quantitative methods of evaluation and performance measurement; the disaggregation of public bureaucracies into managerially autonomous agencies whose responsibilities are defined by 'contracts'; and a 'consumerist' bias expressed through a new focus on the quality of services provided to the citizen-consumer.

These policy similarities attracted much scholarly attention in the 1990s. It is fashionable to think that there is a tide, or sequence, of essentially similar public management changes sweeping through the Western world (Pollitt and Summa, 1997b). In particular, the Public Management Committee (PUMA) of the OECD has played a key role in propagating the uniform, 'one-track' picture of public sector reform (Premfors, 1998). But there are several different reform trajectories in Western-style democracies (Kickert, 1997). And 'rather less discussed', as one of the leading students of the new managerialism argued, 'is the extent to which OECD countries have varied in the extent to which they adopted New Public Management doctrines in the 1980s' (Hood, 1996: 270). As explored in greater detail later, there is wide variation between Britain, Canada, and France not only in terms of *style* as Vincent Wright correctly pointed out (1994), but also in the *degree* to which managerialist ideas were implemented as policy and it is these differences that this book wants to investigate. Why does this matter? Over recent years, the management of the state has increasingly been seen by policy makers almost everywhere as crucial to national economic prosperity. In the new international political economy, the effects of what the state does (and how it does it) are said to have an important impact on the global competitiveness of national economies (OECD, 1995*b*). If, as many policy makers argue, the new managerialism helps to improve the efficiency and cost effectiveness of the state—and thus the competitive advantage of nations as a whole—it becomes crucial to understand why some states have been more able than others actively to pursue new managerialist policies.

State action in the area of bureaucratic restructuring and in the development of managerialist policies during the 1980s generated important new demands for social knowledge about public sector management. Such knowledge had to come from outside the state because managerialist ideas emerged in reaction against the traditional bureaucratic model, discredited by new political leaders who came to office convinced that private business management was superior to public administration and that bureaucracies were inefficient and responsible for the economic problems that gripped their countries (Massey, 1993). Policy ideas and advice about how to reform public administration could no longer be exclusively provided by permanent officials because they were seen by many as part of the 'bureaucratic problem' that Public Choice theorists and New Right politicians helped to popularize in the 1970s (Blais and Dion, 1991). The perception, whether warranted or not, of failure in bureaucratic institutions and the delegitimation of the public service created political space for social groups to advocate new kinds of policy ideas about public sector management.

In the 1980s, government officials and agencies increasingly mobilized management consultants from the private sector in the process of trying to make the administration of the state more business-like. The state's use of management consulting services influenced the growth of the profession and helped consultants to make claim to authority over questions of public administration. During the 1980s, consulting firms expanded their activities in the public sector and many created within their organization 'Government Consulting Divisions'. Consultants were brought into government because of their technical expertise, as well as for political reasons. The use of consultants and of their ideas gave credibility to managerialist policies because they came from the private sector. Consultants brought into the state values and methods from industry and commerce and thus endorsed a major political objective of policy makers. One major conclusion of this book is that the possibilities for consultants to provide advice that can appeal to public officials and enhance the state capacity to pursue managerialist policies depend on how much their services are used by businesses, which in turn are linked to historical patterns of industrial and corporate developme

Unlike the output of think-tanks and other organizations that are part of what is sometimes called 'the policy-ideas industry' (Smith, 1991: 214), the knowledge that management consultants generate is not primarily intended for state consumption. Management consulting firms are profit-based organizations and, traditionally, their main clients have not been state organizations but private sector businesses. Consultants are first and foremost specialists in business management and the existing literature tells us that it is for this reason that they have been increasingly called in by policy makers to help them develop managerialist policies.[1] It is because they are 'experts' in something that largely takes place outside the state (in private sector management) that it becomes possible for consultants to be called in by state officials to provide policy advice on public sector reform. In this sense, the process by which states use management consulting knowledge to develop managerialist policies is largely affected by societal developments that first take place in the private sector. That is to say, the development of managerialist policies grows out of the nexus of state and society.

In trying to explain differences in the acceptance of managerialist ideas across states, I look at the history and development of management consulting and at the pre-existing legacies of bureaucratic reform policies. In particular, I analyse the ways in which the differential access of consultants to strategic policy centres in the state influenced the application of the business management ideas that they bring to the policy process. The explanation that I develop to account for variation in the reception given to managerialist ideas and policies contrasts in five major ways with much of the current literature on bureaucratic reform.

First, like a number of other scholars who are beginning to pay more attention to differences, I seek to explain policy variation and not simply the apparent convergence of the various managerialist initiatives that states have put into place since the late 1980s. I argue that the adoption of new managerialist ideas did not follow a linear path, determined by the fiscal crisis and the process of globalization, but that their influence on policy varied according to institutional and political factors. Secondly, unlike those who believe that the state is becoming increasingly obsolete and is being eroded or 'hollowed out' by the loss of its functions to the market, the approach I take puts a particular stress on the critical role played by the state in the determination of policy. Thirdly, my approach is fundamentally historical, looking for connections among bureaucratic reform policies over time.

---

[1] In his analysis of administrative reform in Britain and the United States, Pollitt found that policy makers had 'repeated recourse to the major consultancies such as Peat Marwick . . . Coopers & Lybrand, Touche Ross and Arthur Young' (1990: 135). With the emergence of the new managerialist paradigm, state officials 'increased their use of this kind of advice because the ideological dominance of private-sector management was such that central departments were less likely to question recommendations from a consultancy than from an internal analysis' (Pollitt, 1990: 136).

Students of public sector reform have often tended to view the rise of the new managerialism as a 'revolution', suggesting that it appeared suddenly in the 1980s in some kind of Big Bang form (Boston *et al.*, 1991; Metcalfe, 1993). But the term 'new' does not mean that the ideas that are part of the new managerialist paradigm all appeared for the first time in the 1980s. On the contrary, many of its principles have been in public administration for a while, at least since the Planning, Programming, and Budgeting System (PPBS) movement of the 1960s. Policy innovations are rarely constituted on a *tabula rasa* and recent developments in public management reforms should be seen as evolutionary rather than simply the product of any new managerialist 'revolution'.

Fourthly, and most importantly, this is the first detailed empirical study of the role of management consultants in the marketization of state bureaucracies. There is no comparative analysis of the role of management consultants in government and about how more or less successful they are in getting their policy recommendations accepted by governments. This is partly due to the fact that the presence of management consultants in central government is regarded as a relatively recent phenomenon. Consultants have long been active in the reorganization of state-owned enterprises because the functioning of these organizations (whose mandate relates to industrial and commercial activities) is closer to the competitive logic of the private sector. Unlike government departments, nationalized industries are not headed directly by ministers and are organized at arm's length from government. The managerial and accountability regimes of state-owned enterprises are much more flexible than those of ministerial departments. The argument is that entities engaged in commercial activities would be at a competitive disadvantage if they were not given more autonomy than is provided in government departments. In this sense, managerialist ideas have always been present in the public enterprises sphere of the public sector and it is this same rationale that policy makers now want to extend to central government.

It is commonly believed that management consultants became more visible at the central government level at the same time that the new managerialism began to emerge in the 1980s (Blymke, 1995; Smith and Young, 1996: ch. 8). But as we shall see, management consultants from the private sector have been actively involved in government restructuring at least since the early 1960s, thus well before the rise of the new managerialism in the 1980s. Those who first noted the growing presence of consultants in government during the 1980s found that their role in the process of administrative reform was 'more opaque' than that of ministers and civil servants (Pollitt, 1990: 135). This book removes some of this opacity and tries to bring the role of management consultants out of the shadows and into the full light of public policy analysis. The involvement of consultants in public sector reform has so far not been viewed in political terms. In public administration, where the policy-administration dichotomy is still influential, management consultants

are seen as providing not *policy*, but essentially *administrative* advice that
is technical or scientific and thus separated from politics. It is true that the
political aspect of the role of consultants has until now been somewhat
'invisible' because governments at both ends of the ideological spectrum
have increasingly used consultants and adopted managerialist policies. After
all, consultants are 'hired guns' whose ideas need to be non-political so that
they can be sold to both the Right and the Left. As one can read in a brochure
produced by the consulting firm that the principal author of *Reinventing
Government* (D. Osborne) founded after having served as senior adviser
in the White House, managerialist ideas 'are post-bureaucratic ideas that
are neither conservative nor liberal'. But does this mean that the ideas that
consultants sponsor are not political? No, because they are contested. The
empirical evidence about whether managerialist principles have made the
bureaucracy more efficient and cost effective is inconclusive (Pollitt, 1995*b*).
Managerialism is also the object of intense political debate between state
managers and public sector unions (Walsh, 1995). When consultants advise
policy makers to marketize or contract out a given field of state activity,
this obviously has an impact on public sector workers. And furthermore, the
managerialist solutions that consultants sponsor are political because, when
translated into policy, they change accountability relationships and affect
the balance of power between the political executive, the bureaucracy, and
the legislature.

Finally, my approach differs from much of the existing literature because
I explain differences in the acceptance of managerialist ideas across nations
by focusing on the interrelations between management consultants and the
state in the process of administrative reform. This means that I also look
outside the state to understand something—public management reform—that
has so far been seen as being almost exclusively internal to the state. Public
administration scholars have traditionally tended to see public management reform as a closed policy sector, located in the command structure
of the state and thus insulated from societal influence. It is true that the
'societal side' of the bureaucratic reform policy sector is not as obvious
or visible as in other policy domains, such as the green movement in the
case of the environment or women's groups in the case of abortion policy.
Management policy is a technical field and issues related to administrative
reform are generally under the responsibility of central agencies, staffed with
'superbureaucrats', whose clients are not members of the public as in the
case of most government departments, but bureaucrats from other ministries
(Campbell and Szablowski, 1979).

On the basis of the cases examined here, we can say, however, that the
bureaucratic reform policy sector has never been as closed as is often
assumed by students of public administration. In other words, bureaucratic
reformers in government have never been completely 'autonomous' from
societal influences and pressures, as state-centric theories would lead us to

believe. The openness of bureaucratic reform policy-making institutions to management consultants from the private sector has varied in time and across space, thereby allowing managerialist ideas to make more rapid inroads in some countries than in others. Thus, the rise of what some have recently called the new 'managerial state' (Clarke and Newman, 1997; Scott, 1992), cannot be fully understood in isolation from societal forces. It has to be understood in relation to the development of modern management consultancy. In this respect, the formation of the new managerialist state and the growth of management consultancy may well represent a major historical change somewhat comparable to that ushered in by the development of the legal-rational state studied by Weber and the rise of lawyers in the last century (Torstendahl and Burrage, 1990). Of course, it is too soon to know. For now, our goal is more modest: it is to examine the ways in which managerialist ideas acquired political influence over state management practices and became a more or less important component of bureaucratic reform policy. Before we proceed, however, our first task is to give an overview of the reform policies introduced in Britain, Canada, and France between the late 1980s and the early 1990s to see how well current approaches explain the reception given to new managerialist ideas. Each approach seems to suffer from important defects, and many of these come from their neglect of the state as a key variable in the structuration of policy outcome.

Explaining the rise and spread of managerialist ideas

There is only a limited number of explanations accounting for the acceptance of managerialist ideas and policies across nations and these have not yet been the object of extensive enquiry and debate. Very little systematic comparative work has been done in this area, partly because of methodological problems (Derlien, 1992). There is no systematic database with which to measure change among countries and the research done so far is based on preliminary and impressionistic analysis (Kettl, 1997). Moreover, 'there is no single accepted explanation or interpretation of why the New Public Management coalesced and why it "caught on"' (Hood, 1991: 6).

Trying to explain how the new managerialism 'caught on' and replaced, or at least challenged, the Weberian model of public administration is, of course, very much like explaining policy change or what Christopher Hood calls 'policy reversal' (1994). A review of the literature on bureaucratic reform suggests that we might distinguish at least three broad approaches explaining the rise of new managerialist ideas and policy change in the area of public administration. The first, which might be termed the 'ideological' interpretation, links the emergence and diffusion of managerialist ideas to the rise of the New Right in the 1980s. The second, which may be called the 'structural' interpretation, relates the rise of managerialism to the process

ɔmic globalization and to rapid developments in information tech-
The third and most recent explanation suggests that the diffusion
of managerialist ideas and policies across nations is essentially a process driven
by the interests of rational and profit-maximizing management consultants
from the private sector.

As causal factors explaining the development of managerialism, these
three approaches are not mutually exclusive, but are in fact interconnected.
There is even a certain sense of continuity among the three explanations. The
globalization approach was developed after the New Right interpretation when
it was noted that left-of-centre parties also embraced managerialist ideas in
reforming their bureaucracy. And in the same way, the consultant-centred
approach emerged after the globalization explanation when, in the early 1990s,
a growing number of analysts started to observe the increasing presence of
external consultants as a source of policy advice in the process of bureaucratic
reform (Halligan, 1995). Because its appearance in the academic literature
is more recent, the consultant-centred approach has sometimes been noted
anecdotally, but it has not yet been the object of empirical examination. This
book fills this gap. The objective is not to argue that consultants are more
important than the New Right or the globalization approaches in accounting
for the influence of managerialism. Rather, the intent is to complement these
approaches and to shed some light on an unknown and neglected aspect
of modern governance. But like the other two approaches, the consultant-
centred interpretation, because of its lack of focus on implementation,
cannot explain policy variation. The New Right, the globalization, and the
consultant-centred approaches are all powerful explanations to account for
the movement to pursue new managerialist policies but these three approaches
have nothing to say about implementation. There is a need to distinguish
between the *movement to pursue a new policy* and the success with which or the
extent to which it is implemented. This distinction may seem familiar to many,
but the factors that often best explain the former are not adequate to explain
the latter, a point not well emphasized in the current literature. But before
I discuss how I intend to illuminate the contents of the policy implementation 'black box' with the help of historical-institutionalist theories, the next
section examines each of the three approaches in an ideal-typical form.

The New Right

Most of the early studies discussing the concept of managerialism in the context of bureaucratic reform and state restructuring linked its development
to the rise of the New Right in the 1980s, as exemplified by the election of
Thatcher in Britain and Reagan in the United States (Aucoin, 1988*a*; 1990).
In most of these studies, the rise of managerialism was perceived as being
linked to the election of anti-statist politicians in the 1980s whose agenda was
to denigrate the role of the public sector and its employees (Hood, Dunsire,

and Thomson, 1988; Peters, 1991). It was generally believed that managerialism had advanced in parallel with New Right ideas and with the desire to replace bureaucratic institutions with market ones (Cutler and Payne, 1994). In his *Managerialism in the Public Services*, Pollitt argued that under Thatcher and Reagan 'managerialism has become a steadily more prominent component in the policies adopted by right-wing governments towards their public services' (1990: 48). 'Managerialism', he wrote, is one central aspect of the 'new-right thinking concerning the state' (Pollitt, 1990: 49).

This is not the place for a detailed account of the rise of the New Right (King, 1987). Suffice to say here that, as a political movement, it emerged in the 1970s following the oil embargo that plunged the world into a slow-down in economic growth, coupled with rising inflation and unemployment. As these events often took place under governments led by the Centre Left, opposition politicians from right-wing parties began to search for an alternative to Keynesianism and saw advantages in a set of ideas associated with monetarism and Public Choice theories (Jenkins, 1987; Kymlicka and Matthews, 1988). The political implications of these new doctrines were clear. They included: a belief that governments had become too large and were consuming too many scarce resources from more productive pursuits in the private sector; that civil servants were too powerful, had too much discretion over policy decisions, and were not sufficiently responsive to political direction; that public services were inferior to those of the private sector because they lacked the incentive and discipline of the market; and that the monopolistic position of the state in the delivery of public services limited the freedom of citizens and their capacities to make choices (Swann, 1998; Taylor-Gooby and Lawson, 1993).

Prime Minister Thatcher in Britain—in part because she was elected to power before Reagan—embodied the resurgence of neo-conservatism in the 1980s to such an extent that many often used the terms 'Thatcherism' and 'New Right' interchangeably as if the two were synonymous (Kavanagh, 1987b; Levitas, 1986; MacInnes, 1987). In the field of bureaucratic restructuring, Mrs Thatcher led the way on many fronts at home and abroad. Compared to other New Right leaders such as Reagan in the United States, Thatcher had more scope to act because the state had the strongest presence in many sectors of the British economy and society. For instance, her government's privatization policy has been tried and emulated in over a hundred countries throughout the world (Savoie, 1994: 10). Under this policy, 46 major businesses were privatized and over 900,000 jobs were transferred to the private sector (OECD, 1992: 324).

But privatization is very different from managerialism. Privatization is the sale of government assets to the private sector whereas managerialism consists in the introduction of private sector management practices into those parts of the public sector that have not been privatized. Privatization returns to the market activities that were once run by the state, while managerialism seeks to facilitate the entrance of market criteria into public administration as a way to allocate public resources and measure the efficiency of public services. In Britain, privatization generally preceded the implementation of new managerialist policies in the public sector (Kirkpatrick *et al.*, 1996: 198; Pollitt, 1990: 48). Once the easier privatizations had been accomplished, it became politically more difficult for policy makers to return to the market public services that do not have mainly commercial objectives such as those dealing with health, justice, immigration, and so forth. The alternative, therefore, was to reform the management practices of the services which escaped privatization by trying to subject their operations to the discipline of the market as a way to do 'more with less'.

This is precisely what the British government sought to do when it introduced the Next Steps initiative in 1989. Next Steps emerged in the wake of a government study which concluded that previous efforts at reducing the size of the public sector had run out of steam (Jenkins, Caines, and Jackson, 1988). The study, known as the Next Steps report, argued that ministries were too big, ministers overloaded, and management neglected and that there were few positive incentives for civil servants to pursue quality of service and value for money. To correct this situation, the report recommended the separation of executive operations from policy work and the 'hiving off' of the former to 'Executive Agencies' that would remain under arm's-length political control but free to operate under business-style regimes. The Cabinet accepted the recommendations of the Next Steps report in 1989. Progress of the Next Steps initiative has been very rapid (Seidle, 1995). Between 1989 and 1998, 112 executive agencies were created. About 77 per cent (355,902) of the total number of civil servants are now working in agencies (Government Statistical Service, 1998: 6). Each Next Steps agency is headed by a chief executive, generally recruited by open competition, and paid on the basis of performance. Chief executives are responsible for managing their agencies within policy and resources frameworks agreed between them, their department, and the Treasury. Within the constraints of those frameworks, chief executives have complete discretion as to whether the services provided by their agency should be carried out by the public or the private sector.

Increasingly, the move is to contract out the responsibilities of agencies, as the Next Steps initiative was followed by two measures setting out proposals requiring departments and agencies to open up many of their functions to competition from private sector or other public sector contractors. Introduced by the Major government in 1991, the Citizen's Charter aims at improving the quality of public services by providing more information on the standards of service people are entitled to expect, and allows for compensation in cases where these standards are not met. The Charter sets out a number of mechanisms and ideas designed to promote better services and customer choice. These include increased privatization; wider competition and contracting out; performance-related pay; published service standards and performance in meeting targets; tougher and more independent inspectorates; more effective complaints procedures; and better redress for the individual when things go wrong.

Part of the Citizen's Charter initiative is the 'market testing' policy outlined in a White Paper put forward in 1991 by the Treasury, entitled *Competing for Quality*. To achieve the Citizen's Charter's goal of improving services and consumer choice, the 'market testing' seeks to increase contracting out in the public sector. The intent is to open up to competition 'new areas, closer to the heart of government' (HM Treasury, 1991: 12). The rationale underlying the 'market testing' policy, is that 'In a free market, competing firms must strive to satisfy their customers . . . Where choice and competition are limited, consumers cannot as easily make their views count. In many public services, therefore, we need to increase both choice and competition' (Citizen's Charter, 1991: 4).

Because of its boldness and radicalism, Britain's programme of bureaucratic reform attracted world-wide attention (Butler, 1994). In the mid-1980s, policy makers in Canada kept a close watch on Britain's managerialist policy innovations. As in the case of Britain, the Canadian bureaucracy was also under the control of the New Right during most of the 1980s. In 1984, Brian Mulroney's Conservative Party came to office convinced that the federal bureaucracy was costly, unresponsive, and ineffective. Like Thatcher, Mulroney was intent on making the public sector behave more like the private sector (Aucoin, 1986). During his first term in office, Mulroney began to restructure the state by putting into place a restraint strategy which resulted in the privatization of more than twenty Crown corporations and in the abolition or transfer to the private sector of 80,000 public sector jobs. Following its re-election in 1988, the Mulroney government pursued a wide range of managerialist changes, the most important being Public Service (PS) 2000, a high-profile and ambitious bureaucratic reform exercise unveiled by the prime minister in 1989. As Peter Aucoin argued, 'beginning in 1989 with its Public Service 2000 program', the Mulroney government 'embraced wholeheartedly, at least at the level of official rhetoric, the new paradigm of managerialism' (1995: 15).

PS 2000 sought to improve service to the public by delegating more authority to managers through the decentralization of administrative controls (Swimmer, 1992; Swimmer, Hicks, and Milne, 1994: 183). PS 2000 borrowed from the business management literature the idea of 'empowerment', which stresses the need for administrative simplification, autonomy, entrepreneurship, risk taking, and being close to 'clients' (Kernaghan, 1992). The idea of 'empowerment' has its roots in the Total Quality Management (TQM) movement of the 1980s (Carr and Littman, 1991). As the most senior civil servant in Canada argued in a report on PS 2000, although TQM comes from business, 'it is an approach to administrative reform that is applicable to the Public Service as well as to the private sector' (Canada, 1992: 16).

PS 2000 tried 'to create a client-oriented Public Service, a major change since the Public Service has not been used to regarding Canadians as clients' (Canada, 1990: 51). To ensure that departments provided their 'clients' with the best possible service, PS 2000 introduced the Service Standards Initiative (SSI). Service standards are performance objectives for the delivery of government services to the public. They specify the quality of services and they help to measure the performance of senior managers in the delivery of services to Canadians. As the government later recognized, the development of its SSI has been modelled on the British Citizen's Charter which, like the Canadian initiative, also seeks to make public services more responsive and accountable to their 'clients' (Canada, 1992: 120; Good, 1993).

As part of the new empowerment culture that PS 2000 sought to introduce in the federal bureaucracy, the government established new organizational forms, known as 'Special Operating Agencies' (SOAs). In developing its SOAs policy, the Mulroney government looked to Thatcher's Next Steps initiative for inspiration. Public officials were sent to London to learn more about the agency concept and 'returned with ideas on how to adapt it to Canada' (Savoie, 1994: 231). Like the British agencies, SOAs are less centralized and more autonomous organizations designed to deliver certain government services that were previously provided by ministerial departments. SOAs have been developed to increase managerial freedom from departments and central controls in return for meeting key operational performance objectives. These objectives are part of a 'Framework Document' negotiated between the agency, its department, and the Treasury Board. SOAs are supposed to allow managers 'to apply more business-type approaches' (Canada, 1992: 38). Among such approaches is the adoption by each SOA of a business plan which establishes operational and financial targets and defines what the SOA needs from its department and from the Treasury Board in terms of mandate, resources, and authorities.

The weakness of the ideological approach
When one looks at how the Mulroney government in Canada often drew inspiration from the administrative policies adopted by the Tories in Britain, the belief that the development of managerialism would have been caused by the election of governments committed to the ideology of the New Right seems to be plausible. As one Canadian official remarked, 'Without any doubt the politician who had the most significant impact in shaping PS 2000 was Margaret Thatcher' (quoted in Savoie, 1994: 247). But a closer look at the Canadian case shows that there is wide variation between Britain and Canada in the extent to which managerialist ideas were adopted as policy. Although they were modelled on the Next Steps and intended to introduce more business-like management practices into public administration, Table 1.1 clearly shows that Canadian SOAs have not been put in place as widely as their British counterparts. There are also important differences between the

TABLE 1.1. Autonomous service delivery agencies, 1998

	Number of agencies	Number of employees	Percentage of total employment
Britain			
Executive agencies	112	355,902	77
Canada			
Special operating agencies	18	4,408	1.8

Source: Civil Service Statistics, 1998 (London: HMSO); and Treasury Board Secretariat website: http://www.tbs-sct.gc.ca.

SSI and the Citizen's Charter (Doern, 1993: 222). By 1992, only five Canadian federal departments and units had adopted service standards and in 1996 the Treasury Board Secretariat found in a survey on the SSI that two-thirds of federal departments and agencies still did not have service standards (TBS, 1996). By the same time, more than forty public service bodies in Britain had adopted their own Citizen's Charter (Cabinet Office, 1998).

The New Right approach does not adequately explain these differences. Why are there variations between the two countries in the degree to which new managerialist ideas were implemented as policy? Why have New Right governments in countries that are said to be part of the same 'family of nations' (Castles, 1993) not laid the same emphasis on managerialist ideas? What is even more puzzling is that differences persist despite a process of policy emulation whereby the New Right in Canada continually imported managerialist policy innovations from Britain. The New Right approach is useful to explain some of the key political and ideological motives underlying the pursuit of managerialist policies. But it says nothing about policy implementation, a process which remains very much like an opaque 'black box'. Equally problematic for the New Right approach is to account for instances where left-of-centre parties, such as the Socialists in France, also adopted managerialist policies when reforming their bureaucracy. As some have argued, 'it is too easy to see [managerialism] as simply a product of governments of right-wing free marketeers. In the Netherlands, New Zealand and Sweden, for example, many of its ideas have been pursued with almost missionary zeal by governments of the center or left' (Gray and Jenkins, 1993: 21).

As the movement towards public management reform proceeded in the 1980s and 1990s, the ideological or political content of managerialism became 'far less visible' because it was adopted by governments of many ideological persuasions (Hughes, 1994: 261). The rise of managerialism could thus no longer be regarded as a distinctly Anglo-American phenomenon of the Reagan–Thatcher era and as a product of the New Right. Political ideology alone was no longer seen by most analysts as a sufficient variable for explaining the diffusion of managerialist ideas (Savoie, 1993: 17). Something deeper, bigger, and more important was taking place that, to some extent, 'forced' political leaders, no matter what their political orientation, to reform their bureaucracy along the lines prescribed by the new managerialist paradigm.

The process of globalization

One important stream of literature on recent bureaucratic reform holds that states increasingly formulate managerialist policy responses to cope with the decentralizing and eroding pressures exercised on their administration by the process of globalization (Belloubet-Frier and Timsit, 1993; Campanella, 1993; Thoenig, 1988). The term globalization is used to cover a dizzying array of phenomena, but it basically refers to a 'macro' process by which something is becoming larger and taking more space than before. To a large extent, that 'something' is the economy or the market (Tooze, 1992; Robertson, 1992: 113). It is the boundaries of the market that are supposedly expanding. They are expanding, for instance, into new geographic areas such as the Eastern European countries of the old communist bloc. In the West, the expansion of the market boundaries has to some extent meant that those of the state, in return, have shrunk; they have been 'rolled back' (Claisse, 1989). Many Western states have thus made more room for the market by reorganizing their activities and responsibilities (Suleiman and Waterbury, 1990).

Because of the process of globalization, the state is believed to assume 'a more dispersed' form (Jessop, 1993: 34). Some have suggested that the state is being 'hollowed out' by the process of globalization (Milward, 1994; Rhodes, 1994) or that 'globalization is eating away the nation-state' (Savoie, 1994: 335). One of the consequences of the pressures exercised by the process of globalization on the state executive arm would be the 'breakdown of the bureaucratic model' (Rosell, 1992: 19). This breakdown, in turn, creates within the bureaucracy the dispersion or the decentralization of responsibility. Indications of such dispersion in the British and Canadian reform initiatives described earlier include measures such as 'empowerment' in Canada or the concept of 'devolution' in Britain. According to British documents, the 'devolution of responsibility' is a key element of the government's reform strategy, which seeks 'to give maximum authority to managers to respond to the demands of the public as effectively as the best private sector managers can' (Citizen's Charter, 1992: 2).

The fact that 'we live in a global market place' means that 'the bureaucratic institutions developed during the industrial era increasingly fail us. Today's environment demands institutions that are extremely flexible' (Osborne and Gaebler, 1992: 15). In this context, managerialism would emerge from the structural changes underlying the process of globalization. Managerialism is 'interpreted as an administrative reflection of that broader set of social changes triggered by post-industrialism or post-Fordism'. Indeed, post-Fordism 'explains' managerialism (Hood, 1990: 207). In the face of economic globalization, states are said to be 'forced' to reform their bureaucracies along the lines prescribed by the new managerialism (Mascarenhas, 1993: 320). It is argued that, 'for the most part, individuals, corporations and governments don't have a choice about it' (Cleveland, quoted in Rosell, 1992: 17). One global economy would thus generate only one global or universal way for the bureaucratic apparatus of the state to adjust to restructuring. As a result of changes in the international economic system, the new managerialist paradigm more or less imposes itself across the globe as the 'one best way' to reorganize bureaucracies (Gray and Jenkins, 1993: 22).

How is it possible for the managerialist paradigm to impose itself as the only solution to reform state administrations? According to proponents of the globalization thesis, this process is in large part driven by technological changes related to the rise of the so-called 'new information society' (Rosell, 1992). To be more precise, there are in fact two ways in which the 'new information society' is related to the demise of the bureaucratic model and the global diffusion of new managerialist ideas. First, there is the 'technicist' position which sees the new managerialism as a form of public management for the information age (Bellamy and Taylor, 1998: 37). According to this view, rapid developments in information technology and the computerization of office work are increasingly making bureaucratic principles useless because they are eroding hierarchies as devices for centralizing and managing information in large organizations (Bailey and Mayer, 1992; Cleveland, 1987; Dobell and Steenkamp, 1993; Taylor and Van Every, 1993; Taylor and Williams, 1991). Secondly, improved communications would now enable one state to know very rapidly what another state on the other side of the planet is doing to reform its management practices. Proponents of this view argue that

the phenomenon of globalization applies to public sector reform itself; reforms implemented in one jurisdiction have spread rapidly to others, spawning imitations and spin-offs throughout the developed world. The similarity of these reforms is partly a response to local conditions and pressures. But it is also a testimony to the phenomenon of globalization itself: the almost instantaneous speed with which information is communicated around the world. (Heintzman, 1993: i)

Refined information technologies have contributed to 'the globalization of approaches to public sector management . . . [In the 1980s] concepts and new approaches to public sector management traveled the Western world as if there were no jurisdictional boundaries' (Savoie, 1992: 8). As communications have developed, there is a more extensive international exchange of ideas between state officials and policy advisers. An example is the Public Management (PUMA) Committee created by the OECD in the late 1980s as a forum where officials meet to discuss their countries' public service reforms. The PUMA Committee publishes yearly reports and studies and has become a key focal point for the international diffusion of managerialist ideas (Halligan, 1996: 297).

The case of France broadly corresponds to the kind of scenario described by the globalization and information technology thesis. As one French colleague noted, the policy of administrative modernization adopted by the Socialists in 1989 'reflects the managerialist fashion of the 1990s' (Rouban, 1993: 404), thus showing, as the globalization thesis suggests, that managerialism is not necessarily a New Right phenomenon. In 1989, the prime minister, Michel Rocard, launched an important policy of administrative modernization known as the *Renouveau du Service public*. The French Renewal policy focused mainly on service delivery, accountability, and evaluation. In the area of service delivery, the government adopted in March 1992 its *Charte des services publics* which seeks to improve relations between the administration and the citizen-user (Pêcheur, 1992). Like its British counterpart, the French Charter sets out a number of measures to make public services more responsive. Some of the more notable ones include mechanisms for monitoring service quality and providing for citizen participation in the organization of services (OECD, 1993: 70).

The issue of accountability, or *responsabilisation* as it is referred to in the French documents, is the central theme of the Renewal policy (MFPMA, 1991b: 4). One of the key initiatives implemented under the theme of *responsabilisation* is the creation of *Centres de responsabilité* (CDR). A CDR is an administrative unit located within a *service déconcentré* (i.e., that part of a ministerial department located at the regional level). As in the case of British executive agencies and the Canadian SOAs, French CDRs are based on a three-year contract, known as *projet de service*, negotiated between the unit, its parent department, and the Ministries of Budget and Civil Service (Bodiguel, 1992). In 1993, there were 207 CDRs representing more than 40,000 civil servants (about 2 per cent of total central public service employment). CDR status constitutes an option open to those units that wish to apply more flexible public management rules. In return, the CDR has to implement a service project, develop a training plan, improve service delivery, reduce processing and waiting time, introduce management control procedures, assess results annually, and report on the experience at the end of the mandate (Bodiguel and Rouban, 1991; Fialaire, 1993; Tonnerre, 1991).

In the domain of evaluation, the government created in 1990 a *Comité interministériel de l'évaluation*, chaired by the prime minister, which selects the policy to be evaluated; a *Conseil scientifique de l'évaluation* to develop the methodology for evaluation, and a *Fond national de développement de l'évaluation* (Commissariat général du Plan, 1991). The creation of this new evaluative machinery is the direct consequence of the emphasis put by the Renewal policy on *responsabilisation*. In his 1989 circular, Prime Minister Rocard noted that 'Il ne peut y avoir ni autonomie sans responsabilité, ni responsabilité sans évaluation' (MFPRA, 1990: 13). *Responsabilisation*, like 'empowerment' in Canada and 'devolution' in Britain, seeks to broaden the responsibility of civil servants by de-bureaucratizing administrative systems and by removing the rules, processes, hierarchies, and other forms of legal and political controls that supposedly limited the extent to which public managers could be responsible or accountable for their actions. These Weberian-type controls are to be replaced or complemented by controls whose content is often specified in 'contracts' (the Framework Agreement of the Next Steps agencies in Britain; the Framework Document of Canadian SOAs, and the *projet de service* of French CDRs) in which performance is assessed through the evaluation or measurement of the results achieved in the management of public programmes.

Differences within convergence

To develop its Renewal policy, the French government sent some of its officials to London to see how certain policy ideas were operating and borrowed a number of managerialist innovations from Britain.[2] This again tends to support the globalization thesis and suggests that improved communications may be leading to a greater awareness about what other states are doing and a keenness to learn from each other's experiences. But contrary to what the globalization thesis suggests, developments in information technology did not lead to uniformity in the management policies developed by the two states. Proponents of this approach believe that 'improved direct communications and exchange of ideas between interested parties in various countries . . . helps to explain not only the uniformity of ideas but also the uniformity of language and practices' (Greer, 1994: 29).

Even from casual observation, it is clear that the British and French reforms are not 'uniform' either in ideas or in language. As Christopher Pollitt and his colleague argued in a recent article, 'a number of commentators have noted that the pervasiveness of New Public Management thinking varies a good deal from country to country, and France is usually cited as a state that has adopted managerialism to only a middling or low extent, while the UK is seen as a true believer' (Pollitt and Summa, 1997a: 333). For instance, a comparison of the French Public Service Charter and the British Citizen's Charter shows that the French initiative does not share with its British counterpart an economistic conception of citizenship. In the UK Citizen's

---

[2] Contacts between British and French officials in the process of bureaucratic change were sufficiently important to justify the publication, by the British government, of a glossy document written in French and entitled *Amélioration de la qualité: Charte des citoyens britanniques et réformes du Service public*. In this document, one can read (in the original English version) that from the outset, the British programme of bureacratic reform has attracted interest not only in France, but throughout the world and that British officials 'played host to Government Ministers, academics and officials from the European Community and from countries such as Sweden, Australia, Japan, India, Cyprus, Hungary, Canada, the United States and Brazil' (Foreign & Commonwealth Office, 1992: 20).

Charter there are many references to customers or 'clients', rather more than there are to citizens, unlike the more state-centred traditions reflected in the French *Charte des services publics*. In France, the *Charte* is clear that the relationship between citizen and the state 'ne peut être assimilée ni à une relation entre deux particuliers ni à une relation de type commercial; les services publics sont en charge de l'intérêt collectif, ce qui les conduit à assurer des prestations d'utilité collective que la loi du marché amènerait à négliger . . . la relation des services publics avec les usagers n'est pas assimilable à celle d'un prestataire avec un client' (MFPRA, 1995: 7–8).

There is also wide variation in the extensiveness of implementation of new managerialist ideas. Even if French reformers used the Next Steps initiative as the basis to develop the *Centres de responsabilité*, only 2 per cent of total central public service employees worked in CDR as opposed to 77 per cent in the case of Executive Agencies in Britain. For proponents of the globalization-information technology approach, such differences are difficult to explain because they tend to point to 'uniformity' or 'convergence' in the bureaucratic changes that states have recently put in place. In the literature on comparative bureaucratic reforms, discussions of policy uniformity or convergence have more or less become a familiar theme (Copper, 1995; Crozier, 1988; Holmes, 1992). Policy convergence is a concept which assumes 'that greater economic integration will encourage closer political relationships among the authorities responsible for the economies affected, and possibly convergence in institutional arrangements' (Coleman, 1994: 274; Bennett, 1991). In concluding his study of bureaucratic reform in Britain, Canada and the United States, one of the leading students in comparative public administration argued: 'There are remarkable similarities in the approaches tried in the three countries, despite their different institutional structures and public service cultures, and the degree of similarity means one can now make the case that globalization is having as much an impact on the public sector as it has on the economy' (Savoie, 1994: 319–20).

Besides its problems in explaining policy variation, the globalization approach has another difficulty: that it focuses too much on the broad 'macro' factors (socioeconomic structures and technological changes) that are supposedly forcing states to marketize or managerialize their bureaucracies. To put it simply, the globalization thesis is based on strong deterministic assumptions. But to the extent that we take seriously notions of human agency as crucial to explaining outcomes, we need to come to terms with the role of policy actors not just as the dependent variable, influenced by globalization and technological changes, but as an independent variable as well. To some extent, the New Right approach addressed that issue more adequately because it at least identified real human beings and not only 'invisible' forces as one of the major causal factors in the managerialization of state bureaucracies. But the New Right approach did not pay much attention to the processes by which the broad political ideas and normative views of New

Right leaders were operationalized or translated into managerialist ¡
The New Right approach focused on the guiding philosophies of righ
political leaders *vis-à-vis* the state but it did not tell us how the anti-
rhetoric and symbols used by the New Right were tied to manage
policy innovations. If the pro-market philosophy of Thatcher and Mulroney
opened a 'political opportunity' or space that made the development of
the new managerialism possible, who provided the more technical or
programmatic ideas on which were based policies such as the Next Steps
initiative and PS 2000?

'Consultocracy'

One approach to have emerged in the literature recently answers this
question by claiming that the global spread of managerialist ideas and
policies across states is a process 'driven primarily by private sector consultants' (Boston, 1991: 9). The 'latest wave of business managerialism', this
third approach suggests, has been 'mainly brought into the public sector
by management consultants' (Foster and Plowden, 1996: 1). 'Management
consultants', others similarly argue,

clearly played an important role in packaging, selling, and implementing the 'New
Public Management' reforms. Management consultancy has become big business
. . . [Consulting] firms have developed into multinational giants which have deeply
vested interests in terms of future work, in selling the ideas, language and methods
of New Public Management. The consultancy firms have highly developed international networks through which many of these profitable ideas have been trans-
mitted and translated. (Greer, 1994: 29)

As rational actors, it is assumed that management consultants have 'deeply
vested interests' (to paraphrase Greer) in pushing for the implementation of
more and more managerialist policies within the state. The state and the
bureaucratic reform policy domain are conceived as a 'competitive market'
in which consultants constantly struggle to aggrandize their share in order
to maximize the profit of their firms (Henkel, 1991b: 129). Accordingly, the
new managerialism is seen as a mere reflection of the material interests of
consultants. It is conceived as 'a vehicle for particularistic advantage' and as
a 'self-serving movement designed to promote the career interests of an élite
group of New Managerialists' which, according to Christopher Hood, is
made of 'management consultants and business schools' (Hood, 1991: 9).
As Hood later explained, consultants are part of a 'new class'—those 'who
colonized the public management from the outside'. They are part of what he
calls 'the "privatization complex"', the management consultants, accountants
and IT specialists who form the contemporary equivalent of the "efficiency"
experts who championed the Progressive Public Administration [model]
eighty years or so earlier' (1994: 138).

According to this 'new class' approach, the relative influence of managerialist ideas on policy is linked to the growing use of management consultants as a source of policy advice in the process of administrative reform. Consultants are said to be called in by government because of their technical knowledge or managerial skills (Henkel, 1991b: 127). As one European official noted, management consultants entered

public administration in a major way in the 1980s. Criticism had mounted against the bureaucracy on several fronts: its working methods, the qualifications of its employees, and its efficiency and rationality. Free and independent consultants were expected to show their worth, drawing from their experience and qualifications from the private sector to improve on the government bureaucracy. (Blymke, 1995: 127)

Those who have underlined the growing role of consultants in public sector reforms shared very differing views of the influence that consultants have on government policy. These positions can be arrayed along a continuum running from least to most influence, although the reality is probably somewhere between these two poles. Management consultants themselves generally argue that they are the 'servants of power' and that they have no influence over policy (Abbott, 1993; 1994). They are in the business of selling ideas and, after all, it is up to their clients to decide whether to translate those ideas into policy. Some consultants are even critical of the fact that they are too often used as 'hired guns' to play a window-dressing role for decisions made by politicians for entirely non-technical reasons (Corneille, 1994). Others, who use the idea of technocracy, contend that the power of consultants in the management of the state is increasing while the power of traditional kinds of politicians is declining. Some coined the term 'consultocracy' to describe this process (Hood and Jackson, 1991: 24), while others talked about the new 'cult of the management consultant' in government (Smith, 1994: 130) or argued that consultants are now part of a 'new nomenklatura' that is being formed in and around the managerialist state (Smith and Young, 1996: 150). A study in Australia goes as far as suggesting that consultants 'reoriented' the nation's social policy framework (Martin, 1998).

Basically, the idea of an emerging 'consultocracy' suggests that consultants have become powerful because, when implemented, the new managerialist model that they advocate tends to remove public administration from politics and thus, from public scrutiny. In the bureaucratic model developed by Weber, most areas of government work traditionally used to take place in organizations placed under the direct control of elected politicians. In that model, everything was 'political' because civil servants were all hierarchically linked to a politician who sat at the top of the organization and who was alone responsible for the work done by the department placed under his or her command. This kind of centralization is said to have been possible because, when Weber wrote his theory of bureaucracy, the state was not as active as it later became and politicians were not as busy as they now are (Blau and Meyer, 1987; Dunleavy, 1991). The new managerialism is based on the assumption that with the rise of the welfare state and the increasing complexity of social problems, politicians have become 'overloaded' (King, 1975). They can no longer be responsible for everything as they theoretically were under the traditional bureaucratic model. The increasing volume of demands on politicians' time tends to encourage the devolution of responsibilities. As a result, public administration is increasingly moving toward 'arm's length government' (Greer, 1994: 2). This results in the depoliticization of public administration or, more precisely, in the subtraction of whole areas of government work from the direct control of politicians (Foster and Plowden, 1996: ch. 4). Once politics is out of public administration, the argument goes on, it should no longer be difficult to import into the bureaucracy management ideas and techniques from the private sector because the presence of politics is the only thing that made public sector organizations different from businesses (Allison, 1982).

Consequently, in the new managerialist model, civil servants are encouraged to become more 'entrepreneurial' and to take risks, just as the best business managers do. They operate in a more decentralized environment where traditional forms of bureaucratic and political controls (hierarchy, rules, processes, etc.) are replaced or complemented by new forms of control based on social knowledge increasingly provided by management consultants (Henkel, 1991a). Consultants are especially involved in promoting and developing the techniques that attempt to reproduce within the public sector the 'bottom line'[3] of commercial enterprises (Plumptre, 1988). Within the state, techniques such as performance evaluation and output measurement are seen as substitutes for the market sector 'bottom line' (Kramer, 1983; Carter, Klein, and Day, 1992). They are conceived as a 'quasi-market discipline' for those parts of the public sector that cannot be privatized or subjected directly to the forces of the market (Pollitt, 1986a: 319).

For instance, in Britain the Treasury published in 1990 a guide entitled *Seeking help from Management Consultants*, the front page of which is reproduced as Figure 1.1. This guide is addressed to managers who are considering using private sector consulting services when devising and introducing output and performance measures and other aspects of improving value for money or management change. According to the guide, management consultants 'can help make dramatic improvements to the work of Departments' by 'importing experience' from the private sector to government (HM Treasury, 1990: 8–9).

---

[3] Broadly speaking, performance indicators try to reproduce within the state the 'invisible hand' type of control that is, in theory, achieved in the private sector through the 'bottom line' (Pollitt, 1986a; 1986b; 1988). This is why in discussing performance indicators and output measures some scholars refer to the notion of 'hands off control' (Carter, 1988). The idea is that through the introduction of such techniques, the bureaucracy would become an almost self-managed and self-controlled institution to some extent similar to private sector enterprises whose performance is evaluated or controlled at the end of the day through the calculation of the 'bottom line'.

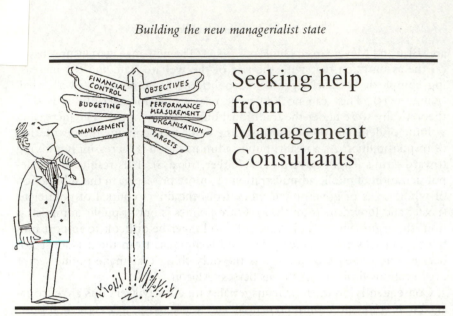

FINANCIAL CONTROL · OBJECTIVES · BUDGETING · PERFORMANCE MEASUREMENT · MANAGEMENT · ORGANISATION · TARGETS

Seeking help from Management Consultants

HM Treasury

FIGURE 1.1. HM Treasury guide on seeking help from consultants

Source: HM Treasury, *Seeking help from Management Consultants* (London, 1990).

In Canada, soon after launching its PS 2000 initiative, the federal government issued a guide on 'Measuring Client Satisfaction' and a new programme evaluation policy which encouraged public managers to 'take full advantage of the benefits of professional evaluation resources outside the government in private sector consulting firms . . . These benefits may include the enhancement of the credibility and objectivity of evaluations—and the perception of these qualities—by involving persons outside the institution who have specialized subject matter or methodological expertise' (OCG, 1991: 4).

In France, the implementation of the new management measures derived from the 1989 Renewal policy has likewise created a situation where, in the central government, 'on fait appel de plus en plus souvent à des consultants' (MFPRA, 1993: 134). As one study on the development of the Renewal policy found, management consultants from the private sector have been 'heavily involved' in the process of administrative reform (Chaty, 1997: 33). In June 1990, the Minister for the Civil Service and Administrative Reform created a working group of senior officials, academics, and private sector management consultants to study the use of management consultants in government.[4] In that study, it was noted that

---

[4] The working group is known as the Groupe de modernisation consultants internes dans l'Administration.

le processus de renouveau dans lequel s'est engagé le service public implique des changements dans de multiples domaines: ajustement des missions, déconcentration, responsabilisation, amélioration de l'efficacité, nouveau mode de management, etc. Pour accompagner et faciliter ce processus, plusieurs administrations . . . ont fait appel aux consultants externes. (DGAFP, 1991: Annexe 1)

The working group found that it was 'not possible' for private firms alone to respond to the state's increasing needs for management consulting knowledge (DGAFP, 1991: 1). It argued that it would be preferable for the state to create its own internal management consulting capacity rather than to rely exclusively on the private sector. As a result, the French state undertook in 1991 to develop, within its administration, the new function of internal management consultant.

The shared limits of existing interpretations
In the three countries, there are a number of signs showing that the development of managerialist policies in the 1980s has been accompanied by the use, or by an encouragement to use, the services of management consultants. These indications are not inconsistent with the interpretation that the rise and spread of managerialist ideas and policies is a process driven by rational and profit-maximizing management consultants. However, the cases of Britain, Canada, and France also show the limits of this explanation. The weakness of the the consultant-centred approach is that it cannot account for variation in the reception given to managerialist ideas, a weakness it shares with the globalization and the New Right interpretations. As a result of policies encouraging the use of private sector consultants, state officials in Britain, Canada, and France may have all been increasingly exposed to the business management ideas that consultants bring into the policy process. But nevertheless, there are important differences in the extent to which policy makers in the three countries embraced these ideas in the process of reforming their bureaucracy. If managerialist ideas simply reflected the material interests of 'rational' consultants, French and Canadian consultants would, to some extent, be 'irrational', because in these two states managerialist ideas have not been as influential as in Britain. Although present in France, managerialist ideas have not yet penetrated deeply into the administrative system, while in Canada managerialist ideas, often directly imported from London, have not been implemented as extensively as in Britain. If the management consultant-centred approach were adequate, there would be less variation between Britain, France, and Canada. Does the fact that managerialist ideas have not been as influential in France and Canada as in Britain mean that French and, maybe to a lesser extent, Canadian management consultants are not as 'rational' as their British counterparts? Or is it that management consultants may have similar preferences cross-nationally but that they cannot influence policy in the same way or to the same extent in different national contexts?

It may well be that in attempting to account for the diffusion of man-agerialist ideas, the structural, ideological, and interest-driven interpretations have neglected an important factor which could explain differences in the reception given to managerialist ideas. This neglected factor is the state. In all these interpretations—and especially in the case of the globalization hypothesis where the state is said to be 'hollowed out' or 'eaten away'—there is no serious examination of the intervening processes by which ideology, interests, or structural factors enter state institutions and shape policies (Peters and Pierre, 1998). In the same way, in the management consultant-centred interpretation the state is also invisible. The state is assumed to be an empty shell through which consulting interests can easily press their views concerning public management issues and get their prefer-ences almost automatically translated into policies. Since the state is not seen as something that could constrain the capacities of consultants to promote their interests, the result is that bureaucratic reform policies throughout the world should converge, because the managerialist preferences of manage-ment consultants are assumed to be everywhere the same. But, to be able to explain policy variation, the state needs to be 'brought back' because one of the reasons for taking the state seriously is to explain cross-national differences in policy.

Consultants, the state, and the politics of managerialism

The role of management consultants in the managerialization of state bureaucracies has not yet been the object of scholarly examination. This is a potentially promising line of explanation that deserves to be seriously examined, especially in light of recent surveys which have found that con-sultants lead ministers and legislators as sources of innovative ideas in public administration (Gow, 1994: 47). However, in order to understand why there is wide variation across nations in the degree to which managerialist ideas were implemented as policy, the consultant-centred approach needs to incorporate a more complete model of the policy-making process as a whole. To do this, I first develop an approach that stresses the interrelations of management consultants and the state, and then outline the method of analysis and plan of the book.

Historical institutionalism and policy variation

The 1980s and 1990s have witnessed a 'rediscovery' of institutions in the study of political phenomena (March and Olsen, 1984; 1989). As is well known, there are a number of different approaches that have been labelled 'neo-institutionalist' (Pal, 1994). Although they may differ in terms of their level of analysis (micro, meso, macro) or epistemological assumptions (rational

choice versus historical-interpretive), what all varieties of neo-instituti
approach have in common is that they developed in reaction to the beha-
vioural perspectives that were influential during the 1960s and 1970s and all
seek to elucidate the role that institutions play in the determination of policy
outcomes. In trying to explain differences between Britain, Canada, and
France, I will use the historical institutionalist stream of the neo-institutionalist
literature. One central theme in the work of historical institutionalists is to
explain 'the persistence of cross-national differences despite common challenges and pressures' (Thelen and Steinmo, 1992: 5). By being situated between
state and society-centred analyses, and by looking at the institutional arrangements that structure relations between the two, historical institutionalism
seeks 'to illuminate sources of variation on a common theme' (Thelen and
Steinmo, 1992: 10). As it has been argued,

> those who advocated 'bringing the state back in' in order to examine cross-national
> differences in policy outcomes were most interested in exploring variations in the
> role of institutions across space. In trying to account for policy differences, they
> emphasized the autonomy of the state from civil society and the independent role
> of policy decision makers . . . they focused on state structures in order to explore
> how politics and policies were jointly conditioned by institutional arrangements and
> social relationships. (Jenson, 1991*a*: 45–6)

In the historical-institutionalist literature, institutions are not only those
associated with a country's constitution and formal political practices. The
historical-institutionalist approach 'ranges more widely to consider the role
of institutions located within society and the economy, as well as less formal
organizational networks, in the determination of policy' (Hall, 1986: 20).
Examples of 'less formal' organizations that are located within society and
the economy, and which will be discussed in the next chapter, include, for
instance, the structure of the consulting market and the organization of the
management consulting industry and profession.

In developing an explanatory framework that stresses the links between
consultants and the state to account for differences in the reception accorded
to managerialist ideas, I will use some of the insights derived from recent
work examining the historically evolved interrelations between states and
knowledge-bearing occupations in public policy making (Furner and Supple,
1990; Rueschemeyer and Skocpol, 1996; Skocpol, 1992). There are in this
body of literature a number of studies from which useful theoretical lessons
can be gleaned. Such studies include, for instance, the comparative research
of Immergut (1992) on the role of the medical profession in the health policy
sector; Jenson's study on the impact of demographers on natality policies
(1986), and the work of Orloff (1993), Steinmo (1993), and Weir (1992) on
the influence of professional economists in the development of pension, tax
and employment policies. In particular, the study by Peter A. Hall (1989) on
the spread of Keynesian ideas, and the concomitant rise of economists within

government circles after the economic depression of the 1930s, provides, for the purposes of this book, an important source of intellectual inspiration to conceive the relationships between the role of management consultants and the rise of new managerialist ideas in the context of the structural changes associated with the process of 'globalization'.

The organizational development of management consultancy

One important factor that often stands out from these studies is that in a technically complex policy domain, ideas are more likely to influence policy and to be better received when they are advocated by a relatively well-developed group of specialists or professionals (Ziegler, 1995; 1997). For instance, Hall has suggested that one important factor which affected the speed with which Keynesian ideas were diffused and assimilated into policy making concerned the 'organization' of the economics profession. 'Not surprisingly', he argues, Keynesian ideas and 'concepts spread more slowly in nations where the economics profession was small' (1989: 365). Likewise, Weir and Skocpol's comparative study of Keynesian responses to the Great Depression underlines the need for an analysis of the growth and structure of the economics profession to understand the state's capacities for socio-economic interventions (1985). Although he does not look at the impact of ideas on policy—but rather at their influence on the models of management predominant in industry—Guillén also uses a strategy which consists in studying 'the relative strength and influence of different professional groups and their contribution to the adoption and implementation of organizational paradigms' (1994: 26–7).

None of these authors is of course trying to reduce the influence of ideas simply to the organizational characteristics of knowledge-bearing groups. Ideas have a causal power and a persuasiveness of their own. However, when attempting to explain their influence, ideas and organizational factors should not be treated separately (Laumann and Knoke, 1987). And 'neither can ideas and self-interest be successfully disentangled theoretically. People need to attach meaning to their behavior, even if that behavior is motivated by self-interest' (Kingdon, 1994: 223).

The influence of ideas does not depend on the innate qualities of those ideas alone. Influence is a relational concept determined as much by the content of the ideas themselves as by the organizational status of their advocate. As Judith Goldstein has argued, 'it is not only the content of an idea which influences whether or not it is "consumed" . . . the status of the idea's bearer will [also] be important' (1993: 15). Thus, in trying to see whether the differences in the acceptance of managerialist ideas that were noted earlier can be linked to the role of consultants in the process of bureaucratic reform, one of the first tasks that needs to be undertaken is to study the organization of the management consulting profession and industry in the three countries

under investigation. To do so, I will borrow the concept of 'orga
development' from the works of policy network analysts who ha
patterns of relations between societal interests and state institution.
policy domains (Katzenstein, 1978; Knoke, Pappi, Broadbent, and Tsujinaka,
1996; Marin and Mayntz, 1991; Schmitter and Streek, 1981).

In studying the organizational development of management consultancy,
one crucial element deserving careful attention is the extent to which the
services of consultants are consumed by the private sector (Alvarez, 1998).
To the extent that managerialism consists of the importation of business
management ideas and techniques into the public sector, the experience that
consultants have of private sector administration becomes a key factor in
determining the possibilities for managerialist ideas to be used by state officials
as the basis for bureaucratic reform policy. The specialized knowledge that
consultants have of private sector management and, consequently, the extent
to which their expertise can be seen by policy makers as useful for improving the administration of the state by importing business management ideas
and practices into the public sector partly depend on how much their services
are used by businesses (Clegg and Palmer, 1996).

But this does not mean that states use consulting services to reform their
bureaucracy only when consultants belong to a relatively well-developed
industry that has already acquired a 'good' reputation among the business
élite. Government agencies and officials have, for their own policy purposes,
mobilized and contributed to the development of management consultancy. This happened in at least two ways: by adopting industrial policies
designed to stimulate the penetration of management consultancy in small
and medium-sized enterprises (SMEs), and by using the knowledge and ideas
of business consultants to reform the public sector. During the 1980s, in the
context of changes in the international political economy (i.e. the formation
of the European Union and of the North American Free Trade Agreement),
the British, Canadian, and French states all adopted various initiatives to
encourage the use of consultants in SMEs as a way to improve their efficiency
and competitiveness through the implementation of new management
models (OECD, 1995a). It is often in conjunction with the adoption of such
initiatives that the state began to develop new managerialist policies and to
increase its use of private sector consultants. Initiatives adopted in the field
of industrial policy helped to shape the state's own thinking about bureaucratic reform policy. This underlines the need for an analysis that also looks
at policies formally classified in other sectors if the growth of the new managerialism in public administration is to be fully understood.

The openness of policy-making institutions to outside expert advice

Of course, the organizational development of management consulting does
not alone determine the acceptance of managerialist ideas and policies by

states. Managerialist ideas can be present in a given national setting and they can be advocated by a well-developed and strong management consulting industry, but to become policy, ideas must first enter state institutions. As has been suggested, 'Ultimately, the promotion of ideas also involves placing their proponents in government positions, where they can shape policy' (Smith, 1991: 207). This does not mean that policy ideas automatically become influential when their advocates obtain prestigious positions in government, although this is certainly an important part of the equation. To become policy, ideas must come to the attention of those who make decisions in centres of national power. Two elements play a critical role in this process: the relative openness of policy-making institutions to social knowledge generated outside the state and expert access to decision-making centres (Weir and Skocpol, 1985: 109).

The issue of institutional openness or permeability has often been discussed by comparing the American presidential model with parliamentary states. As is well known, the American president can bring a wide range of outside advisers into his administration (Busch, 1997). The American practice of recruiting 'inners and outers' means that policy-making institutions are more or less constantly refreshed with ideas from outside government (Mackenzie, 1987). In parliamentary states, policy advice has traditionally come from an echelon of permanent civil servants who have a virtual monopoly on access to official policy information and to the ultimate decision makers. But this monopoly is one of the main aspects of the Weberian bureaucratic system that the new managerialism seeks to transform (Boston, 1994). In the late 1970s, in the context of the fiscal crisis, the monopolistic and closed character of the public service became key themes in the challenge mounted by Public Choice theorists and New Right politicians against the bureaucratic state (Niskanen, 1971; 1973). They argued that because of the monopolistic character of public services, politicians were the victims of bureaucratic manipulation and exploitation. The BBC series *Yes, Minister* popularized that view by portraying politicians as the helpless hostages of their bureaucratic subordinates (Borins, 1988). Accordingly, in nations where the new managerialism 'caught on', there has been a tendency to bring in more outside consultants and experts as a way to challenge the monopoly of the bureaucracy by multiplying the sources of policy advice (Halligan, 1995).

But this trend is not new, and did not develop suddenly with the emergence of new managerialist ideas in the 1980s. In the 1960s, there were attempts to make the standards of recruitment to administrative posts more flexible in order to allow governments to bring in more outsiders from the private sector. Talking about the 'new' managerialism implies that there was an 'old' managerialism; but, as noted earlier, many 'new' managerialist ideas have their roots in the planning and rational management (i.e the Planning, Programming, and Budgeting System) movement of the 1960s. The 'new' managerialism emerged largely in reaction against the 'old' managerialism

(Dunleavy and Hood, 1994). After the failure of the PPBS movement, the 'old' managerialism and the idea that politics could be reduced to a quantitative science were criticized for being 'hyperrational', too abstract, and theoretical (Braybrooke and Lindblom, 1963; Wildavsky, 1984). Indeed, the appeal of the 'new' managerialism lies exactly in those things that the 'old' managerialism was said to lack: common sense or practicality. Although much of its ideas can be found within the academic literature, the popularity of the new managerialism comes from the fact that it has been packaged in ways that have addressed issues from the perspective of management practitioners rather than from the perspective of the theorist or social scientist, as was often the case with the 'old' managerialism (Aucoin, 1990: 118). Christopher Pollitt summarizes the periods of the 'old' and 'new' managerialism in the following way: 'First' he argues,

came an Age of *Enlightenment*, lasting from the mid-1960s to the soaring oil prices of 1973. This was a period when . . . government was fertile with new, more analytical approaches to the business of making and implementing policies . . . The main intellectual influences of this period were American . . . Corporate planning was an approach which had first been developed in large US private-sector companies between the World Wars, while articles on PPBS and the American use of cost-benefit analysis were widely prescribed readings . . . The second period can perhaps be christened one of *Dire straits*. The global economic upheaval of the mid-1970s swept away many of the hopes for rationalistic analysis entertained during the preceding period . . . Policy analysis was guilty by association: it was portrayed as one more symptom of the arrogance of government, of a mistaken belief that the state was capable of large scale social engineering on the basis of rationally worked-out plans. [It was believed] that government had taken on more than it could handle, that the decentralised decisions of the market-place should whenever possible replace the inevitably inadequate plans of government. (1993: 354–5)

As can be seen from the above quotation, the 'old' managerialism is generally associated with the 'rationalistic' thinking of the 1960s (Van Gusteren, 1976). A central theme of rationalism and the 'old' managerialism was how to use social scientific knowledge and techniques to rationalize public policy in order to keep in check the irrational aspects of politics (Ezrahi, 1990: 263). In the 1960s, in the context of President Johnson's Great Society initiative, the United States became the cradle where new management techniques, often rooted in engineering (systems analysis, cybernetics, etc.) were first developed (Beer, 1966; Berlinski, 1976). As a result of Washington's fascination with 'rational management' some argued that the American management consulting industry—which is the oldest and most strongly developed in the world—became in the 1970s a 'shadow government' to which the White House was giving away its policy-making powers (Guttman and Willner, 1976).

Following the example of the United States, many OECD governments in the 1960s imported from Washington new management techniques that sought to strengthen the executive and rationalize the intervention of the state in society (Wildavsky, 1975). They created new central capabilities and used outside management consultants and other policy experts to help build these new organizations. This was later seen by some (in parliamentary states) as evidence of the 'Americanization' or 'presidentialization' of their government (Jones, 1991).

Policy legacies and the 'old' managerialism of the 1960s

Thus, if we want to understand whether it has been possible for consultants during the 1980s to enter state institutions and advocate new managerialist ideas in the process of bureaucratic reform, it is necessary to go back to the 1960s because it was then that policy-making structures became more open to advice from outside management experts. It is necessary to go back and study the institutions and the reactions of policy actors to the reform initiatives associated with the period of the 'old' managerialism. One has to see if there are any connections over time between the policies derived from the periods of the 'old' and the 'new' managerialism. To do this, I use the idea of 'policy legacy' that Weir and Skocpol developed to study the history of social policy (1985: 119).

But bureaucratic reform is very different from social policy and, when using the concept of policy legacy, one must take these differences into account. For one thing, as a policy area, bureaucratic reform is much more technical and less 'political' than social policy. It is less political not because it does not involve ideologies, values, and struggles over resources, but because it is primarily targeted to a much smaller group—civil servants—over whom the state, as an employer, has enormous powers. Citizens do not go out on the streets to protest against or to support a management reform policy as they sometimes do when important changes are made to social programmes. Of course, public service unions can go on strike to protest, for instance, against management policies designed to increase competition in the delivery of government services, but the state can legislate them back to work—something that it cannot do (at least in a democracy!) with the movements and groups that oppose a certain course of action in the field of social policy. As a policy sector, bureaucratic reform is both less 'democratic' (i.e. more technocratic) and much less inclusive than social policy. It does not involve representatives of women, the youth, senior citizens, or the unemployed. It has traditionally been restricted to the officials who work in the agencies that have jurisdiction over management policy issue. Over the years, it has become more open to outside management experts, as well as to their associations and to reform-minded organizations promoting the adoption of certain management techniques in the public sector. And along with this increased openness has come a greater politicization of public management issues. Since the 1980s these issues have been among the top items on the agenda of political leaders. The effective management of the public sector is now seen as an important component of economic recovery strategies. Likewise, the numerous versions of the 'Citizen's Charter' that many countries have adopted are not only managerial but also political tools designed to address the 'democratic deficit' by bringing the state closer to the citizen-user and by making it more responsive to his or her needs. But nevertheless, bureaucratic reform policy issues do not arouse intense popular concern. In the field of bureaucratic reform, unlike most other policy areas, ideas are not primarily judged by reference to their ability to forge the large coalition of social groups that politicians often need to sustain their policy initiative. Policy ideas are judged by reference to their perceived technical credibility, and this is why the 'politics of expertise'—as opposed to the 'street politics' of social movements—often tends to prevail over questions of public administration reform (Beneviste, 1977; Tarrow, 1989). In brief, different policy sectors have different 'politics'.

With these distinctions in mind, 'policy legacy' is generally defined as a concept that focuses on two main themes: policy or social learning processes and the impact of inherited policy structures (Pierson, 1994: 40). It starts with the insight that policy making is inherently a historical process in which actors define their responses to a particular policy on the basis of their prior experience with similar measures. Policy actors will be more or less predisposed towards policies (i.e. they will reject or support them), depending on what they have learned from previous governmental efforts dealing with the same (or similar) problems. But this learning process is never purely 'rational' or intellectual. Contrary to what rational choice theorists argue, it is shaped by the practices, norms, and institutional context left by past policies. Accordingly, my approach will focus on the legacies of past bureaucratic reform initiatives that: (a) influenced the political predisposition of policy actors towards strategies designed to improve the management of the state; and (b) affected the participation of consultants in the process of bureaucratic reform and their access to decision-making centres through which managerialist ideas did (or did not) enter into the formulation of policy. Schematically, the framework that this book proposes to account for cross-national variation in the reception given to managerialist ideas is represented in Figure 1.2.

Let me briefly illustrate the model of causal interrelationships sketched in the diagram by using examples drawn from the three cases discussed in the following chapters. When they came to power during the 1960s after a long period out of office, the Conservatives in Canada and the Labour Party in Britain both distrusted the bureaucracy they inherited from their predecessors. Prime Minister Diefenbaker in Canada viewed the civil service as inefficient and too close to the Liberals who had ruled the country for almost thirty consecutive years. In Britain, Prime Minister Wilson saw the bureaucracy as an elitist institution made of 'Oxbridge' graduates who, because of their class origins, were expected to be hostile to the policies of a socialist

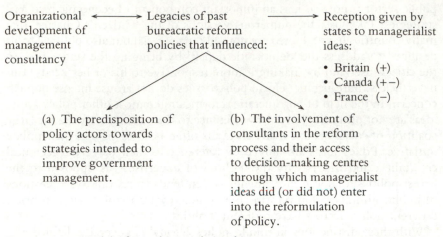

Organizational ⟷ Legacies of past ⟶ Reception given by
development of bureacratic reform states to managerialist
management policies that influenced: ideas:
consultancy

• Britain (+)
• Canada (+−)
• France (−)

(a) The predisposition of　　　　　　(b) The involvement of
policy actors towards　　　　　　　　consultants in the reform
strategies intended to　　　　　　　　process and their access
improve government　　　　　　　　　to decision-making centres
management.　　　　　　　　　　　　through which managerialist
　　　　　　　　　　　　　　　　　　ideas did (or did not) enter
　　　　　　　　　　　　　　　　　　into the reformulation
　　　　　　　　　　　　　　　　　　of policy.

FIGURE 1.2. Model of causal interrelationships

government. In reaction against the administrative and recruitment policies that their predecessors had adopted and which, in their view, had made the civil service either 'inefficient' or 'elitist', Diefenbaker and Wilson set up, soon after their election, public commissions to reform the administration of government. The two commissions (Glassco in Canada and Fulton in Britain) saw the need to learn from the private sector in order to rationalize the management of the state. Both Glassco and Fulton recommended that private sector consultants be brought into the civil service as a way to internalize their knowledge of business management within state structures. In Canada, Glassco argued that consultants would help bring some order in the financial management of the state, while in Britain, consultants were part of the new group of middle-class experts that the Labour government sought to promote as a way to abolish the 'amateur' model that the 'Oxbridge' bureaucrats were believed to have imposed on the British civil service. Fulton and Glassco were able to recommend the appointment of outside consultants because there existed at that time, in both Britain and Canada, a management consulting industry that was beginning to grow and to become more organizationally developed. As a result of Fulton and Glassco, British and Canadian consultants were given an institutional and professional hold on bureaucratic reform policy issues and it is in these two countries that managerialist ideas subsequently made their fastest inroads into policy. As we shall see later, the 'politics' of how consultants entered state institutions and of how their ideas about government management influenced policy was, of course, more complex than this. But these examples at least highlight a key aspect of our model, which is that there exists a close relationship between the development of a given field of social knowledge—in our case management consultancy—and the openness of state institutions to the use of that knowledge. To make a simple analogy, this relationship is to some extent similar to the dynamics of supply and demand in the economy: 'supply' understood in terms of the organizational development of management consultancy and 'demand' as the state's need for managerial knowledge. Whether supply drives demand or vice versa is an empirical question but what we know is that the two go together and need to be studied in a *relational way*.

What about the French case? Managerialist ideas penetrated only slowly in France, where management consulting is much less developed than in Britain and Canada, and where the legacies left by post-war reforms (the creation of the École Nationale d'Administration) made the civil service more impermeable to policy advice generated outside the state. In France the ÉNA is the central source of expertise for policy makers in the field of administrative reform. In Britain and Canada, there is no comparable institution. In this institutional vacuum, business consultants have become since the 1960s an increasingly important source of management expertise for policy makers. By comparison, French consultants began to play a role in the process of administrative reform only in the 1980s; first in local governments following the 1982 decentralization, and then in the central administration at the same time that the management consulting industry became stronger as a result of state initiatives designed to stimulate its development.

Method of analysis: Mill's two comparative logics

Britain, Canada, and France were selected as case studies to examine the relationship between the role of management consultants in the bureaucratic reform policy process and the reception given by states to managerialist ideas for two main reasons. First, we saw earlier that the wide-ranging programmes of bureaucratic reforms introduced since the end of the 1980s in these three countries have all more or less been influenced by managerialist ideas. Secondly, it was also noted that there existed a comparable trend where, in the process of developing and implementing bureaucratic reform policies, British, Canadian, and French public administrators have been encouraged to use the services of management consultants.

Britain, Canada, and France thus all have in common the phenomenon that this study is trying to explain (the presence of managerialist ideas) and there is evidence suggesting that the three cases also have in common one of the hypothesized causal factors (the presence of management consultants). At first glance, the three cases look as if they could be investigated by using Mill's 'Method of Agreement'. However, although Britain, Canada, and France may all have in common the phenomenon to be explained, there are variations in the character or in the intensity of the phenomenon because there are differences in the reception given by each state to managerialist ideas, and these differences are especially noticeable in the French case. In

France, managerialist ideas are not absent but they are not as influential as in Britain and Canada. Furthermore, the 'form' of one of the hypothesized causal factors (the presence of management consultants) is also different in France. While in the early 1990s both Britain and Canada took steps to encourage the use of private sector consultants, the French state internalized the management consulting function.

Because of these differences, I use France as a contrast to the British and Canadian cases because in terms of the 'presence of managerialist ideas' and the 'presence of management consultants', there is less difference between the British and Canadian cases than there is between these two countries and France. Mill labelled this procedure the 'Method of Difference'. Taken alone, it is a more powerful method than the 'Method of Agreement' for attempting to establish valid causal links (Skocpol and Somers, 1994: 81). The major point of contrast between the methods of 'Agreement' and 'Difference' is that the latter uses negative instances to reinforce conclusions drawn from positive instances (Ragin, 1987; Tilly, 1984). The method of analysis used in this study will therefore combine Mill's two comparative logics. This will be done by using Britain and Canada as 'positive' or similar cases with the French case used as a contrast.

Without entering immediately into a detailed discussion of the specific characteristics of each of the three cases, suffice it to say for the moment that differences between Britain and Canada in the acceptance of managerialist ideas and policies have not primarily been caused by differences in the strength of their management consulting industry. Although both Britain and Canada have a well-developed management consulting industry, managerialist ideas in the two countries have not been equally influential. In Britain, managerialist ideas have been embraced more enthusiastically than in Canada because of differences in policy legacies and the access of management consultants to decision-making centres. In Britain, management consulting interests under Thatcher were institutionalized in the Prime Minister's and Cabinet Offices, where they had direct access to decision-making centres and where their ideas received strong government support. By contrast, the primary entry point of consultants to the Canadian state since the 1970s has been in the Office of the Auditor General (OAG). As a result, their access to decision-making centres and their influence on policy are more limited than in Britain, because the OAG is attached to the legislature and thus separated from the executive.

As for the French negative case, there is less of a 'story' to tell concerning the relationship between managerialism and the role of consultants in the bureaucratic reform policy process. Because the organizational development of management consultancy in France is at a much earlier stage than in the two other cases, and because of the post-war legacy of statism, managerialism penetrated French state institutions later than in Britain and Canada. Unlike their British and Canadian counterparts, French consultants did not start to become involved in the process of administrative reform in the 1960s, but only after the 1982 decentralization, when the ideas that they first advocated in local governments later spread into the central administration. However, managerialist ideas did not take hold in the central administration as much as they did in local governments. Senior civil servants in the central administration resisted the managerialist solutions advocated by consultants and, as a result, the French state decided in 1990 to create its own internal management consulting services.

Plan of the book

This study relies on several types of evidence. To evaluate the organizational development of management consultancy I have primarily used data pertaining, for instance, to the size of the management consulting market and the size of membership of management consulting associations. Since the role of management consultants in the process of bureaucratic reform is a topic for which there exist no serious studies, I have relied on primary sources from the state agencies that have jurisdiction over bureaucratic reform policy issues and from the records of management consulting organizations (professional and business associations as well as individual firms) in London, Paris, and Toronto. I also conducted interviews with civil servants and management consultants involved in the process of bureaucratic reform. When available, I have used quantitative evidence (e.g. public expenditure) to measure the importance over time of the participation of consultants in government administration.

This book is divided into six chapters. Chapter 2 examines the history and structure of the management consulting industry and profession in Britain, Canada, and France. A major finding of this chapter is that management consulting has become an important industry in those countries where it has developed as the extension of the institutionalized relationship that accounting firms have historically established with their audit clients. Chapters 3, 4, and 5 consist of a retrospective examination of the history of bureaucratic reform since the period of 'rationalism' and the 'old' managerialism, beginning with the introduction of the British, French, and Canadian versions of PPBS in the early 1960s up to the early 1990s and the period of the 'new' managerialism. The purpose of these three chapters is not to analyse in great detail all the particular aspects of the recent history of administrative reform. Rather, the intent is to examine whether past bureaucratic reform experiences have left legacies that influenced the predisposition of key policy actors involved in the reform process and affected the access of consultants to decision-making centres. Chapter 6 turns to a comparison and interpretation of the observations and findings made in the previous chapters and discusses the implications of this book.

The management consulting industry: History and structure

In trying to explain differences in the reception given by states to manager-ialist ideas, this study relies on a two-step causal model. The first and the more 'structural' or 'society-centric' step focuses on the development of mod-ern management consultancy. The second and more 'state centric' looks at the legacies of past bureaucratic reform initiatives and how these affected both the predisposition of policy actors towards administrative modern-ization strategies and the access of consultants to decision-making centres. But before we look at the role of management consultants in the history of bureaucratic restructuring since the period of the 'old' managerialism in the 1960s, our first task is to study the organization of management consultancy in each of the three countries. Obviously, the mere existence and degree of development of management consultancy is likely to affect the extent to which states can use the services of management consultants in reforming their bureaucracies. Although in the 1980s it may have seemed 'normal' or 'logical' for policy makers to call on management consultants to help them reform their bureaucracy to deal with the consequences of the fiscal crisis or global economic restructuring, the possibilities for doing so depended on the presence of a consulting industry, its maturity, size, and reputation. Reputation is crucial to the extent that public policies generally need input from recognized experts if they are to be regarded as credible (Margolis, 1973; Larson, 1984). It is one thing to argue that it is 'the widely acknowledged expertise of consultants' that makes it legitimate for governments to use their services (Martin, 1998: 1). But it is quite another to ask the question of how expertise is constructed and acquired. The recognition of expertise is some-thing that becomes established in society at large through processes that are largely social, cultural, and political in character. The following pages show how both business and the state played a key role in the social and institutional construction of management consulting expertise.

This chapter examines the history, structure, and growth of the manage-ment consulting industry, both globally and with respect to each country. It begins by providing a definition of management consulting and a brief sketch of the current world market for consulting services. This is followed by a discussion of the origins of management consulting, from the creation of the first consulting firms in the United States at the turn of the century to the entry of the large international accounting firms in the 1960s. These firms, today known as the 'Big Five', dominate the world management consulting market. The second part of the chapter analyses the emergence and growth of modern management consultancy in Britain, Canada, and France. In making this analysis, I borrow the concept of 'organizational development' from the works of policy network analysts to shed some light on the internal organization and structure of the management consulting sector (Atkinson and Coleman, 1989; Coleman and Skogstad, 1990; Grant, 1987; Wilks and Wright, 1987). Organizational development can be broadly defined as the degree to which the organizations of private actors within a given policy sector are well resourced, formalized, mature, autonomous from state direction, and capable of providing specialized and policy-relevant knowledge. It is a concept which assumes that there is an almost reciprocal link between the extent to which societal interests can participate in the policy process and have their ideas come to the attention of those who make policy, and their level of organizational sophistication.

One key element that needs to be taken into account when studying the organizational development of management consultancy is the extent to which the services of consultants are used by the business sector. This is an important factor because, historically, it is the production needs of the private sector, and especially the growth of the large modern business enterprise, that first instigated the creation and development of management consulting (Chandler, 1977: 468). Although the state has become since the 1980s an increasing source of income for consultants, the private sector still provides around 80 per cent of the total revenues of the global management consulting industry (Wooldridge, 1997: 5). Consultants are first and foremost specialists in business management and this is why policy makers have used their services to help them develop administrative policies that sought to make the management of the state more business-like (McKenna, 1996). This means that the possibilities for consultants to enter the state and form what can be termed a 'managerialist policy network' with those agencies that have jurisdiction over bureaucratic reform policy partly depends on how much their services are used by the private sector. When the use of consulting services by businesses is not a relatively widespread practice, this affects the level of knowledge that consultants have of private sector management and their ability to be seen by policy makers as 'experts' who could improve the efficiency of the state by transplanting and adapting business management ideas and techniques in the public sector.

In this sense, 'business' or the 'private sector' is an institution that *mediates* the relationship between management consultants and bureaucratic reformers in government. Business is a mediating institution that plays a 'social legitimation' role *vis-à-vis* management consultancy (Alvarez, 1996; 1998). The passage through the private sector—in terms of making consultants more knowledgeable about business administration—makes management consultancy more relevant in the eyes of policy makers in government who want to make the functioning of the state more business-like. It is important to stress the legitimating role of business in the social construction of management consulting expertise particularly because management consultancy is not a real profession. Unlike other fields of social scientific knowledge, the credibility or relevance of management consulting is not established through professionalization processes: the existence of professional associations that would license—on behalf of the state—as competent only those who have the proper qualifications. There are long-established prejudices against consultants in general (Roberts, 1996a: 77). Management consultants are often regarded with 'mistrust and suspicion' (Davidson, 1972). Their claims to authority are often disputed and this has a major impact on whether their ideas and advice will be taken seriously and adopted by managers in the private sector or policy makers in government. In the absence of a real professional status that would help consultants to deal with the credibility problem they often face, the social legitimation role of business becomes crucial in establishing the relative authority of management consultancy. It is essentially through the consumption of their services by administrators in the private sector that management consultants can establish the relevance of their knowledge. To put it simply, if business people in the private sector—and especially the large and organizationally complex firms that are more comparable to government organizations—often use management consulting knowledge to reform their management structures and processes, reformers in government are more likely to find the consultants' claim to expertise more credible and to think that consultants have the right to speak more or less authoritatively on the subject of management reform, particularly in the case of reform that seeks to make the administration of government more business-like.

As we shall see, British and Canadian business managers consume more consulting services than their French counterparts and as a result, management consultancy is much more developed in Britain and Canada than in France. In Britain and Canada—but not in France—management consultancy has been developed as the extension of the institutionalized relationship that accounting firms have historically established with their audit clients. In these two countries, management consulting started to grow in the 1960s when accountants moved into consultancy. In Britain and Canada, the development of the accounting profession is closely linked to the history of the British colonial empire, in that UK accountants, following the trail of UK investment in the colonies, started to set up offices and create professional associations of accountants in North America towards the end of the nineteenth century. Today, there are approximately 167,000 professional accountants in Britain and about 85,000 in Canada. In Britain and Canada, the accounting professions are wholly self-regulating bodies which do not prohibit their members from providing management consulting services to their audit clients. By comparison, there are only 21,000 accountants in France and their first professional associations were created only fifty years ago. There are fewer accountants in France because of historical patterns of industrial and corporate development (i.e the prevalence of small and medium-sized family-owned businesses). In France, the accounting profession is placed under the authority of the state and French accountants are legally restricted from performing management consulting work for their audit clients. Thus, in moving into consultancy, British and Canadian accountants have had a key organizational advantage over their French counterparts because they have been able to use their existing audit client contacts as a platform on which to build their management consulting businesses.

If the status of those who advocate ideas in the public policy process is important in determining whether an idea will appeal to policy makers, the historical and institutional link with accountancy—which enhanced the social prestige and professional reputation of management consulting— then becomes a key variable in understanding the possibilities for consultants to sponsor managerialist ideas that can enter into the formulation of bureaucratic reform policy.

The boundaries of management consulting

In part because it is a young and diverse industry, it is important to be aware that there is not much published information on the topic of management consulting (Kubr, 1993). Very few practitioners and academics have written about it (Peet, 1988: 4). Management consulting is also a very secretive industry. Management consulting firms rarely reveal the names of their clients, although recently, partially in reaction to growing competition, large firms have asked and received clients' permission to advertise some of their major assignments. Most management consulting firms are private partnerships, meaning that all are owned by the firm's senior executives, which also means that none of the firms is required to report its profits (Kepos, 1994: 198). The materials they publish about themselves are generally intended to improve their public relations and contain very little quantitative financial data. As noted in a United Nations survey of the management consulting industry and its largest firms, reliable figures on revenues, and especially on profits or market share, are difficult to obtain (United Nations, 1993: 2). And when they can be obtained, various inconsistencies sometimes exist because management consulting is defined in many different ways and its boundaries are unclear (Wilkinson, 1986).

In 1986, the International Labour Office (ILO) in Geneva identified the main features of management consulting (Kubr, 1986). First, consulting is an independent service provided to a range of different clients. The management consultant is detached from the employing organization and is urged to retain a degree of objectivity. Secondly, consulting is an advisory service. The management consultant's recommendations do not have to be implemented; they give an account of the problems that are perceived to exist and then provide advice. Thirdly, management consulting is a knowledge-based activity, providing ideas and skills which are applicable to problems of management. The ILO definition (used in this study) includes strategy advisers, management information systems (MIS) consultants, accounting firms, and human resource specialists. It excludes head-hunters and public relations advisers since they do not deal with mainstream management problems. It also does not cover consultancy services such as engineering consulting or technological, scientific, and legal services.

Business or profession?

Management consultants are part of new occupations, their bodies of knowledge undefined and their claims to authority often disputed. They have been variously defined as consisting of people in the knowledge industry or as technocrats dealing with the production and distribution of non-material goods and services (Kellner and Heuberger, 1992). Unlike that for the older or liberal professions, in most countries the market for management consultants is almost unregulated; an affiliation with some governing association is not mandatory to conduct business and management consultants do not need to be licensed (United Nations, 1993: 1). This is why management consultancy is often seen as a 'quasi-profession' (Aucoin, 1995: 68). There are low barriers to entry to the management consulting industry: anyone can hang out a shingle bearing the title 'Management Consultant' (Pal, 1992: 72). Qualifications are thus not easy to determine.

   In many countries, including those studied in this book, there have been some developments towards certification where management consulting institutes or associations establish and apply admission criteria indicative of their members' competence (Kubr, 1986: 104). Certification is seen by many practitioners as a step towards recognition of management consulting as a true profession (Kinard, 1986). However, some argue that certification cannot really guarantee anything more than the application of a few general and rather elementary criteria of admission to the practice (Moore, 1984). The product management consultants sell is ideas, and because ideas are intangible it is difficult to establish objective means for certifying the competence of consultants and the quality of their services (Clark, 1995). Certification cannot show whether a consultant is actually suitable for a complex job, and after all, the argument continues, consulting to management is a business and if a consultant finds enough clients, his or her service is regarded as technically valid by those clients (Klein, 1977). This reflects the ongoing and unresolved controversy among firms and practitioners as to whether management consulting is really a business or a profession (Tisdall, 1982: 78).

Over the years, management consultants have followed different strategies in trying to validate their knowledge base. Historically, management consultancy first tried to establish its authority by claiming that management was a 'science' (Roberts, 1996a). Claims to scientific status were particularly strong among early management theorists such as Taylor, with his 'scientific management' approach. Taylor—who is regarded as the founding father of management consultancy in the United States—sought to buttress the authority of management with the claim of its being 'scientific'. He thereby capitalized on the achievements of natural sciences in the nineteenth century (Banta, 1993). Taylor's approach was also legitimated through state sponsorship. In the United States, 'scientific management' took shape in close interaction with early American attempts to build a new administrative state (Haber, 1964; Skowronek, 1982). Management's claims to objectivity and scientific status, although still present, have become less predominant (Scott, 1992). Over the years, research has shown the ideological and normative basis of management and today, it is more often seen as 'an art not a science' (Mintzberg, 1973: 174). Nowadays, the processes by which the authority or credibility of management consultancy is being established are to a large extent commercial in nature. As an industry, management consulting is made up of profit-based organizations and the knowledge and ideas that these organizations generate are first and foremost intended to increase revenues. As a business, the ideas of management consultants become valid and relevant when they are used and bought by an increasing number of consumers. To put it simply, the ideas that consultants sell are perceived as being 'good' or useful when more and more people buy them. This was the case in the 1980s when consultancy became a major growth industry (Golembiewski, 1993).

The world market for management consulting

In the last half of the 1980s the management consulting market in Europe and North America grew at a rate between 25 and 30 per cent a year (Rassam and Oates, 1991: 1). Rapid change in information technology, downsizing, and outsourcing created perfect conditions for consultancy-fee income to increase in the 1980s.

In 1995 the size of the world market for management consulting services was estimated at $US40 billion and was expected to exceed $98 billion in 1999 (Kennedy Research Group, 1999). The United States is by far the largest market for management consulting services in the world. The importance of the US market is highlighted in Table 2.1.

The rapid growth of the 1980s has been accompanied by increasing concentration, with the world's 40 largest management consulting firms accounting for approximately 60 per cent of the world market in 1991. During the 1980s, many of the large international management consulting firms grew by 30 per cent annually (United Nations, 1993: 12). Transnational

TABLE 2.1. Global management consulting markets by revenue share, 1995

Region	Share (%)
USA	52
Canada	6
Europe	32
Asia	7
Latin America	2
Rest of the World	1
Total value	$US40 billion

Source: Industry Canada, 1997, *Key Points About the Management Consulting Industry*. Retrieved from the Internet: http://info.ic.gc.ca/ic-data. See the 'Strategis' programme.

corporations based in the United States strongly dominate the management consulting industry in most countries and most major international consulting practices have their head offices in North America. Although several European-controlled firms operate in the North American market, few have made significant inroads.

The global management consulting market consists of large transnational and independent firms, but also of certified public accountants and thousands of freelance practitioners, as well as business-school professors and in-house consultants (Barcus and Wilkinson, 1986).

As Figure 2.1 indicates, in the European Union in 1992, Britain was the first and France the third (after Germany) most important market for

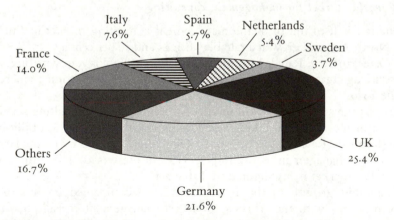

FIGURE 2.1. The Western European management consulting market

Source: *Financial Times*, Survey: Management Consultancy, Section IV, 21 October 1992, p. 2. Reproduced with permission.

management consulting services. The British management consulting market is nearly twice as large as that of France (25.5 as against 14 per cent). A 1999 survey of the European management consulting market, conducted by the European Federation of Management Consulting Associations, shows that the situation described by Figure 2.1 has not changed, and that Britain and Germany are still the leaders in Europe. According to the survey, 'The UK and Germany continue to earn a higher proportion of the overall revenues than their share of European GDP would suggest, indicating that these are mature markets for consultancy. For France, Italy and Spain, the revenues remain disproportionately smaller' (FEACO, 1999a: 1).

The American origins

Management consulting has both an accounting and an engineering background and, historically, there has always been some animosity between the two professions in their attempts at controlling the development of consultancy (Jeans, 1993; Wilkinson, 1986). It was in the United States that modern management consulting was first developed (McKenna, 1995). In the United States, management consulting had its origins in engineering and time-and-motion studies and was first concerned with issues such as employee output, machine efficiency, and factory productivity. Management consulting began around the turn of the century with Frederick Taylor and his 'scientific management' approach to the work process (Pattenaude, 1979: 203). None of the early American practitioners described themselves as management consultants; they were usually known as 'industrial engineers'.[1] Most of their work related to work-method improvements in factories. They were mainly interested in exploring new methods for saving resources. They believed that one could define a universal set of management rules, principles, and activities.

The first management consulting firms emerged in the United States with the creation of Arthur D. Little in 1886, Booz Allen in 1914, and McKinsey in 1926. As has been noted, 'American practice in the 1920s was also influential outside the USA, most noticeably in the UK' (Rassam and Oates, 1991: 3). The creation in the 1920s of Urwick Orr (one of the first and most important consulting firms in Britain) was inspired by the early industrial engineering work of Taylor (Rassam and Oates, 1991: 3–4). American practitioners also brought their experience of consulting over to Britain, and sometimes founded their own firms (Kipping, 1996). One such firm was Bedeaux Consulting which later spawned major firms in Britain

---

[1] In the United States, industrial engineering firms created the first association of management consultants in the world. Founded in 1929, the Association of Consulting Management Engineers (ACME) did not begin to admit to membership the management consulting arms of accounting firms until 1982 (Mellett, 1988: 7).

such as PE Consultants in 1934 and the PA Consulting Group in 1943. Today, these firms are among the top 10 management consultancies in Britain.

Although the early years of management consulting were relatively success-ful, with several firms emerging both in North America and in Western Europe, consultants were often viewed with scepticism (Mellett, 1988: 3). In the 1930s it was considered a disgrace for a company president to hire a management consultant. It was an admission that s/he did not know how to run a business. A business employing management consultants appeared weak or sick in the eyes of its competitors, shareholders, and customers. Similarly, management consulting was often perceived as a threat by employees, who believed that companies only employed consultants when they had difficulties. Furthermore, consultants had to deal with the bad reputation the industry began to earn in the 1940s and 1950s because of incompetent or fraudulent practitioners.[2] As a result, management con-sultants became known 'as people who borrowed your watch to the tell you the time and then walk off with it' (Townsend, 1971: 89). The negative reputation of management consulting as a field of activity 'attractive to charlatans and quacks who preyed upon the gullible' started to hit the consultancy companies in their balance sheets (Mellett, 1988: 5). Thus, in the 1960s began the quest for professional recognition which coincided with the entry of accountants into the management consulting field.

The entry of accounting firms into management consulting

The entry of major accounting firms into management consulting was one of the main developments to take place in the 1960s. Management consult-ancy really started to establish itself as a multi-billion-dollar industry and as a professional body selling expertise in the 1960s when the large inter-national accounting firms started to move into consulting (Arnstein, 1967). In the 1960s, the growth of audit work had slowed and accounting firms were looking for new fields. Faced with intense competition and low pro-spects for growth in the marginally profitable mature tax and audit sectors, the international accounting firms attempted to expand their services into management consulting (Higdon, 1969: ch. 13). These firms, which were then known as the 'Big Eight', included: Arthur Andersen, Coopers & Lybrand, Ernst & Whinney, Arthur Young, KPMG Peat Marwick, Deloitte, Haskins & Sells, Touche Ross, and Price Waterhouse. Although these firms are now all American owned, most of them were originally British and

---

[2] The reputation of management consulting suffered from the activities of a number of unqualified and unscrupulous practitioners. For instance, a 1953 *Fortune* article reported that the management consulting firm, George S. May of Chicago, encouraged its employees 'to overstate the size of the savings possible by its methods and to overstate the time really needed to accomplish such savings' (quoted in Mellett, 1988: 5).

TABLE 2.2. Revenues of the Big Eight firms, consolidated data, world-wide ($USm.)

	Tax, accounting, and audit		Management consulting	
	1983	*1988*	*1983*	*1988*
Arthur Andersen	909 (74%)	1,692 (60%)	329 (26%)	1,128 (40%)
Coopers & Lybrand	n/a			
Ernst & Whinney	836 (86%)	1,708 (78%)	136 (14%)	482 (22%)
Arthur Young	903 (90%)	1,642 (80%)	100 (10%)	410 (20%)
KPMG Peat Marwick	2,011 (91%)	3,330 (86%)	218 (9%)	570 (14%)
Deloitte, Haskins & Sells	851 (91%)	1,652 (86%)	84 (9%)	269 (14%)
Touche Ross	806 (89%)	1,509 (82%)	98 (11%)	331 (18%)
Price Waterhouse	901 (90%)	1,623 (81%)	111 (10%)	386 (19%)

n/a: data are unavailable for Coopers & Lybrand.

Source: Moody's Investors Service and United Nations Centre on Transnational Corporations, 1990, *Directory of the World's Largest Service Companies*.

emerged during the mid-nineteenth century when British accountants, following the trail of investment from the City, established offices in North America (Hussein and Ketz, 1980).

In moving into management consulting, accountants improved its image considerably. Accountants brought with them a certain aura of respectability, seriousness, and professionalism (Mellett, 1988: 6). Unlike that of the efficiency measurers or the industrial engineers, the involvement of accountants in management consulting was not seen as that of an 'intruder or snoop' in the operations of a company, since accountants had already developed an organized relationship with their audit clients (Mellett, 1988: 5). In addition, the capital that the large accounting firms provided, along with their international reputation, was a key factor in the rapid growth of their management consulting divisions. As the auditors to blue chip North American and European businesses and industries, many of the Big Eight firms had earned a reputation for being the world's premier accountants. The prestige accompanying this reputation helped the Big Eight to become the world leaders in management consulting services (Hanlon, 1994).

Although most of them had started to enter management consulting in the 1960s, it was in the 1980s that consulting became as important as auditing for many big accounting firms. As Table 2.2 shows, during the 1980s management consulting revenues grew from 9 per cent to 40 per cent (depending on the firm) of Big Eight revenues. During that period, losses in audit and accounting revenues were compensated by increases in management consulting fee income.

TABLE 2.3. The world's 10 largest management consulting firms, 1994 ($USm.)

Rank	Firm	Consulting revenues*
1	Arthur Andersen & Co.	4,285
2	McKinsey	1,500
3	Ernst & Young	1,181
4	Deloitte Touche	1,061
5	Coopers & Lybrand	1,049
6	Booz-Allen	950
7	Mercer Consulting	933
8	KPMG Peat Marwick	875
9	Towers Perrin	766
10	Price Waterhouse	755
Total Big Six		9.206 bn.
Total Top 10 Firms		13.355 bn.
Total World Market		33.000 bn.

* This amount excludes accounting revenues.

Note: Arthur Andersen & Co. (or Andersen Worldwide) comprises two separate units, Andersen Consulting and Arthur Andersen (Burke, 1995: 11). In 1989, following a series of lawsuits, the big accounting firm Arthur Andersen decided to separate its management consulting activities from its accounting work by creating Andersen Consulting. But the accountants in Arthur Andersen still sell management consulting services to their clients, meaning that there is some overlap between the activities of the two halves of Arthur Andersen & Co. (*The Economist*, 1997: 64). This is why the amount showed in Table 2.3 includes the management consulting revenues of both Arthur Andersen and Andersen Consulting.

Source: *Management Consultants International*, June 1995, p. 11; and *The Economist*, 1997, Survey of Management Consultancy, 22 March, p. 4.

In 1989, following the megamergers uniting Ernst & Whinney with Arthur Young and Touche Ross with Deloitte, Haskins and Sells, the oligolopoly of the Big Eight was reduced to six firms. In another round of mergers in 1998, the Big Six were reduced to five with the fusion of Price Waterhouse and Coopers & Lybrand. Well before these mergers took place, some commentators were already suggesting that management consulting was becoming 'a highly concentrated industry' (Peet, 1988: 7). The Big Six (now five) operate within international networks which are essentially an affiliation of independent firms. They emerged during the twentieth century as behemoth professional firms with nearly ten thousand partners among them and aggregate revenues in 1991 of nearly $US30 billion world-wide (*The Economist*, 1992: 19). As illustrated in Table 2.3, in 1994 the top 10 management consulting companies in the world shared 40 per cent of the world market. These dominant firms are all American. In 1994 the Big Six alone controlled around 28 per cent of the world management consulting market. More recent data indicate that the large accounting firms, together, still share more than a quarter of the world market management consulting revenues (Rassam, 1998: 18). The top largest consultancies also include non-accounting firms such as McKinsey, Mercer, Towers Perrin, and Booz-Allen. Unlike the accounting firms, which specialize in financial management and in management information systems (MIS) consulting, these companies specialize in management/strategy consulting and are generally referred to as the 'strategy consultancies' (Collis, 1994). Their practices focus on business strategy, diversification strategies, human resources consulting, logistics, and so forth.

When the accountants arrived in consulting in the 1960s, they had an organizational advantage over existing consultants. This was their long familiarity with audit clients. In order to be competitive and be able to maintain their share of the market in the face of the Big Five, the strategy consultancies have increasingly been involved in the last twenty years in research and development and in the production of new management ideas and theories. Whereas the Big Five's comparative advantage lies in the relationship with their audit clients, that of the strategy consultancies lies in their research and marketing capacities. As discussed next, the ideas that increasingly came to influence the management practices of several states during the 1980s were often produced and marketized by the strategy consultancies.

The strategy consultancies and the production of management ideas

It is estimated that large strategy consultancies such as McKinsey spend $US50 to $US100 million a year on research. McKinsey also publishes a review (the *McKinsey Quarterly*), and has produced 54 books on management since 1980 (*The Economist*, 1995: 57). The most famous book produced by two management consultants from McKinsey is the best-selling *In Search of Excellence* by Peters and Waterman (1982). This book, which sold more than five million copies, has been described as one of the 'most influential' sources of ideas in the development of the new managerialism in public administration (Aucoin, 1990: 117). Similarly, in studying the origins of managerialism in Britain, Pollitt found that

in the mid-1980s, notions of excellence drawn from Peters and Waterman's *In Search of Excellence* became a very popular component of seminars and conferences for managers in the U.K. state sector. Subsequently, the public services served as test beds for a series of management techniques drawn from U.S. private sector practice, including performance-related pay, total quality management (TQM), benchmarking, and most recently, re-engineering. (1996: 84–5)

For large consultancies such as McKinsey, Booz Allen, Gemini, and Arthur D. Little, one of the key instruments for disseminating ideas is the publication of articles or books, which has become a favoured marketing tactic in the firms' attempts to increase their share of the market (Dwyer and

Harding, 1996). The book is a tool of the consultant. As one can read in a 'how to' manual on management consultancy, 'a book can create wide exposure, immediate credibility and generate revenue' (Blumberg, 1994: 46). For instance, since its publication in 1993, *Re-Engineering the Corporation* by Champy and Hammer has sold nearly two million copies world-wide. Subsequently, the management consulting firm that employed the two authors increased its annual revenues from $US70 million in the year preceding publication, to more than $160 million the year after (*The Economist*, 1995: 57).

Organizational sociologists interested in the study of management innovations have argued that management consulting firms are 'fashion-setting organizations' whose missions involved the creation and/or dissemination of new administrative ideas and models (Abrahamson, 1991; Hirsch, 1972). This research shows that new administrative ideas do not become fashionable by direct popular demand but that 'fashion setters', such as consulting firms and business mass media, play active roles in developing organizations' awareness and tastes for these models in order to render them fashionable and to prompt their diffusion (Blumer, 1969). Abrahamson suggested that business schools and consulting firms, because of their expertise, dominate in the selection of fashionable management models (1986). Many of the consultancies that are part of the 'strategy' category are keen to be seen at the forefront of management thinking. Some firms have formed alliances with business schools by sponsoring research on issues such as the future shape of companies or the changing role of the chief executive (Wooldridge, 1997: 17). Consultants are often seen as the conduit between the business schools and the business world. It is largely the management consultants who transfer new ideas from the academic world out to the commercial one. This is especially true of the American-owned consultancies (McKinsey, Boston Consulting Group, etc.) which have always had strong links with the leading US business schools (Rassam and Oates, 1991: 23).

In the search for new, ground-breaking ideas, consultancies offer their brightest consultants time to write books, and then the firms throw the full weight of their marketing divisions behind the final products. Consultancies arrange for such books to be serialized in magazines, advertised in newspapers, and endorsed by well-known business persons or even by the President of the United States. On the front cover of Osborne and Gaebler's *Reinventing Government* (1992), a best-seller written by two management consultants, there is a quotation from Bill Clinton saying that this book 'should be read by every elected official in America'. *Reinventing Government* has been a major source of new managerialist ideas across the Western world in the 1990s, with Osborne and Gaebler giving speeches to senior government officials in places such as Ottawa and London (Kamensky, 1996).

A common practice among the strategy consultancies, and increasingly also among the accounting firms, is to buy large quantities of books written by their employees to pass along to clients as 'gifts'.[3] This practice provides consulting firms with a means by which they can have their ideas come to the attention of those they want to influence. For example, in 1991 Coopers & Lybrand published *Excellence in Government*, which advocated the application of Total Quality Management (TQM) ideas (first developed in business) to the American government. In the introduction, the authors wrote that

We hope this book will help promote TQM in government, because we see it as the best way to improve public services . . . To this end we are giving copies of *Excellence in Government* to Members of Congress, the President, federal cabinet secretaries, the heads of major independent agencies, and the governors of all states . . . We address the last chapter of the book to them: they must lead the way to government excellence. (Carr and Littman, 1991: 1)

The accountants' organizational advantage

Since the 1980s, the big accounting firms have climbed up to the top of the list of large companies that dominate the world's management consulting market. This has happened essentially because the accounting firms had an immediate advantage over management consultant competitors since they had long familiarity with their audit clients, many of whom found it convenient to buy both audit and management consulting services from the same company. Possession of the audit contract enhances the possibility for the accounting firm of attracting further work from the client, for two main reasons (Ridyard and de Bolle, 1992: 65). First, the accountant is likely to have a cost advantage over his or her competitors for the management consulting business originating from the audit client firm. Execution of the audit involves the accounting firm in developing a significant body of inside knowledge about the client's business. Consequently, for management consultancy projects which require the consultant to acquire such knowledge, the accountant clearly enters any competition with other consultants with an in-built advantage. This advantage applies mainly to those areas of management consulting for which the accounting firm can use the same personnel to conduct both the audit and the consultancy projects. The need to duplicate learning costs is thus avoided, and the accounting firm can pass some of the savings along to the client. In addition to the learning cost advantage, the long-term nature of the relationship between the accounting firm

---

[3] However, that practice raised a number of questions in 1995 when it was discovered that *The Discipline of Market Leaders* by Treacy and Wiersema (1993), had been artificially maintained on the *New York Times* best-seller list for 15 weeks because its authors, associated with the consulting firm CSC (the twelfth-largest management consulting firm in the world), had bought tens of thousands of copies of their book in small bookshops all around the United States, particularly in those thought to be monitored by the *New York Times*. In addition, many other copies (between 30,000 and 40,000) were bought by third parties who were reimbursed by CSC (*The Economist*, 1995: 57).

TABLE 2.4. Big Six presence by country, 1989

	Britain		Canada		France	
	Offices	Partners	Offices	Partners	Offices	Partners
Arthur Andersen	14	125	8	50	3	40
Coopers & Lybrand	41	365	24	245	14	58
Ernst & Young	48	469	96	931	11	94
KPMG	59	506	28	257	28	596
Deloitte Touche	n/a					
Price Waterhouse	23	364	24	242	12	48

n/a: data not available for Deloitte Touche.

Source: Moody's Investors Service and United Nations Centre on Transnational Corporations, 1990, *Directory of the World's Largest Service Companies.*

and its audit clients confers a 'reputation' effect which means that the client may be more likely to use the known firm for consulting work than to risk giving the contract to an outside firm of which it has no direct experience.

Thus, in moving into management consulting, accountants had a head start since they already knew their audit clients and were party to their business secrets. At the same time, however, they faced potential conflicts of interests between their roles as certified public accountant and management consultant. An accountant may feel he or she cannot comment on a management information system installed by a consultant employed by the same firm. Accountants argue that the proportion of 'dual' clients is exaggerated: some estimate that fewer than a quarter of their consulting clients are also their audit clients (Peet, 1988: 9). A 1991 survey of public accounting by Industry, Science and Technology Canada indicates, however, that 30 per cent of the consultancy clients of the large international accounting firms are also their audit clients (ISTC, 1991b: 4). A survey done for the European Union shows that in Britain, 35 per cent of the big accounting firms are dependent on their audit clients for consulting and other non-audit incomes, while 'dependence on audit clients for such income appears to be the lowest in France' (Ridyard and de Bolle, 1992: 70). In France, this situation is due to the fact that the independence restrictions imposed by the state on accountants are stricter than in Britain and Canada.

And partly because of these legal restrictions, as Table 2.4 shows, in terms of the number of offices and partners, the big accounting firms have a much greater presence in Britain and Canada than in France. In 1989, they had only 68 offices in France as compared to 185 in Britain and 180 in Canada. They are less established in France because, unlike their British and Canadian counterparts, French accountants are legally prevented from performing management consulting work for their audit clients. The rationale for restricting management consulting work done by accountants for the audit clients is to ensure that their independence is not compromised by the financial incentives derived from consultancy work (Ridyard and de Bolle, 1992: 80). In France, the accounting profession is state regulated, whereas the British and Canadian accounting professions are wholly self-regulating bodies (OECD, 1980). In these two countries, the independence of the accountants is not guaranteed by state regulation, as in France, but by ethical guidelines issued by accounting bodies, and these guidelines do not restrict the ability of accountants to provide consulting services to their audit clients.

The historical and institutional link between management consulting and accountancy

This second part of the chapter analyses the development of management consultancy in Britain, Canada, and France. It explores the relations between accounting and consulting and explains why consulting became more developed in countries where the state does not prevent accountants from performing consulting work for their audit clients. Because of such restrictions, the French consulting industry is less developed than that in Britain and Canada. In these two countries, accountants played a leadership role in the creation of business and professional associations of management consultants in the early 1960s. By contrast, in France management consulting is an occupation whose organizational and professional development has taken place only recently and which has, to a large extent, been state led.

To highlight the historical and institutional link between accountancy and consultancy, each of the following sections on Britain, Canada, and France starts by describing the history of accountancy and then turns to the analysis of the organizational development of management consultancy. This allows us to identify, for each case, the factors that made possible the involvement of accountants in the development of management consultancy in Britain and Canada and their absence in France. The most important of these factors pertain to differences in historical patterns of industrial and corporate development, in the importance and size of the accounting profession, and in the ways accountants are regulated—an aspect that is closely linked to broader issues dealing with the state's relationship with professional groups.[4]

[4] In the literature on professions there are basically two models of state-professions relations: the Anglo-American and the Continental models. The first assumes that professions have historically developed independently of the state and stresses the autonomy of the professional to regulate his or her own working conditions. In the Continental model, it is believed that professional development and dependence on the state go hand in hand. The Continental model emphasizes the protective role of the state in the supervision of professional authority. The state represents a defender of professional groups rather than something to be suspected (Geison, 1984; Suleiman, 1987; Torstendahl and Burrage, 1990).

Britain

The history of accounting in Britain is inextricably linked to the history of the Industrial Revolution (Jones, 1981: 19). In Britain, the early creation and growth of accounting firms, as well as the establishment of a well-developed accounting profession, was due to the process of industrialization which began in the eighteenth century. At this time, the corporate form of ownership began its rise to prominence, and there was a corresponding separation of management and ownership. It is this separation that was to stimulate the growth of the accounting profession (Bailey, 1984; Carey, 1969; Puxty, 1990).

The separation of management and ownership

In eighteenth-century England, the Industrial Revolution remained limited in its impact, with small-scale workshops, artisan technology, and restricted family and partnership enterprise still characterizing the organization of business (Jones, 1981: 23). In the eighteenth and early nineteenth centuries, industrial units remained relatively small, which meant that they could be managed on a family or close partnership basis. Such a structure of business organization did not provide strong incentives for the employment of specialist accountants. During that period, most entrepreneurs did not feel the need for an independent accountant. Undertaking 'simple book-keeping in the counting house, they were capable of performing virtually all the calculations required for the practical operation of their business' (Jones, 1981: 25). But later, as many companies expanded and became more complex, with much of their capital no longer provided by families but subscribed by outsiders, specialist accounting skills were increasingly demanded. As Stacey mentions in his history of English accountancy, there is an important difference 'when the capital of a company is owned by members of a family or group of families, and companies where the capital is owned by a large number of small or medium-size shareholders without any direct participation in the organization or direction of the company whose funds they have collectively contributed' (1954: 82).

The divorce between capital ownership and management thus made it necessary that accountants be called upon to examine the accounts of companies and to report on what had been found (Bailey, 1990). It was only with the advent of shareholders or partners outside the family circle, and the need to calculate their dividends or profits share, that accountants tended to be called in to verify and report on a company's or firm's accounts (Jones, 1981: 55). The most critical decade for the development of the accounting profession in Britain was the 1840s (Stacey, 1954: 36; Jones, 1981: 28). In those years, the accounting profession started to blossom as a result of the conversion of family-owned businesses into public companies that required examinations of their records and financial statements (Armstrong, 1987). The creation of many of these public companies was related to the completion of Britain's railway network (Littleton, 1966). Parliament granted railway companies the right to raise the vast sums of money needed for their construction by the sale of shares to the public. In terms of organization and finance, these large firms were the antithesis of small family businesses, as joint stock companies were controlled by managers and financed by investors, remote from the board of directors and anxious to see a return on their capital. Before the 1840s, few safeguards existed in law against the fraudulent use of money subscribed by shareholders. The government recognized that vast enterprises such as the railway companies, with capital often running into millions of pounds, 'had overstepped the traditional family partnership and hence required greater public controls' (Jones, 1981: 29).

For instance, the joint stock company legislation of 1844–5 included mandatory provisions regarding the keeping of books of account, the preparation and registration of annual balance sheets, and the appointment of auditors (Edey and Panitpakdi, 1956). It provided companies with an administrative and financial framework which required, among other things, that the auditors, 'one of whom at least shall be appointed by the shareholders', be given open access to the company's books while compiling their report on the balance sheet (Jones, 1981: 30). The 1856 and 1862 Companies Act allowed companies to sell shares to the public in order to raise capital for improvements and expansion with the protection of limited liability for shareholders (Stacey, 1954: 36–7). These two Acts resulted in the formation of hundreds of joint stock companies each requiring an annual audit, thus opening the doors for accountants to this kind of work (Jones, 1981: 50).

Following the trail of UK investment: Internationalization and professional consolidation

The second half of the nineteenth century also witnessed the establishment and the internationalization of a number of leading accountancy practices which today are part of the Big Five international network. For instance, Deloitte was created in 1845 and Price Waterhouse in 1849 (Allen and McDermott, 1993; O'Malley, 1990). In fact, four of the Big Five trace their origins to chartered accountants from the United Kingdom who first came to the United States at the end of the nineteenth century to oversee the commercial interests of British industrialists and entrepreneurs (Stevens, 1991: 18). The first international accounting firms began to emerge then, as UK accountants, following the trail of UK investment, set up offices in North America (Wootton and Wolk, 1992). As the profession grew and expanded on both sides of the Atlantic, further offices were established throughout the world. The result was that the professions of both continents soon became dominated by a relatively small number of firms, from which evolved the Big Five international accounting firms of today.

British accountancy firms benefited from London's position as the finance capital of the world, picking up the audit of a number of companies based overseas and throughout the colonies, but controlled from the City (Jones, 1981: 61). British accountancy firms followed a parallel path to that of the evolving businesses which they served. British accountants followed British business overseas, operating wherever important clients became established in the world. In the nineteenth century, they started to cross the Atlantic because at that time large sums of British capital coming from the City were invested in the newly industrializing countries of North America (Adler, 1970).

The second half of the nineteenth century was also an era of professional consolidation for accountants in Britain. During that period, six professional associations of accountants were created (Willmott, 1986). There are more than 167,000 professional accountants in Britain (*Revue française de comptabilité*, 1989: 34–6). Britain accounts for about half of the total number of professional accountants in the European Union (Ridyard and de Bolle, 1992: 142).

The British accounting profession is a self-regulating body that formulates for itself the basic principles that guide the conduct of the accountant (Briston, 1979; Cooper, Puxty, Lowe, and Willmott, 1990). The profession does not forbid its members to provide management consulting services to their audit clients (Lee, 1984: 263). British professional bodies issued ethical guidelines to ensure that the independence of their members is not threatened by commercial considerations associated with the provision of management consulting services to audit clients (Ridyard and de Bolle, 1992: 144). These ethical guidelines 'are relatively relaxed, relying upon fairness, reasonableness, and high standards of conduct, rather than harsh prohibitions' (Lee, 1984: 263). As discussed below, it is because they were not prohibited from performing consulting work for their audit clients that British accountants were interested in playing an important role in the organizational development of management consultancy in the 1960s.

The management consulting industry and profession
In Britain, management consulting is represented by two main organizations: the Management Consultancies Association (MCA) and the Institute of Management Consultants (IMC). The MCA is comprised of companies while the IMC is comprised of individuals (Hook, 1994). The MCA is the main UK trade association and the IMC is the British industry's professional body. The MCA has 34 member firms, including all the Big Five and the other large firms, while the IMC has 3,600 individual members (James, 1994; IMC, 1994: 31).

The MCA was formed in 1956 by the four largest British-owned consulting companies: PA Management Consultants, PE Consulting Group, Urwick Orr, and Inbucon (Davidson, 1972). In 1956, these four companies alone accounted for three-quarters of all consultancy work, at a time when it was estimated that about £4 million annually was being spent on management consulting assignments and there were about 1,000 practising consultants (Tisdall, 1982: 9). Part of the impetus for British consultancies to organize themselves into a national association came from the fierce competition that British firms were starting to meet from their American counterparts following the Marshall Plan (Carew, 1987; Kipping, 1996). Under the Plan's Technical Assistance Programme several million dollars were spent on the transfer of managerial knowledge and know-how from the United States to Europe, and it is in this context that American firms such as McKinsey and others arrived in the the the UK during the 1950s (Locke, 1996: 41–2; Tiratsoo and Tomlinson, 1993; 1998). The influx of American consultants into the management consulting market was much resented by UK firms. In the 1960s no fewer than 32 of the largest 100 business firms in Britain were known to have called management consultants in, to assist in the reorganization of administrative structures. In 22 of these cases, the consulting firm called upon was McKinsey & Co. (Channon, 1973: 239). When the Bank of England gave an assignment to McKinsey this became front-page news and caused a national furore. So strong was the feeling that representatives of the leading UK firms wrote to the Bank of England's governor and the prime minister. The issue was even discussed in the House of Commons (Rassam and Oates, 1991: 5).

It is noteworthy that the four firms that founded MCA in 1956 were all industrial engineering firms (PE Consulting, 1985). At its founding the MCA did not admit the management consulting practices of accounting firms. Engineers saw accountants as unfair competitors (because they were using their contacts with their audit clients to enter into management consultancy). The MCA started to admit accounting-related firms in 1962, after the creation of the Institute of Management Consultants (IMC), established as a result of pressures exercised on the MCA by chartered accountants (Mellett, 1988: 7). Although it was formed without a single accounting firm on its register of members, in 1986 the MCA numbered 15 accounting consultancies amongst its total membership of 27 (Gopalan, 1986: 10). The engineering firms that founded the MCA did not want it to be a professional institute. The MCA's founding companies wanted to create a business association; they were looking for co-operation, mainly for promotional reasons. The association did not attempt to set itself up as a professional body which would examine individuals or provide them with qualifications (Tisdall, 1982: 80). The engineering profession believed that it would be inappropriate for the MCA to act as a qualifying body. The engineers maintained that 'there were no appropriate grounds for a "Professional Institute" [because] there were no means of establishing a proper qualification' (Tisdall, 1982: 84). Chartered accountants thought otherwise, however. The MCA had been approached by accountants who desired a professional institute, separate from the MCA, which would be comprised of individuals rather than firms (Cheadle, 1994). Accountants thought that the MCA had given itself terms of reference which were too narrow (Tisdall, 1982: 80). The IMC was formed in 1962 by the MCA in response to a threat posed by accountants who were ready to start the IMC themselves, in competition with the MCA (Mellett, 1988: 15). The MCA decided to create the IMC because its members were concerned that they could be embarrassed by the creation of such an institute if the MCA was not itself responsible for its formation. It is reported that 'the Institute of Chartered Accountants welcomed the arrival of the IMC from the start' while the 'reaction by the engineering institutions was one of disapproval' (Tisdall, 1982: 84).

Following the formation of the MCA and IMC, the British market for management consulting services increased steadily and was estimated in the 1970s at £200 million annually and consisting of 5,000 consultants (Tisdall, 1982: 9). The British management consulting industry can be divided into at least two broad categories: global firms and smaller firms consisting of individual practitioners (Studer and Walters, 1994). The first category is dominated by the Big Five but also includes the major 'strategy' consultancies such as McKinsey, Mercer Consulting, and PE International. In the second category, the number of small firms grew importantly during the recession of the late 1980s as experienced managers made redundant moved into consultancy, and consultants released by the larger firms set up their own consulting practices. The total number of businesses registered as management consultants rose from 12,000 in 1988 to nearly 20,000 in 1990. During this period, total turnover for the management consulting industry increased from £1.3 billion in 1988 to £2.9 billion in 1992 (Efficiency Unit, 1994: 32). In 1998, the British market was estimated by the MCA to be around £5 billion and employing 35,000 consultants. This meant that the top 10 firms listed in Table 2.5 held in 1998 more than a third of the British management consulting market.

The British state contributed significantly to the expansion of management consulting in the late 1980s and early 1990s (Abbott, 1993). Growth partly came from policies that sought to create a new 'entrepreneurial culture' in private industry (Hughes, 1993). In 1988, the Department of Trade and Industry (DTI) launched the Enterprise Initiative which provided financial support for the provision of management consulting services to raise the competitive ability of small businesses (Atkinson and Lupton, 1990). The Enterprise Initiative was part of the DTI's new industrial policy which sought to reverse Britain's economic decline by stimulating a more efficient and productive market. This was to be achieved by emphasizing the importance of management, education, and technological innovations.

Between 1988 and 1995, the DTI received over 138,000 applications from small businesses seeking financial assistance for the use of management consulting expertise. During this time, the government spent more than £300 million on the Enterprise Initiative (OECD, 1995b: 145). Under the

TABLE 2.5. Revenue of the top 10 management consulting firms in Britain (£m.)

Firm	1998	1997	1996	1995
PricewaterhouseCoopers	420.0	393.0	n/a	n/a
CAP Gemini	236.1	149.3	101.1	69.0
KPMG Consulting	217.0	153.2	115	109.3
Andersen Consulting	201.6	164.5	129.5	118.4
PA Consulting Group	170.5	124.0	70.3	86.4
Ernst & Young	151.1	108.0	77.4	55.2
Deloitte Consulting	150.5	129.9	112.0	88.0
McKinsey	122.8	103.2	86.0	76.0
Sema Group	104.0	87.0	72.0	51.0
Gemini Consulting	95.0	100.0	96.0	88.3

n/a: data not available.

Source: Management Consultancies Association, 1999, '1998 Management Consultancies Magazine League Table', *News*, 25 July.

Initiative (which was later renamed the 'Consultancy Scheme'), management consulting firms could bill up to around £5 million a year for consultancy assignments carried out for the DTI. This is why some argued in 1988 that 'management consultancy services have recently been given a considerable shot in the arm through the launch of the Enterprise Initiative to provide financial assistance for firms with a payroll of fewer than 500 to use the services of consultants in various areas' (Burt, 1988: 98).

The British government encouraged the use of management consultants in private industry but also in its own sphere. Greater efficiency was the key motive at work. The government basically applied to the public sector the same logic that it promoted in private industry and during the 1980s, and as will be discussed in the next chapter, policy makers increased their use of management consultants in their attempts at making the administration of the state more business-like. Articles appearing in various issues of *Management Consultancy*, a monthly journal published by the MCA, noted that 'public sector consultancy is big business' (Corneille, 1994: 27), and that government has become 'the most important source of fee income to the consultancies' (Abbott, 1994: 1). In the late 1980s, public sector consultancy grew faster than private sector business and now provides around 25 per cent of the total fee income of the largest consulting firms (MCA, 1998).

Canada

The historical development of the accounting profession in Canada has been strongly influenced by the tradition of the pioneering practitioners who came from Britain in the latter part of the nineteenth century (AICPA, 1964: 6). The first of the colonies to form an association of accountants was the Dominion of Canada (Brown, 1905: 253). The Association of Accountants in Montreal, today known as the Ordre des comptables agréés du Québec, was the first official accountancy organization in North America (Collard, 1980: 18). In June 1879, a preliminary meeting was held in Montreal to consider the advisability of forming an association of accountants and of applying to the legislature of the Province of Quebec for an Act of Incorporation (Brown, 1905: 253). The meeting had been organized under the leadership of James Court and Philip Ross. Both Court and Ross were accountants from Britain who arrived in Montreal in the mid-1800s. Court and Ross first arrived in Montreal to oversee the commercial interests of their clients because, during the 1850s, the Canadian Dominion was witnessing a spectacular period of railway investment dominated by British capital (Mackintosh, 1964: 36). In 1858, Ross founded the accounting firm P. S. Ross (Collard, 1980: 21). In 1899, P. S. Ross merged with Touche & Co. creating Touche & Ross, which is one of the predecessor firms of Deloitte Touche, one of the Big Five international accounting firms (Kepos, 1994: 167).

Like other Commonwealth countries, Canada shares the heritage of the British accounting tradition (Carrington, 1984). Canadian accountants share the British 'philosophical attachment to the notion of professional self-regulation' (Standish, 1990: 168). In Canada, accounting professions are self-regulating entities that formulate for themselves the basic principles that guide the conduct of their 85,000 members (Anderson, 1984: ch. 2; ISTC, 1991b: 1). And like their British counterparts, professional accounting bodies in Canada allow their members to perform management consulting services for their audit clients.

The management consulting industry and profession

The oldest management consulting organization in Canada is the Canadian Association of Management Consultants (CAMC) created in 1963.[5] The group that organized the preliminary meeting in 1962 that led to the establishment of a national association of management consultants consisted of the heads of the six major consulting practices associated with accounting firms in Canada.[6] They met under the sponsorship of the Management Consultants Committee of the Quebec Institute of Chartered Accountants (Mellett, 1988: 2). Unlike Britain, industrial engineering companies did not play a role in the development of management consulting. As noted, the early 'involvement of the chartered accounting profession has been a distinguishing

---

[5] The following paragraphs discussing the origins of the CAMC draw heavily on a document describing the history of the first 25 years of the CAMC (Mellett, 1988).

[6] These were: Woods Gordon, Peat Marwick, Urwick Currie, P. S. Ross, Price Waterhouse, and Riddell Stead (Mellett, 1988: 8).

feature of management consulting in Canada' (Mellett, 1988: 2). The membership of the CAMC has traditionally been dominated by accounting firms (Despatis and Tunney, 1987: 32).

In the immediate post-war period, the accounting firms' first ventures into management consulting were informal and tentative (Leach, 1976). For instance, Price Waterhouse created its management consulting arm in 1945, and in 1954 a chartered accountant from Britain (G. Coperthwaite) emigrated to Canada to begin the management consulting practice of Peat Marwick (Mellett, 1988: 6). In Canada, the consulting services offered by accounting firms were performed for their audit clients, not being seen as a distinct service from the accounting work.

Among the concerns that led accountants to found the CAMC was the desire to improve the reputation of a field that they thought could become highly profitable and change the view that American firms such as Booz Allen and McKinsey were more capable of handling large assignments than Canadian firms (Mellett, 1988: 6). James J. Macdonell of Price Waterhouse has been the driving force behind the movement that sought to extend the professional reputation of accounting into the field of management consulting. Macdonell 'was convinced that consulting was destined to enjoy the professional status accorded to auditing, to law and medicine' (Mellett, 1988: 7). In December 1957, he published an article entitled 'The Professional Practice of Management Advisory Services' in *Canadian Chartered Accountant*. In that article, Macdonell (who would later become the third president of CAMC in 1965–6 and Auditor General of Canada in 1973) called for the establishment of a Canadian organization of management consultants. At the time, Macdonell was serving as chairman of the Management Consulting Committee of the Quebec Institute of Chartered Accountants, which had been formed in 1956 to study 'ethical and other considerations relating to management consulting practices' conducted by accountants (Mellett, 1988: 8).

Besides the CAMC, the other organization representing consultants in Canada was the Institute of Management Consultants (IMC) founded in 1969. The IMC was the pan-Canadian organization that represented the professional institutes of management consultants first established by the CAMC in the provinces of Ontario and Quebec (Mellett, 1988: 23). The provincial institutes were created in response to the CAMC's recognition that there was a need for a professional organization to complement its commercial and industry-oriented activities.

The fact that management consultancy had, from the start, always been dominated by accountants in Canada and that industrial engineers played no role in the development of consultancy (as this happened in Britain), meant that there was no opposition concerning the creation of a professional institute that would set the standards to be met by individual practitioners who wanted to be recognized as professional management consultants. In Britain engineers saw management consulting primarily as a business. But one consequence of their absence in the organization of the field in Canada is that management consultancy has tended to be viewed more as a profession than a commercial activity. And in 1990, the main leading business association of consulting firms, the CAMC, merged with the IMC, creating the new Institute of Certified Management Consultants of Canada (ICMCC). The structure of the new body reflects the federal nature of the Canadian state as the ICMCC is now organized into six provincial and one regional (Atlantic Canada) institutes. The goal of the ICMCC is to promote the development of professional management consulting. The ICMCC confers the designation, 'Certified Management Consultant' (CMC), on practitioners who successfully complete its course of studies and practical experience requirements and adhere to a uniform code of professional conduct. The professional movement in Canada is highly regarded internationally for its leadership role in seeking legislation and setting standards. Ontario was the first jurisdiction in the world to grant legal protection to the title and designation, Certified Management Consultant (CMC) (Robinson, 1984).

The Canadian management consulting market was estimated at $Can.3 billion in 1995 (Industry Canada, 1997). There are more than 20,000 practitioners working in the management consulting industry in Canada. Ontario, Quebec, and British Columbia account for about 80 per cent of industry revenues and employment. In 1991, a survey by Industry, Science and Technology Canada found that the consulting industry was very fragmented. Firms with fewer than five employees constituted in 1986 the greatest number of consulting businesses, accounting for 84 per cent of establishments but only 24 per cent of industry employment. Management consulting firms with fewer than 20 employees accounted for 97 per cent of the establishments that year, but only 49 per cent of employment. Establishments with 100 employees or more in 1986 represented less than 1 per cent of management consulting businesses but accounted for 27 per cent of employment (ISTC, 1991*a*: 3).

The Canadian management consulting industry has become increasingly polarized, characterized by a few very large firms and a large number of small firms (ICMCC, 1995). Many small management consulting firms consist of sole practitioners, often providing unique services to niche markets. According to the Industry Canada study, 'many of the consultants in this category were formerly associated with government' (ISTC, 1991*a*: 5). None the less, the big international accounting firms are the major players in management consulting in Canada (Despatis and Tunney, 1987: 32). They have the fastest growing consulting practices (ISTC, 1991*a*: 3). Accounting firms are estimated to hold an aggregate market share of the Canadian management consulting market in the 40–50 per cent range (Despatis and Tunney, 1987: 32). In 1989, the revenues of the management consulting practices of accounting firms in Canada was estimated to be in excess of $600 million (ISTC, 1991*b*: 2).

In recent years, public sector consulting work has become increasingly important for a number of management consulting firms. It has been estimated that government contract work (provincial, federal, and local) accounted for 40 per cent of the Canadian management consulting revenues in 1988 (ISTC, 1991a: 9). This figure is more important than in Britain where, as indicated earlier, public sector consulting (central and local) accounted for 25 per cent of firms' income in the mid-1980s.

Data in Figure 2.2 from a 1995 ICMCC survey of the Canadian consulting market show that government clients form a higher proportion of total consulting revenues as firm size increases. Among firms with one consultant, government clients comprise 29.6 per cent of revenue whereas government clients comprise 80.4 per cent of revenue for firms with 50 to 149 employees. For firms like the Big Five with more than 150 consultants, the public sector represents 52 per cent of revenue.

France

The development of the French accountancy profession reflects the overall pattern of French industry and the capital market (Forrester, 1985). In the late 1940s, France was still a nation of small producers, heavily agricultural and industrially stagnant (Lauber, 1983). The French industrial structure has long been characterized by small and medium-sized family-controlled businesses. Also, the Bourse has not played an important part in company financing. Until recently, the stock exchange has not been important as the channel for corporate financing and the number of listed companies has been comparatively small.[7] Consequently, there has not been a large body of shareholders, and this is one of the most important reasons for the underdeveloped state of the accounting profession in France (Lafferty, 1975: 1).

The prevalence of family-controlled businesses

The development of French commerce and industry in the nineteenth and early twentieth centuries differed significantly from the major nations of the English-speaking world. France was not touched as deeply nor as soon by the Industrial Revolution. Until recently, businesses with closely controlled ownership, often within families, were prevalent (Standish, 1990). Thus, in France, the demand placed on accountants for audit services has traditionally been low because of the small number of publicly owned companies. Corporate finance has generally come from family members. This implies that the major financiers are 'insiders' and that they can obtain up-to-date detailed information as owners of the companies. As a result, there has been

---

[7] The number of domestic companies listed on the stock exchange in Canada and Britain is much more important than in France. In 1991, there were 1,804 such companies listed on the London stock exchange, as compared to 1,147 and 459 for the Toronto and Paris stock exchanges respectively (Nobes, 1991: 26).

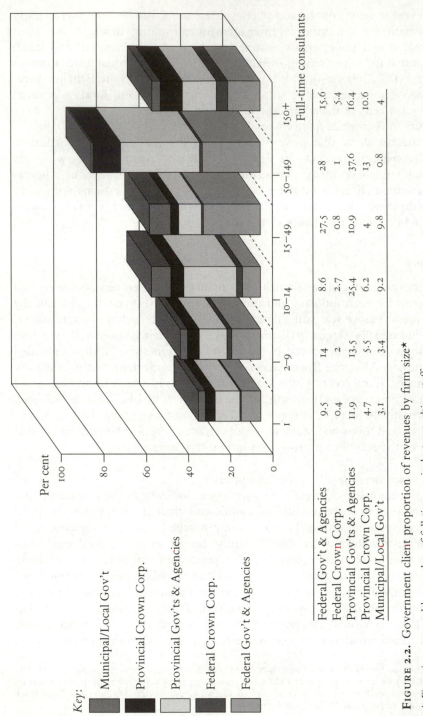

	I	2–9	10–14	15–49	50–149	150+
						Full-time consultants
Federal Gov't & Agencies	9.5	14	8.6	27.5	28	15.6
Federal Crown Corp.	0.4	2	2.7	0.8	1	5.4
Provincial Gov'ts & Agencies	11.9	13.5	25.4	10.9	37.6	16.4
Provincial Crown Corp.	4.7	5.5	6.2	4	13	10.6
Municipal/Local Gov't	3.1	3.4	9.2	9.8	0.8	4

Key:

■ Municipal/Local Gov't

■ Provincial Crown Corp.

□ Provincial Gov'ts & Agencies

■ Federal Crown Corp.

■ Federal Gov't & Agencies

FIGURE 2.2. Government client proportion of revenues by firm size★

★ Firm size measured by number of full-time equivalent consulting staff.

Source: Adapted from: Institute of Certified Management Consultants of Canada, *Consulting Industry Survey* (Toronto, 1995).

no great demand for publication of financial reports or for external audit. The interweaving of these elements in French experience explains why the French accounting profession 'has never attained the status and influence which it enjoys in other countries' (Lafferty, 1975: 24). In 1905, a Scottish account-ant comparing the development of accountancy throughout the world wrote that in France

the profession of accountant is considered by the public as something altogether inferior. With a few exceptions it is practised by people of little education, and of a generally mediocre standing, both intellectually and socially—people who tried, without special training, to gain a livelihood by this means after having failed in other careers. As a matter of fact, commerce and all that relates to it has no pres-tige in the eyes of the Frenchmen, and accounting can not fail to suffer thereby. (Brown, 1905: 290–1)

After the Second World War, the French state initiated a wide-ranging programme to rebuild the economy and intervened in the business sector through nationalization and direct investment (Hayward, 1986). As a re-sult, large-scale commercial and industrial organizations were created. These large, publicly owned organizations no longer relied for corporate financ-ing on family members but on banks and the government which demanded financial reports and audited published information. This situation created a demand for statutory auditing knowledge and although the French accounting profession had existed since at least the 1940s, its members had no experience in that field of activity. Because corporate financing has traditionally come from family members, the demand for audit services has been weak and consequently, French accountants did not develop a strong expertise in statutory auditing. To compensate for this situation, the French state sought in the 1960s the constitution of a separate body for statutory auditors distinct from the organization representing the account-ing profession (Standish, 1990: 169).

The dualism of French accounting
In 1969 the state created the Compagnie Nationale des Commissaires aux Comptes (CNCC) with statutory audit functions reserved to its members. The other professional organization that represents accountants in France is the Ordre des Experts-Comptables et des Comptables Agréés (OECCA) established by law in 1942. The CNCC represents the accountant in his or her capacity as statutory auditor appointed by the shareholders, and OECCA in his or her capacity as a professional whose services are contracted by the management of a particular company. The CNCC is placed under the authority of the Ministry of Justice and the OECCA comes under the auspices of the Ministry of Finance (Most, 1984). In 1989, there were 10,692 *commissaires aux comptes* and 11,018 *experts-comptables* (*Revue française de comptabilité*, 1989: 34–6).

The position of the accounting profession in France is notable in at least two respects. The first is the separation of the auditing and accounting activities[8] that took place in 1969 with the creation of the CNCC (Nobes, 1991; Scheid and Walton, 1988). The second is that it is the state (i.e. the departments of Justice and Finance) and not the profession that formulate the basic principles guiding the rules of accounting and auditing (OECD, 1980). Some have argued that the accounting profession is 'weaker' in France because the 'government or government-run committees control most of the rules of accounting and auditing' (Nobes, 1991: 26).

The CNCC is the professional body of official statutory auditors. The primary responsibility of a *commissaire aux comptes* is to certify the regularity and legal correctness of companies' financial statements. To ensure their independence, *commissaires aux comptes* are restricted to statutory audits and they cannot provide management consulting services (Campbell, 1985: 61). The rationale for restricting consulting work by auditors is to ensure that the auditor is above all suspicion of being influenced by other interests.[9] It is sometimes argued that different rates of profitability between audit and non-audit work (such as consulting) where both are done for the same client run the risk of threatening this independence, since the accounting firm is in some sense under pressure to please the client on the audit in order to keep the (sometimes more profitable) non-audit work. In these conditions, it might be argued, the auditors' freedom to say no to the client, on which independence is ultimately dependent, is compromised (Ridyard and de Bolle, 1992: 80).

The OECCA includes all qualified *experts-comptables* (Moliterno, 1992). The *expert-comptable* primarily provides accounting, taxation, financial, and general business and management consulting services (Blake and Amat, 1993: 115). An *expert-comptable* is the equivalent of a certified public accountant with the notable exception that he or she cannot perform a statutory audit unless qualified as a *commissaire aux comptes*, but most *experts-comptables* are also *commissaires aux comptes* (and vice versa). However, when acting as *commissaires aux comptes* to perform a statutory audit, the *experts-comptables* cannot provide consulting or other type of services to the audit client (Barrington, 1989: 19).

[8] Although accounting and auditing are sometimes believed to be the same thing, there are some basic differences. Accounting can be described as measuring and reporting the effects of economic activities of individual entities. Auditing, on the other hand, involves an independent examination to determine the propriety of accounting processes, measurements, and communication. Stated simply, the accountant prepares financial information; the auditor checks it (AICPA, 1977: xii).

[9] The only other European country where the instruments used to regulate auditor independence are stricter than in France is Greece. To ensure that the auditor can have no direct financial interest in whether the audit client is pleased with the outcome, in Greece audit services are provided by the state. In Europe, the states where restrictions on the extent to which auditors can perform management consulting work are the most liberal are Britain, Ireland, and The Netherlands (Ridyard and de Bolle, 1992: 80–1).

Thus, both *experts-comptables* and *commissaires aux comptes* are not totally forbidden to be management consultants. However, they are prohibited from performing consulting services to their audit clients, and it is precisely the link with the audit client that has served as the platform on which accountants in Britain and Canada have developed their lucrative management consulting businesses (Welchman, 1983). In France, this institutional advantage is not present because of the separation between the accounting and auditing activities established in 1969 with the creation of the CNCC (Wyman, 1989). In most countries, including Britain and Canada, there is no such separation because the statutory audit function has historically come to be occupied by accountants. But in France, accountants had no developed expertise of statutory auditing because of the prevalence of family-controlled businesses (Lafferty, 1975). If the statutory audit function had fallen under the control of the professional association representing accountants, there would probably be no prohibition concerning the provision of consulting services to audit clients because, like their British and Canadian counterparts, French *experts-comptables* are not prohibited from providing consulting services. They are only prohibited from doing so when they act as *commissaires aux comptes* and perform a statutory auditing role.

The management consulting industry and profession

For reasons that should now be clear, the accounting profession has not been involved in the organizational development of management consulting in France (ISÉOR, 1993). Historically, French engineers played a more important role in the development of consultancy as many of them showed an early interest in Taylorism and created—generally with the help of American colleagues—the first consulting firms in France in the 1920s (Kipping, 1996).

Nowadays, management consultants in France are represented by two main organizations: Syntec Management, which is a committee of the national organization Syntec Conseil; and the Office Professionnel de Qualification des Conseils en Management (OPQCM). Syntec Management is a trade association representing management consulting firms and the OPQCM is the profession's certifying body. Syntec Management is made up of companies, not individual practitioners (Shays, 1985: 52).

Syntec Management is one of the four committees which compose Syntec Conseil (the other three being Market Studies, Recruiting, and Public Relations). The Marshall Plan played an important role in the formation of the first associations of consultants in France (Sauviat, 1991: 20). As has been argued, 'It is no exaggeration to claim that the French discovered "management" during the Marshall Plan' (Kuisel, 1993: 84). In 1948 the French state introduced its 'programme for productivity' and, using funds provided by the Marshall Plan, sent 'productivity missions' to the United States to study the secrets of American prosperity. Under the programme, more than 450 productivity missions were organized, involving over 4,000 members, bosses, engineers, and trade union representatives (Boltanski, 1990: 345). Within the French state, these missions were organized and co-ordinated by the Planning Commission, the body created after the war to help reconstruct the economy and modernize industrial production (Ullmo, 1974). As is well known, the process of industrial planning and the nationalization policy gave the government considerable control over the economy (Andrieu, Le Van, and Prost, 1987). The creation of many State Owned Enterprises (SOEs) and the growth of the industrial public sector after the war generated new demands for management knowledge—part of which was supplied by American consultancies expanding their operations to Europe in the 1950s and 1960s (McKenna, 1995). A study conducted by management researchers in the early 1970s argued that the growing presence of US firms in France was the result of the under-development of the French management consulting industry. The study concluded that 'American consulting success clearly shows up an absence of French-grown managerial skills' (Dyas and Thanheiser, 1976: 247). But this conclusion seems somewhat excessive because several French 'home-grown' firms emerged after the war to help develop the managerial infrastructure of the expanding industrial public sector. For instance, Bossard was created in 1956; CEGOS changed its status in 1948; SEMA was established in 1957; and Eurequip in 1961. The expertise and services provided by these firms tend to focus more on the 'human relations factor'—that is, industrial psychology as opposed to the Taylorian focus on organizational structures and processes (Henry, 1994). Interestingly, the reason why knowledge of the 'human relations factor'was thought to be important had to do with the political context of post-war France, where many believed that the new techniques of industrial psychology could help to foster more harmonious social relations between labour and business, and established a stable social order capable of restraining the rise of the French Communist Party (Boltanski, 1990: 345).

As in Britain, the growing presence of US consultancies on the European scene was a major factor in the decision of French consulting engineers to form Syntec Conseil. Syntec Conseil was created in 1958, and its Management Consulting Committee was set up in 1973. Unlike their British and Canadian counterparts, French management consultants do not have their own national association to promote their interests. What they have is a committee within a broader structure (Syntec Conseil) that represents the interests of a wide variety of practitioners who are in the consulting business.

In 1992, Syntec Management represented 50 firms employing 3,200 professionals, most of whom have a professional background in engineering (Syntec Management, 1994: 8). Membership in Syntec Management is limited to companies which are at least three years old and employ more than five people. Management consulting must be the firm's main activity for membership in Syntec Management and at least one of its directors must have a minimum of five years' experience in the profession (Stern and

Tutoy, 1995: ch. 1). The professional body for management consultants in France is the OPQCM. The OPQCM is a certifying agency. Its purpose is to promote the management consulting profession and to act, *vis-à-vis* potential clients, as a point of reference to facilitate the selection of management consulting firms. It was founded by the Ministère de l'Industrie and Syntec Management member firms. In the early 1980s, the Ministère de l'Industrie ordered a study to encourage the penetration of management consulting into small and medium-sized enterprises to help them modernize administrative practices and increase efficiency and competitiveness in the context of the developing European common market (Salvall, 1988: 268).

Submitted to the Ministère de l'Industrie in 1984, the report concluded that, compared to those in other European countries, small and medium-sized enterprises in France did not use management consulting services very widely. To change that situation, the report suggested that the state should act to stimulate both the demand for and the supply of management consulting services. To stimulate demand, the report recommended the creation of Fonds Régionaux d'Aide au Conseil (FRAC) that would provide money to small and medium-sized enterprises so that they could buy consulting services. The lack of professionalism in consulting was identified in the report as one reason why the demand for such services was not strong in industry (Sauviat, 1991). To increase the supply of consulting services, the report proposed to develop the professionalism of consultants (Salvall, 1992). It was thus that the operation *Développement du professionnalisme des consultants* was born in 1985 and that the OPQCM started its activities in 1987.

What has been the impact of these policies? In the 1980s, the management consulting market in France grew steadily from one billion francs in 1982 to seven billion in 1992 and 1993, or 13 per cent of the European market (Gastou and Thévenet, 1990: 24; Syntec Management, 1994: 7). Table 2.6 indicates that the top 15 firms hold more than half of the French consulting market. It is estimated that Andersen Consulting alone holds more than 12 per cent of the French market (Basini, 1994: 72). The second largest consultancy in the market is Bossard, a French-owned firm. Bossard claims to be number one in consulting services to local governments (Crawford, 1991: 11). But according to Bossard, consulting for central government is not as well developed as in other countries, although 'recent reforms are increasing demand from government ministries' (Crawford, 1991: 11). In the early 1990s, it was estimated that public sector consulting (for both local and central government) represented less than 10 per cent of the total market for management consulting services in France (Bruston, 1993: 180).

Although the market increased a great deal during the 1980s, a 1994 survey of the French association of management consulting firms noted that management consultants are still 'an underused asset in France' (Syntec Management, 1994: 7). The survey indicated that management consulting

TABLE 2.6. The top 15 management consulting firms in France

Rank	*1993* *Revenue (F.m.)*	*1992* *Revenue (F.m.)*
1 Andersen Consulting	900	858
2 Bossard	500	455
3 Peat Marwick	258	217
4 Gemini Consulting	217	139
5 Sema Group	200	210
6 Price Waterhouse	200	192
7 Coopers & Lybrand	199	176
8 McKinsey	196	n.a.
9 Solving International	195	190
10 Cegos	160	175
11 Boston Consulting	158	n.a.
12 Ernst & Young	135	145
13 Deloitte Touche	124	120
14 Eurogroup Consultants	110	105
15 Eurosept Associés	107	106

n.a.: not available.

Sources: Chevilly, P. (1994). 'Andersen, Bossard et Peat Marwick en tête du marché français du conseil', *Les Échos*, 17 June; Kileen, R. (1994). 'France endures another sluggish year', *Management Consultant International*, April.

services are used almost twice as often in Britain as they are in France, and that American managers use consultants five to ten times more frequently than their French counterparts. While average growth for the European Community in 1992 was estimated at 8 per cent, during the same period, the French market grew by only 3 per cent (Syntec Management, 1994: 7). The study concluded that 'France, which is not a major consumer of consulting services, seems to be accentuating its lag with respect to other large European countries' (Syntec Management, 1994: 7). Similarly, a study of the Fédération Européenne des Auditeurs et Conseils found in 1992 that France allocated only 0.15 per cent of its GNP to management consulting services as compared to 0.26 per cent in Britain and 0.29 in the United States (Basini, 1994: 72).

Conclusion

The development of accounting and management consulting must be understood in relationship with each other. The evolution of the former to

TABLE 2.7. Summary of key factors affecting the relationship between accounting and consulting

	Britain	Canada	France
Number of firms	20,000 (1990)	12,955 (1986)	3,000 (1993)
Revenues generated by consulting firms	£3 bn. (1992)	$Can.3 bn. (1995)	F.7 bn. (1992)
Lead role in organizational development	Engineers/ accountants	Accountants	Engineers/ state
Year of creation of business or professional association	1956 1962	1963 1969	1972 1987
Existence of 'Government Committee'	YES	YES	NO
% of revenues from public sector	25% (1993)	40% (1988)	10% (1991)

a large extent shaped the development of the latter. As Table 2.7 clearly shows, the two countries where accountants played a leadership role in the organization, legitimation, and professionalization of management consultancy—Britain and Canada—are the countries where that industry is more developed. Management consulting is less developed in France, where accountants were not involved in organizing the consulting industry and profession. In France—and at least initially in Britain—engineers were involved in developing the consulting industry but engineers do not have the organizational advantage (the link with the audit client) that made it possible for accountants to play a key role in the growth of management consulting.

In France, the development of management consulting largely came through state sponsorship, both through the post-war expansion of the industrial public sector around which many consulting firms grew and through the role of Industry Department in the mid-1980s. In the two other countries it is not the state but the accounting profession that took the lead in the professionalization of management consultancy. But as in the case of France, the British state also adopted in the late 1980s policies that provided financial assistance to small businesses for the use of management consulting services. These policies clearly show that the validity and relevance of any given form of social knowledge—in our case management consultancy—are matters that become established in society through processes that are often political in character. With these policies, the state undoubtedly helped to consolidate the authority of consultants by making a causal link between the use of management consultants and increased productivity and wealth. In Britain and France, the development of these policies was linked to the construction of the common European market. They were intended to help small and medium-sized firms to become more competitive in Europe. In Canada, the federal government does not provide direct financial assistance to help small businesses buy consulting services but Industry Canada provides a number of resources (guides, 1–800 phone numbers, internet links, etc.) to facilitate the exchange of ideas between consultants and businesses.

Because of the federal structure of the state, Canada is the only country where management consulting organizations are divided into regional and provincial associations. In terms of mobilization, such division may make it more difficult for Canadian consultants to have a single association that would speak for the management consulting sector as a whole, although this is also the case in Britain and France where management consultancy is divided into professional associations representing individual practitioners and business associations representing the commercial interests of large firms. As we have seen, management consulting is an oligopolistic sector and all the heavyweight firms that dominate the market are organized into a 'league of their own' (James, 1994). They have more capacities and resources than the associations representing individual practitioners and thus more means of securing influence.

This chapter provides the background for the subsequent comparative-historical analysis of the role of management consultants in the process of bureaucratic reform in Britain, Canada, and France. We saw in Chapter 1 that managerialist ideas were more influential in Britain and Canada in the 1980s, and it is in these two countries that the management consulting industry is the most developed because of its link with the accounting profession. France is the only one of the three cases where management consulting has not evolved as an extension of the accounting profession and it is also the country where the consulting industry is the least developed. Therefore, the possibilities for French policy makers to reform their bureaucracy by using the services of consultants to import business management ideas and practices into public administration are not as great as they are for their British and Canadian counterparts. This is in part why managerialist ideas have been less influential in France than in Britain and Canada. In attempting to reform their bureaucracy along the lines prescribed by the new managerialism, British and Canadian policy makers have had the possibility to use the services of a well-developed management consulting industry that has existed since the early 1960s and which has enjoyed a certain reputation of professionalism derived from its links with accounting.

The weakness of the French consulting industry, and the relative absence of managerialist ideas in French public administration, is why I use France as a negative or contrasting case to underline the links drawn from the British and Canadian cases between the strength of the management consulting industry and the influence of managerialist ideas on policy. In France, managerialist ideas only started to become influential in the mid-1980s, first in local governments and then in the central state, at the same time that the management consulting industry became stronger as a result of government initiatives designed to stimulate its growth. As for the two other cases, managerialism has been less influential in Canada than in Britain, even though the empirical evidence gathered in this chapter clearly shows that the management consulting industry is as well developed in Canada as in Britain. Indeed, the revenues derived from government consulting are more important in Canada than in Britain (40 per cent of total revenues as compared with 25 per cent), implying that managerialism should be more influential in Canada. But this is not the case. Therefore, there must be something else than just the strength or weakness of the management consulting industry to explain differences in the acceptance of managerialist ideas and policies. The theoretical framework presented in Chapter 1 assumes that the state, and its prior experience with administrative reform policies, shapes the possibilities for consultants to promote managerialist ideas that can appeal to decision makers and influence policy. One of the main differences between Britain and Canada is the way in which management consulting interests have historically been institutionalized in the state apparatus. As discussed next, in Britain consultants from the private sector were first co-opted into the Civil Service Department and then, following its abolition in 1981, into a number of small units located at the centre of government, where consultants were able to make their voices heard in the inner circles of policy making.

3

Britain: Providing management policy advice through the centre of government

Britain has one of the most mature and well-developed management consulting industries and professions, but this alone is not sufficient to understand why, during the 1980s, British policy makers embraced managerialist ideas more enthusiastically than their Canadian and French counterparts. The impact of managerialism on policy cannot be simply determined by the strength or weakness of the management consulting industry. To explain the impact of managerialism on public administration, we also need to examine the institutional processes by which consultants, as the bearers of managerialist ideas, entered state agencies and helped shape bureaucratic reform policy.

To do so, this chapter analyses the policies of bureaucratic reform that preceded the more recent initiatives (Next Steps, the Citizen's Charter, and Market Testing) discussed in Chapter 1. These past bureaucratic reform policy experiences are: the 1968 Fulton Committee Report on the Civil Service; the 1970 White Paper on the Reorganization of Central Government; the 1979 Rayner efficiency scrutinies and the 1982 Financial Management Initiative. The analysis of these reform policies is not intended as a review of all their detailed aspects or as a critique or assessment of their performance, as this has already been done in a number of important studies (Aucoin, 1995; Campbell and Wilson, 1995; Greer, 1994; Metcalfe and Richards, 1987; Pollitt, 1990; Savoie, 1994; Zifack, 1994). Rather, the purpose is to examine whether these administrative changes left legacies that affected: (a) the predisposition of policy actors towards strategies to reform the state; and (b) the access of consultants to decision-making centres through which managerialist ideas did (or did not) enter into policy.

One of the most critical events accounting for the entry of consultants and the rise of managerialist ideas in the British state was the election of Labour in 1964 and the creation of the Fulton Committee in 1966. The Fulton report, which some have compared to 'the public administration equivalent of the the Bible' (Theakston, 1992: 113), was very much a product of its time. This was the period of Harold Wilson's scientific and technological revolution where faith in rational planning and in the capacity of social sciences and technical expertise to solve public or political problems was relatively high. To strengthen and rationalize the intervention of the state in society and the economy, Fulton recommended to the prime minister that he modernize the management of the bureaucracy by importing ideas and techniques from the private sector. Fulton argued that the American practice of bringing in outsiders provided a useful way for constantly refreshing the civil service with ideas from outside government. As the commissioners wrote in the report, 'in making our proposals for reform we have been influenced by what we have seen in foreign countries . . . e.g. the contributions of the "in-and-outers" in the United States' (Fulton, Lord, 1968a: 13).

To implement Fulton's proposals, the Labour government created the Civil Service Department (CSD) which was to be the lead agency in the area of administrative modernization. The CSD was intended to break the dominance of the Treasury over state management policy and to provide, with other new departments, openings for the appointment of outside 'experts' who had not been able to rise through the senior ranks of the 'amateur' civil service. Following its creation, the CSD went through an important process of institution building and subsequently became the main access point through which management consultants were linked to the British state. To build its expertise, the CSD institutionalized links with the consulting industry and co-opted management consultants from the private sector. However, in contrast to what Fulton had expected, the CSD never had the political clout needed to fight the Treasury. It remained under the control of Treasury officials and 'generalist' bureaucrats whose position Fulton wanted to undermine. As a result, the CSD presented throughout its existence a relatively strong obstacle to managerialist-style policies.

Later in the 1970s, in a process initiated by Edward Heath and pushed much further by Margaret Thatcher, a different type of organization was used to bypass the established bureaucratic hierarchy and to bring in private-sector allies and consultants to provide advice on management policy. This involved the development of a number of small organizational units, such as Heath's Businessmen's Team and Thatcher's Efficiency Unit. Often situated at the centre of the executive machinery and generally composed of a mix of career civil servants and external management consultants, these units were close to the Prime Minister's Office and had direct access to centres of decision-making power. Under Thatcher, such units were in part created to replace the CSD she abolished in 1981. Thatcher dismantled the CSD because it was perceived as impeding the emergence of managerialist ideas and policies within the British bureaucracy. In abolishing the CSD and in centralizing its responsibilities for bureaucratic reform issues in the Cabinet Office, the Thatcher government brought the institutional channel through which consultants had entered into the bureaucratic reform policy process since Fulton closer to the political direction of the Cabinet and the Prime Minister. The management consulting industry link with, or its primary access point to, the British bureaucracy shifted from the CSD to the Cabinet Office. This political centralization of authority for issues dealing with bureaucratic reform greatly facilitated the implementation of managerialist innovations by the Thatcher government in the 1980s. But as we shall see, it also brought consultants closer to 'politics' and politicized the relations between the government and the management consulting industry. After a period of backlash against management consultancy led by the Labour opposition and the media in the mid-1990s, the government reduced its use of consulting services, and thus reduced the possibilities for consultants to influence the process of administrative reform by having their ideas come to the attention of those who make policy.

Labour's scientific revolution and the need for 'opening up' the civil service

The early 1960s saw the British economy expanding at a slower rate and increasingly lagging behind its European competitors. The economy was trapped in a vicious circle, as crises in the balance of payments led to deflation and slow growth (Blackaby, 1978). This, in the eyes of the Labour opposition, was caused by the incompetence, archaic attitudes, and failure of the Conservative government to make the economy more dynamic by using new social scientific knowledge. At a time when Labour was trying to modernize its attitude toward the mixed economy, the new leader, Harold Wilson published in 1963 *Labour and the Scientific Revolution*. The document did not talk about the overthrow of capitalism, but rather offered the vision of a rejuvenated, modern economy under dynamic management. 'A new deal for the scientists and technologists' and 'a new status for scientists in Government' were the essential requirements for reviving the economy.

Wilson's call for a science-based government and a non-ideological approach to policy had to do with the so-called revisionist movement inside the Labour Party and with intra-party conflicts over issues related to the future of social-ism and public ownership (McKibbin, 1974; Smith, 1972). As Samuel Beer wrote, 'the new technocratic rationale gave the party leadership cause to separ-ate itself from the party orthodoxies of nationalization and class struggle' (1982: 125). After 13 years in opposition and three successive defeats, Wilson wanted to fight the 1964 election by creating a wider political coalition that would appeal to the new professional middle class (Cliff, 1988: 280).

In the early 1960s, there was plenty of hostility in the Labour Party towards the Treasury and many were questioning its ability to conduct what they saw as its most important function: the management of the economy (Ponting, 1989). Labour politicians saw the the civil service—and especially the Treasury—as part of a conservative establishment that would absorb and deflect radical socialist policies (Pollitt, 1984: 48). In 1964, the Fabian Society, a group of thinkers and intellectuals close to Labour, produced an influential pamphlet, *The Administrators*, which advocated the reform of the civil service and argued that the dilettantism of the mandarinate was partly responsible for Britain's poor economic performance and its failure to obtain membership in the EEC in 1963 (Fabian Society, 1964). Before the 1964 election, Harold Wilson said in a BBC interview that, if elected, his party would set up a new ministry that would take over the Treasury and have responsibility for economic planning (Hunt, 1964). Wilson believed that a new department was needed if the 'Treasury view' was to be shaken. Besides national economic planning, Labour also promised to stimulate growth by 'injecting modern technology into our industries' (Labour Party, 1964). To a large extent, this interest in technology as a way to improve productivity was a continuation of the concern with management that Labour had developed in the 1940s (Tiratsoo and Tomlinson, 1993).

Once in power, Prime Minister Wilson created the Department of Economic Affairs (DEA) and the Ministry of Technology (Min-Tech), both of which were to be the corner-stone of Labour's attempts at setting up a British version of the French national planning system (Hall, 1986: 88). The new ministries, especially the DEA, were to counterbalance the Treasury and to challenge its monopoly in the public policy process (Brittan, 1970: 311). To do so, the new departments were thought to need 'a powerful injection of business thinking to bridge the communications gap between Whitehall and industry' (Lester, 1970: 49). In the words of Harold Wilson's assistant, this was to be done 'by opening up the civil service' to multiple sources of external policy advice (Williams, quoted in Fry, 1993: 7).

Fulton and the technocratic attack on the generalist administrator

It was in this context that the Committee on the Civil Service chaired by Lord Fulton was established in 1966 with the mandate 'to examine the structure, recruitment and management, including training, of the Home Civil Service and to make recommendations' (Fulton, Lord, 1968a: 2). The Fulton inquiry was not a Royal Commission but a departmental committee of 12 members including civil servants, MPs, academics, and industrialists.

Wilson told the House of Commons that the decision to create the Fulton Committee had been made because of new demands placed upon the civil service and that the time had come to ensure that the British administration 'was properly equipped for its role in the modern state' (724 *H.C. Deb.* 5s, cols. 209–10). Published in 1968, the Fulton report contained 158 recommendations. Many of the policy proposals made by Fulton were developed in reaction to the legacies left by the civil service reforms of the nineteenth century (Christoph, 1984). In the 1850s, the Northcote-Trevelyan report recommended that entry and promotion in the civil service be made on merit rather than patronage. The report set the stage for a civil service that favoured recruits educated in the humanities and that promoted an attitude of 'gifted amateurs' (Balogh, 1959). The first chapter of the Fulton report opened by saying that the civil service was 'still fundamentally the product of the nineteenth-century philosophy of the Northcote-Trevelyan Report when the tasks it faces are those of the second half of the twentieth century. This is what we have found; it is what we seek to remedy' (Fulton, Lord, 1968a: 9). The report asserted that the civil service was still based too much on the model of the 'amateur, generalist or all-rounder' and that 'too few civil servants are skilled managers' (Fulton, Lord, 1968a: 11–12).

The 'generalist model' was very much a product of a period where the role of the state was limited (Parris, 1969). It was a model that neglected managerial tasks and skills, and because of this, Fulton believed that the senior civil service had become incapable of managing the large public sector created by the rise of the Keynesian welfare state. This is what the Committee sought to change. To professionalize government management, Fulton saw the need to learn from the private sector. The report argued that the civil service was too closed: 'there is not enough awareness of how the world outside Whitehall works' (p. 12). Fulton wanted to break down the barriers between Whitehall and the world of industry and commerce by encouraging 'the free flow of men, knowledge and ideas between the Service and the outside world' (p. 13). In arguing in favour of more efforts to promote the 'interchange of staff with private industry and commerce' Fulton evoked the Second World War: 'War-time experience proves beyond doubt the value of such a movement in promoting mutual knowledge and understanding' (p. 45). During the war the whole of Whitehall was opened up and as Margaret Weir showed, these changes eventually paved the way for the entry into the bureaucracy of Keynesian economists and for the acceptance of demand-management ideas (1989: 65).

Because it argued that civil servants needed to adopt a more business-like approach, the Fulton report has been described as 'the high-water mark of managerialism' and as being imbued with a 'business-managerial philosophy' (Drewry and Butcher, 1991: 195). The Fulton report said that although public administration was different from private administration, the managerial problem was the same. Fulton defined management as 'being responsible for organization, directing staff, planning the progress of work, setting standards of attainment and measuring results, reviewing procedures and quantifying different courses of action' (Fulton, Lord, 1968a: 12). Fulton found that too few civil servants saw their role in those terms. In particular, senior officials still perceived themselves as policy advisers to ministers above them, rather than as managers of organizations below them. Fulton attempted to establish within Whitehall the idea that civil servants were and should be managers (Robertson, 1971). As someone who would later become Prime Minister Thatcher's key adviser on public administration reform argued, Fulton wanted to 'make room for managers in Whitehall' (Rayner, 1973). The report sought to create more opportunities for accountants, engineers, consultants, and other specialists 'trained in management' by giving them more responsibilities and authority (Fulton, Lord, 1968a: 12).

The management consultants' report

One of the two pieces of evidence[1] commissioned by the Fulton Committee which 'heavily influenced its report' was a study by a Management Consultancy Group (Garrett, 1980: 13). The Fulton Committee on the Civil Service was the first committee in British administrative history to investigate the civil service by commissioning outside research (Chapman, 1973: 17). Unlike any previous consideration of the civil service, the Fulton Committee decided to carry out its own investigation of what civil servants were doing by establishing a Management Consultancy Group in 1966. The Group examined the management and organization of each block of work in the civil service, comparing these with the best practice in business firms. The Group's study was published as Volume 2 of the Fulton report. Many of the Fulton report's 'ideas were taken from the Management Consultancy Group's report' (Garrett, 1972: 53).

The idea of creating a management consulting group attached to the Fulton Committee came from Dr Norman Hunt of Oxford University.[2] As one participant in the Fulton inquiry later observed, 'the use of management consultants was relatively rare in the public sector in those days' (Garrett, quoted in Fry, 1993: 57). Hunt and other members of the Fulton Committee wanted to commission private sector consultants to carry out the Committee's research because they feared that the Committee's agenda would be captured by bureaucrats and made dependent on official evidence if its research was carried out by civil servants (Fry, 1993: 60). An acquaintance of Prime Minister Wilson, Dr Hunt was appointed as member of the Fulton Committee in February 1966 and the Management Consultancy Group was placed under his responsibility (Garrett, 1972: 40). Originally, Hunt wanted the American firm McKinsey to carry out the Committee's research. He was aware that the Post Office and Shell had employed McKinsey consultants in the mid-1960s and thought that the use of business experts would prevent public criticism if Fulton had a study made by 'management consultants with general experience' of analysing work in large organizations (Fry, 1993: 59). McKinsey was eventually ruled out because they were too expensive and because, politically, 'it would have looked bad to employ an American firm' (Fry, 1993: 60). The Committee offered the job to Associated Industrial Consultants (AIC), a management consultancy based in Britain.

[1] The other piece was a social survey of the civil service based on nearly 5,000 replies to questionnaires analysed by two social scientists from Oxford and the University of Lancaster (Garrett, 1972: 51).

[2] Later Hunt wrote a book about his experience on the Fulton Committee in which he argued that many of Fulton's ideas were not translated into policy because of the resistance of the senior official in charge of the Civil Service Department, which was to be the main driving force for implementing the Fulton recommendations (see Kellner and Crowther-Hunt, 1980: ch. 4: 'How Armstrong Defeated Fulton').

The Management Consultancy Group was thus staffed by AIC consultants and one Treasury official. The Group had an important impact on the Fulton Committee's thinking because the Committee was not organizationally 'separated' from the Group and was thus able to keep in constant touch with the day-to-day investigations of the management consultants. There were regular and informal weekly meetings between the Group and Committee members, enabling management consultants 'to have a constant and continuous impact on the thinking of the Committee whilst this was still in a relatively formative and fluid state' (Kellner and Crowther-Hunt, 1980: 32).

In creating its own consulting group, the Fulton Committee recognized that the services of private sector consultants could be useful for dealing with issues pertaining to bureaucratic reform. Through Fulton, the British state contributed to the legitimization of management consultancy and, as seen in Chapter 2, this followed the efforts of accountants who had attempted to enhance the professional standing of management consulting by playing a leadership role in the creation of the Institute of Management Consultants in 1962. A permanant secretary noted that, before Fulton, 'the idea of asking management consultants to examine our Civil Service had not yet crossed our minds. No doubt', she said, this was 'partly because management consultancy has not yet achieved the standing in Britain that it has in North America' (Sharp, 1967: 283).

Class politics and support for Fulton's policy proposals

The fact that Fulton relied on outside management consultants for advice on bureaucratic reform issues greatly facilitated the entry into the policy process of innovative ideas concerning state administration. As one of the consultants involved in the Fulton report later said, 'what we recommended was the introduction into the Civil Service of attitudes of mind and practices that were common in private industry and commerce and the adoption of which we believed would make for a more efficient Civil Service' (Ferguson, quoted in Fry, 1993: 66).

Among the principal measures that Fulton recommended to increase the professionalism of the civil service and to keep departmental organization up to date with management developments in the private sector were: (a) the creation of departmental Management Services Units and the use of outside management consultants; (b) the establishment of a new Civil Service Department and of a new Civil Service College; and (c) the application of the principle of 'accountable management' in the organization of executive activities (Fulton, Lord, 1968a: chs 5 and 7). These recommendations, which are discussed below, were all based on ideas derived from the work of the Management Consultancy Group. These ideas were initially well received by the Labour administration (Chapman, 1973). Fulton, a personal friend of Prime Minister Wilson, lobbied senior members of the Labour Cabinet to have the government commit itself early to supporting the report or, failing that, at least some of its key recommendations on the day of its release (Savoie, 1994: 70). The prime minister circulated a memorandum to the Cabinet recommending 'that we immediately accept the main recommendations of the Fulton report' (quoted in Kellner and Crowther-Hunt, 1980: 56). As it happened, the prime minister announced his support the day the report was published. He said that this would embrace, if not the entire report, at least most of the key recommendations designed to strengthen the management capacity of the civil service, such as the creation of the Civil Service Department and the Civil Service College.

While the Fulton report gained valuable support from the Labour government, it faced strong bureaucratic opposition from the senior civil service. In a prestigious bureaucracy staffed by intelligent amateurs or educated laymen, self-assured officials tended to view management as an esoteric field of knowledge or as little more than common sense disguised in repulsive jargon and were, therefore, unwilling to listen to Fulton. In particular, Fulton's strong critique of the 'amateurish' character of the senior bureaucracy generated discontent among high-ranking civil servants and this affected support for managerialist ideas and policies in the civil service. The establishment of the Management Consulting Group sent a signal that Fulton did not trust the bureaucracy. One Treasury official said that the creation of the Management Consulting Group 'is evidence of the Committee being unwilling to trust us [the Treasury] to say what happens in the Civil Service' (Caulcott, quoted in Fry, 1993: 60). But politically, Fulton's ideas about the need to replace 'amateurs' by 'specialists' appealed to Labour's socialist egalitarian ideology because the debate about the 'amateurs' was very much a debate about social class. The 'amateurs' were said to come from the upper classes and to be mainly recruited from Oxford and Cambridge. Many inside Labour believed that because of their bourgeois origins, 'Oxbridge' civil servants would be hostile to the policies of a socialist government (Morgan, 1984). This is why Fulton's call for greater 'specialism' among public administrators was favourably endorsed by the government because it was intended to break the dominance of the 'amateurs' in Whitehall and to create a more socially representative senior bureaucracy. This was to be done by widening the access of entry to senior positions and by bringing in people with relevant professional and managerial skills (Jones and Keating, 1985: 143). Fulton believed that the dominance of the 'generalist' in the most senior positions of the bureaucratic apparatus represented a strong block against the entry into policy of management ideas imported from the private sector. This is why it recommended the recruitment of people from outside Oxford and Cambridge and outside the civil service as a way to produce lasting management policy innovation. However, these suggestions were strongly resisted by 'generalist' bureaucrats and most collapsed at the implementation stage.

Management services units and the use of external consultants

In order to ensure that each department kept its organization informed of management developments in industry, Fulton proposed that the Organization and Methods (O and M) divisions of departments be replaced by new Management Services Units which would have 'wider responsibilities and functions than are given to O and M divisions today' (Fulton, Lord, 1968a: 55). This suggestion came from the study of the Fulton Committee's Management Consultancy Group, which found that the staff engaged in O and M 'are not sufficiently expert; they are frequently "generalists" who lack the necessary qualifications' (Fulton, Lord, 1968a: 55). To help departments apply the best available management methods and techniques from the private sector Fulton suggested that 'the use of outside consultants . . . should be an effective spur' (Fulton, Lord, 1968a: 54). The Committee recommended that the staff of these new Management Services Units should be drawn 'from appropriate specialists, including accountants, and from those with experience of similar work outside the Service, including with some practical experience of management in industry' (Fulton, Lord, 1968a: 56). More specifically, the Report urged that 'The qualifications and training of the management services staff of the Civil Service must compare favourably with those doing similar work outside, e.g. in large management consultancy firms' (Fulton, Lord, 1968a: 56).

Of course, Fulton was able to recommend the use of consultants in government and to make comparisons with management consulting firms because, as we saw in Chapter 2, there was at that time in Britain a management consulting industry that was beginning to grow and to become more organizationally developed. If management consultancy had not existed, Fulton would not have been very likely to recommend managerialist reforms. When the knowledge base needed for implementing a given line of policies does not exist, policy makers are less likely to pursue them (Skocpol, 1992: 42).

In the mid-1960s, following a review of the expenditure process (known as the Plowden Committee)[3] recommending that greater attention be given to management, the Treasury issued a report on the use of management consultants in government departments (*O&M Bulletin*, 1966). The Treasury report studied the questions of when and how to use, and how to select, management consultants. In the course of effecting the study, Treasury officials met several times with representatives of the British management consulting industry. As the Treasury recognized in its presentation to the Fulton

---

[3] The Plowden report anticipated much of Fulton's call for the construction of more effective channels of communication between business and the civil service: 'We must emphasize the advantage of seizing every opportunities for interchange of ideas and experience with people in commerce and industry. These are subjects in which the Civil Service can learn from experience in the private sector' (para. 58).

Committee, 'Recently, there has been an increase in consultation with the management services departments of larger firms and particularly with management consultants' (Fulton, Lord, 1968c: 614). For instance, in December 1965 a seminar was held at the Treasury with representatives of about twenty management consulting firms and organizations such as the Management Consultancies Association and the Institute of Management Consultants which, as seen in Chapter 2, were established in 1956 and 1962 respectively (Archer, 1968: 25). These meetings led to the formalization of selection procedures for the engagement of consultants and to the establishment, within the Treasury, of a register of management consultants (including about 125 firms) that government departments were required to consult before selecting and using external consulting services (Archer, 1968: 25).

Under the selection framework for the use of consultants that the Treasury developed with the help of management consulting associations, departments were asked to consult the Treasury before engaging consultants and to supply confidential reports on performance. Departments interested in commissioning consultants drafted a letter of invitation defining as precisely as possible the scope and nature of the assignment, together with a background paper giving further information on the problem and the department. These drafts were then discussed with the Treasury and a list of appropriate firms of consultants was drawn up. The department would send letters of invitation to two or three firms, asking if they wished to be considered for the assignment, and if so, to come to a meeting to discuss it. Treasury officials normally joined with the department in interviewing the consultants, who were often asked to carry out a short unpaid preliminary survey of the problem. Treasury and departmental officials made their final decision based on the preliminary survey report, the impression made by consultants, and the references from previous clients (Archer, 1968: 26). Later, at the end of the 1960s, responsibility for managing the selection process for the engagement of management consultants moved from the Treasury to the newly created Civil Service Department.

The Civil Service Department and the Civil Service College

On the day the Fulton Report was published, Prime Minister Wilson announced the establishment of the Civil Service Department (CSD) in response to the Committee's call for the establishment of a central department separate from the Treasury which would have responsibility for all aspects of pay, manpower, personnel, and civil service management. The Fulton Committee had reported that while, historically, the Treasury had held joint responsibility for public expenditure and civil service management, this arrangement had been to the detriment of the development of the managerial skills of the civil service (Gray and Jenkins, 1985: 96). In fact, Fulton accused the Treasury of being responsible for the underdeveloped state of management in Whitehall (p. 13). In the Treasury, management policy was much less glamorous than economic policy. Management was not highly regarded by Treasury officials, who preferred to work on economic policy issues to ensure their way to the top of the bureaucratic hierarchy (Chapman, 1983: 57). Fulton sought to take management policy out of the Treasury control. It recommended separate responsibilities for public expenditure and civil service management, and the transfer of the latter to a new Civil Service Department (CSD). The Committee concluded that the new department should report directly to the prime minister to secure the necessary political clout to ensure its success. It was also suggested that the CSD be responsible for implementing the recommendations made by Fulton, and this is why Fulton urged that it report to the prime minister, since 'No other minister could assert the needs of the government service as a whole over the sectional needs of powerful departmental ministers' (*The Civil Service*, 1968a: 84). Upon its creation, the CSD was thus placed under the formal responsibility of the prime minister, but in practice the day-to-day running of the department was delegated to a junior minister (Gladden, 1972).

After the establishment of the CSD in 1968, the head of the civil service moved from the Treasury to take charge of the new department. Upon its creation, the CSD took over the Treasury's Pay and Management Division. The CSD was not, therefore, a completely new department with a new staff because many of its most senior officials came from within the civil service, especially from the Treasury. However, the Fulton report had made it clear that this new department should not simply be the existing Pay and Management side of the Treasury hived off and expanded so it could then masquerade as the new CSD. The report emphasized that 'the staffing of this new department will be of critical importance'. It said that it was important that a number of appointments 'within the new department be made from outside the Service of people with appropriate knowledge and experience of managing large organizations' (*The Civil Service*, 1968a: 82). Fulton believed that if the CSD was allowed to bring in outsiders, this would create a more hospitable setting for the implementation of its innovative management policy proposals (Pollitt, 1984: 77).

Following the creation of the CSD, the head of the department reported that in its first year, the CSD had a hundred new entrants, all from within the civil service, and especially from the Treasury.[4] 'In fact', some later argued, 'the new department turned out to be very much like the old Pay and Management side of the Treasury' (Kellner and Crowther-Hunt, 1980: 80). By comparison, during that period, the CSD brought in only twenty-three people from outside the civil service, including eight from universities and

---

[4] As has been noted, because the CSD resulted from a 'hiving off process of a section already existing in the Treasury', it 'did not bring in the new men [*sic*] the Fulton Committee believed were needed if the reforms they recommended were to be implemented' (Armstrong, quoted in Pollitt, 1984: 77).

ten from private industry, including five from management consulting firms (Armstrong, 1970: 79). As new entrants to the civil service, they were appointed to middle and lower level positions and placed under the authority of an under-secretary in charge of the new consulting services that Fulton had recommended be put in place.[5] In Fulton's view, the CSD was to be the government's main internal management consulting service. The idea of establishing within the government a central management consulting unit came from the Fulton Committee's Management Consultancy Group, which argued in its report that the 'need for an awareness by management of developments outside the Service' required the creation of 'a highly professional internal management consultancy service' (Fulton, Lord, 1968b: 98). The Group recommended that this service be responsible for consultancy training, research into the development of new techniques, interdepartmental and high-level assignments, and reviews of the efficiency of the management of departments as a whole.

The Fulton Committee also recommended the establishment of a Civil Service College under CSD direction to provide management training courses. The College was intended by Fulton to be the source of the new professionalism in government administration, teaching the new style of management and 'spreading new ideas throughout the Service' (Garrett, 1980: 37). In opening the college in June 1970, the prime minister said that it was intended to promote 'cross-fertilization' and 'exchanges among the world of business and the civil service' (reported in Hayzelden, 1972: 21). The college offered training in cost accounting and control, planning and programming, and management consultancy (Garrett, 1972: 56). Courses on managerial techniques offered to civil servants by the college were taught by management consultants and practitioners from private industry (Grebenik, 1972: 129). With the CSD, the college provided another route through which new ways of looking at state management could be disseminated in the civil service by consultants.

Fulton's policy inheritance

In the second volume of his *Power, Competition and the State*, British historian Keith Middlemas argued that in the 1960s, Labour 'was unusually receptive to a business-oriented view of where the national interest lay' (1990: 179). As we have seen, this view was not absent from Fulton's policy proposals. Fulton's reforms need to be seen in the broader context of Labour's

---

[5] In the CSD, the under secretary responsible for management consulting services was not a professional consultant recruited from the private sector but rather, as he described himself, a 'general administrator who moves about in the Civil Service from one kind of job to another. I have no formal training in management, and I had had no experience of taking part in management consultancy assignments until I was put in this job where I have to supervise them' (Wilding, 1976: 60).

modernization platform and its attempts at mobilizing new social knowledge to support the institutionalization of rational planning within the British
state. To do so, the Wilson government sought to reduce the influence
of the Treasury in Whitehall by creating new departments such as the
DEA, Min-Tech, and the CSD—each of which was to be staffed, in part,
by recruiting outsiders from industry and commerce. In Labour's view, these
outsiders would help to build channels of communication between the state
and the private sector. This was necessary, because, politically, Labour wanted
to project a business-friendly image and to reassure industrialists that its new
planning system was not meant as a takeover of the economy by the state.
But as is well known, Labour's planning system was not to prove a lasting policy innovation (Leruez, 1975). Economic problems, and the failure
of the DEA and Min-Tech to establish themselves in Whitehall and to
confront the Treasury, led to the abolition of the two departments in the
late 1960s. As for the CSD, it was not abolished but as discussed next, even
under Edward Heath—who shared Labour's view that a more technocratic
approach was needed in Whitehall—the CSD never became the managerialist
powerhouse that Fulton believed was needed to make the administration of
government more businesslike. This happened in part because the outsiders
recruited to the CSD—who were supposed to be the advocates of managerialism in the civil service—did not occupy strategic posts where they could
influence policy. Because its senior echelons was colonized by the Treasury,
the CSD did not have the autonomy required to fight the Treasury view. At
its minimum, managerialism implies the decentralization of administrative
and financial responsibilities. But as long as management policy remained
under the influence of a body like the Treasury where arguments for economy
are paramount, such decentralization was not likely to take place.

Although they may not have had an immediate influence on the policies
adopted by the Wilson government, Fulton's ideas nevertheless shaped much
of the discussion about civil service reform that took place in the 1970s and
1980s (Drewry and Butcher, 1991: 54). As has been argued, the 'Management
Consultancy Group's report changed the climate and the agenda within which
the reform of the Civil Service was thereafter discussed' (Garrett, quoted
in Fry, 1993: 65). The impact of Fulton and of its Consultancy Group on
subsequent reform policies has been most important in the conceptualiza-
tion of the 'problems' that were believed to plague the administration in the
1960s, and in the definition of the solutions deemed appropriate for coping
with them. Fulton and its Group argued that the 'problems' of the British
bureaucracy in the 1960s were the lack of managerial skills in the civil
service, and the archaic character of the methods used to manage the state.
In this context, the idea that the government should emulate business management emerged from Fulton as the best solution to solve the deficiencies
of the British bureaucracy. That this solution was made available to policy
makers at that particular moment was not a coincidence. This was possible

because management consultancy was starting to grow and because consultants were able to make their views known within the government of the day through their presence on Fulton's Management Consultancy Group. Consultants played an influential role on Fulton. Sociologists have argued that 'the situation that is most congenial to expert influence is at the time of the discovery of problems and the founding of institutions [when] . . . professionals can move into unorganized policy fields that are later legitimated by law' (Brint, 1994: 139). This is exactly what happened after Fulton. By creating the Civil Service Department the British government formally recognized bureaucratic reform as a policy domain and publicly acknowledged management consultants as domain participants, thereby giving them a professional and institutional hold on management policy issues.

Heath and the White Paper on government reorganization

The implementation of Fulton's recommendations had hardly begun, when the Labour government was defeated in the June 1970 election. Under the leadership of the new Conservative government of Prime Minister Edward Heath administrative change took a different direction (Theakston and Fry, 1994). In the field of bureaucratic reform, the Heath government is intriguing because it promoted elements of both the 'old' and 'new' managerialism. It was in office as one paradigm was beginning to lose its hold, but the other model had yet to secure intellectual credibility or political backing (Seldon, 1996). Heath was a 'rational managerialist' (Hennessy, 1986: 74). Like the Wilson government, Heath thought that those trained in commerce and industry possessed skills which the civil service lacked (Bruce-Gardyne, 1974: 17). But Heath's government also embraced elements of the market model that some in Tory ranks (including Thatcher) began to promote in the early 1970s. A policy document published by the Conservative Party one month before the June 1970 election stated that

There is all the difference in the world between reform of government machinery and procedures under a party which believes in more government and under one which believes in less. Under the former it develops, automatically, as an aid for improving control of an ever-growing empire of functions and responsibilities. Under the latter it becomes . . . a key instrument in the drive for public economy and in the process of transferring functions and activities back to the private sector or running them down altogether. (Conservative Central Office, 1970: 8)

As part of what he called his 'quiet revolution' in government (Bruce-Gardyne, 1974), Prime Minister Heath issued on 15 October, less than four months after the election, an ambitious plan for bureaucratic reform in a White Paper on *The Reorganisation of Central Government* (Cmnd 4506, 1970).

Five days earlier Heath had told the Conservative Party conference that his goal was to produce a 'rational structure of government' and a better way of taking decisions (quoted in Theakston, 1996: 89). The White Paper argued that Whitehall was 'overloaded' and was critical of the fact that 'government has been attempting to do too much' (Cmnd 4506, 1970: para. 2). As stated in the opening paragraph of the White Paper, 'This Administration has pledged itself to introduce a new style of government' (Cmnd 4506, 1970: para. 1). This 'new style of government', which sought to strengthen the decision-making capacity of the centre by overcoming 'departmentalism', was to be based on what the White Paper saw as a 'functional' and 'analytical' approach to policy formulation.

Departmentalism and the creation of new central capabilities

In arguing in favour of a new style of government, the White Paper contained a criticism of the traditional 'departmentalist' style of British government. This style of government stresses the autonomy of the ministerial department and the weakness of the co-ordinative capacity of the centre (Radcliffe, 1991: 30–1). Of course, this autonomy is very much reinforced by the convention of ministerial responsibility which places accountability for departmental activity in the hands of the minister and of his/her permanent secretary (Marshall, 1989). But to a large extent, departmental autonomy is also closely linked to the dynamics of party politics (von Beyme, 1983). In parties where MPs have a political base of their own and have deep roots in their constituency, they have more autonomy from the party leadership than in leader-centred parties where MPs are dependent on the popularity of their leader for election (Laver and Budge, 1992). Once MPs are appointed ministers, those who have been elected on the coat-tails of the party leader—who, in the meanwhile, has become prime minister—have much less autonomy from the centre than ministers who do not owe their election to the party leadership (Franks, 1987: 110–15).

As we shall see in the next chapter, 'departmentalism' is best understood when contrasted with 'prime ministerialism', the model prevalent in the Canadian case where the prime minister and central agencies closely co-ordinate the activities of line departments (Campbell and Wyszomirski, 1991). As a result of the division of powers between federal and provincial governments, Canada has developed, at the national level, a complex bureaucratic system where the power of the prime minister and the centre has generally been strong as a way to counterbalance the centripetal forces inherent in a federal and multinational state (Aucoin and Bakvis, 1986). In Britain, we have almost the opposite situation: a centralized state has given rise to a more decentralized style of governance. This has been characterized as 'Whitehall as a federation of ministries' (Dunleavy and Rhodes, 1990: 18). As Bruce Heady concluded in his study of how British ministers understood their role in government, 'in Britain we have departmental government' (1974: 60). In this model, ministers regard their departmental work as the most important way to make an impact and promote their political career. This view fits with the picture of the 'Whitehall village' described by Heclo and Wildavsky where the prestige of ministers is determined by their success in bringing their departments resources (1981). In this model, the Cabinet is seen not merely as a forum by which the prime minister and central agencies impose their views on departments, but more as 'an inter-departmental battleground' (Heady, 1974: 60).

It was this type of interdepartmental politics and compromise that Heath wanted to eliminate by strengthening the centre. The 1970 White Paper underlined the need to remove areas where ministerial departments overlapped, causing delay and conflict in decision making. It announced the formation of two giant departments (Trade and Industry, and Environment) as an illustration of the new functional approach which aimed at creating more strategic units of government. The White Paper stated that the aim of creating functionally integrated departments was to reduce 'parochial' departmentalism. A large department would have 'less need to fear and defend its interests against other interests so that in the formative stages of policy it must and will be ready to discuss issues with other departments' (Cmnd 4506, 1970: para. 13). Another reason was that large departments 'would have greater control over resources and be more efficient at achieving broad objectives within the government's overall strategy' (Radcliffe, 1991: 2).

The desire to develop a more strategic form of decision making shaped the analytical approach advocated in the White Paper. As one observer noted, in 'the White Paper's managerialist language . . . the words "strategy" or "strategic" were used seventeen times in a slim document of only sixteen pages long' (Theakston, 1996: 89). The emphasis on the need to increase the capacity of the centre for strategic management resulted in the implementation of the British version of PPBS, the system of Programme Analysis and Review (PAR). This sought to assess the relevance of departmental policies to the government's broader objectives. The PAR system was designed to analyse and review: (a) the goals of the programme; (b) the amount and use of allocated resources; and (c) any alternative means of achieving programme goals.

The White Paper also created the Central Policy Review Staff (CPRS), an organization located in the Cabinet Office designed to provide ministers with a non-departmental source of advice (Pollitt, 1974). The CPRS was intended to aid the government collectively and to relate departmental policies to the broader government strategy (Barnes and Cockett, 1994). It was seen as an instrument of the Cabinet as a whole. The rationale behind the creation of the CPRS was the need to develop a new 'central capability' able to provide to the Cabinet strategic analysis of policy across departmental boundaries (Pollitt, 1984: 87). This was in order that long-term goals should not be lost sight of due to the pressure of day-to-day departmental activity (Radcliffe, 1991: 161). The CPRS, known as the 'think tank', was composed of about twenty members: 'about half of them were career civil servants seconded from departments, the rest recruited from outside: business, management consultancy, the universities' (Plowden, 1991: 229). Because it consisted of a mix of external advisers and civil servants, the CPRS was seen as an interesting experience in the importation of 'outside ideas into a traditionally closed system of government' (Drewry and Butcher, 1991: 89). Heath is said to have appointed outsiders to the Whitehall bureaucracy 'in far greater numbers than had ever occurred before' (Campbell, 1993: 325). This situation gave rise to criticism that Heath was 'presidentializing' the Westminster system of government (Campbell, 1983: 4). This is not totally surprising given the fact that the context for the ideas that underlay the creation of the CPRS was the reform of the US government that led to the establishment of the Office of Management and Budget and the increased importance of White House advisers under President Nixon (Baston and Seldon, 1996: 48). But Heath's desire to strengthen the centre and to rely on outsiders for policy advice generated some tensions within the Conservative party. There was some back-bench resentment towards Heath and a feeling among Tory MPs that the prime minister was paying more attention to his advisers and the CPRS than to the views of his party (Norton, 1978).

Institutional innovation and the origins of PAR ideas

The ideas that went into PAR and that informed the Conservative government's 1970 White Paper came from a variety of sources (Pollitt, 1984: 88; Gray and Jenkins, 1985: 106). First, there was Fulton. 'The White Paper had some links with issues raised by the Fulton report . . . There was a general sense in which both documents saw the need to learn from the private sector' (Radcliffe, 1991: 70). The PAR system was also influenced by rationalist innovations such as PPBS which in Britain had been applied selectively and incrementally, first in the Ministry of Defence in 1963, and then in other high-spending departments such the Home Office, Education and Science, Transport, and Health (Else, 1970).

The main origins of the White Paper and PAR can be traced back to work begun inside the Conservative Party's policy-making bureaucracy, especially in the Public Sector Research Unit (PSRU) and the Businessmen's Team, two new organizations created by Heath in the mid-1960s (Radcliffe, 1991: 61). On becoming leader of the Conservative Party in 1965, Heath established an elaborate policy-making exercise, at its height involving over thirty separate policy groups with a combined membership of well over 200 MPs and outside experts, including academics and management consultants (Johnman, 1993: 187; Kavanagh, 1987a: 221; Seldon, 1994: 56).

Under Heath's leadership, a policy group on Machinery of Government and a privately financed body, the Public Sector Research Unit (PSRU) were created within the Research Department of the Conservative Party (Campbell, 1983: 213; Ramsden, 1980: 254). The work of the PSRU 'was to be very influential with Edward Heath' (Radcliffe, 1991: 68). The primary input of the PSRU into the 1970 White Paper was a concern with policy analysis and policy review outlined in a Conservative Party publication called *A New Style of Government* (Conservative Central Office, 1970; see also Radcliffe, 1991: 68; Ramsden, 1980: 257). The main task of the PSRU consisted of commissioning research by management consulting firms on specific aspects of government activity (Butler and Pinto-Duschinsky, 1971: 85). These included research reports on government procurement procedures, and especially studies on machinery-of-government questions (Pollitt, 1984: 84). For instance, one such study produced in 1965 recommended the creation of a new management consultancy central unit to be charged with improving the efficiency and effectiveness of Whitehall as a whole. This unit, known as the 'Crown Consultants Unit' is said to be 'the direct progenitor' of the Central Policy Review Staff created by the White Paper (Pollitt, 1984: 84).

Many of the studies prepared by management consultants for the PSRU suggested 'that considerable savings could be made by the introduction of more businesslike management into several sectors of the public service' (Butler and Pinto-Duschinsky, 1971: 85). In *The Private Government of Public Money*, Heclo and Wildavsky report that one important source of advice which served as a basis for PAR and the ideas introduced in the 1970 White Paper was 'the nation's leading firms of business consultants [which] were hired to advise the [Conservative Party] leadership' on public management issues (1981: 271). Management consultants were hired for particular projects: RTZ Consultants produced a study entitled *Decision-Making in Government* and Arthur D. Little and Booz-Allen looked at public procurement (Pollitt, 1984: 84).

Heath's Businessmen's Team

A final source of ideas for PAR was the 'Businessmen's Team', a group of advisers to the Conservative leader Edward Heath created in 1969 (Pollitt, 1984: 85). The work of the Businessmen's Team was 'closely directed by Heath' and thus its ideas could feed their way directly into the inner circles of the Conservative Party policy-making machinery (Theakston and Fry, 1994: 394). Two firms of management consultants, PA Consulting and Booz-Allen, were employed by the Conservative Party to recruit the individuals who would become members of Mr. Heath's Businessmen's Team (Butler and Pinto-Duschinsky, 1971: 86). Those recruited included business persons from large companies such as Shell (Richard Meyjes), a merchant banker from Hambros (H. R. Hutton), and senior partners from the firms RTZ Consultants (Ken Lane) and PA Consulting (Alan Fogg). The Business-men's Team also included Derek Rayner from Marks & Spencer who would later become Prime Minister Thatcher's main adviser on efficiency (Jones, 1970: 19).

The businessmen worked for Heath in their spare time on the understanding that if and when the Conservatives won the election their companies would lend them to the government for two years. In the meantime their efforts were devoted to developing specific proposals for bureaucratic reform; some members of the Businessmen's Team worked on the development of output-oriented decision-making systems, and others on computer utiliza-tion, public purchasing, and so on (Hennessy, 1989: 212). By the spring of 1970, in collaboration with the Conservative Party policy-making machine, the Businessmen's Team had helped produce a 'Black Book', an internal party document containing the strategy that informed the 1970 White Paper and with which the Conservatives took over the Whitehall policy-making machine (Pollitt, 1984: 86).

According to Heclo and Wildavsky, it was the Businessmen's Team which 'pulled together the ideas that eventually became Programme Analysis and Review' (1981: 272). In order to know more about planning and PPBS, some members of the Businessmen's Team were dispatched to the United States (Heclo and Wildavsky, 1981: 272; Pollitt, 1984: 84). Once in Washington, the Businessmen's Team liked what they saw but soon discovered that some of the bloom was already off PPBS (Heclo and Wildavsky, 1981: 272). Almost at the same time, Treasury officials also sent emissaries to the United States to study PPBS. They returned full of caution at the immense size of the task and the strong resistance to be encountered in introducing PPBS. Consequently, British policy makers did not enthusiastically embrace PPBS ideas.

The result of the research work done by the PSRU and the Businessmen's Team was that, in 1970, the 'Conservative Party entered office armed with an unprecedented volume of advice on improving administrative structures' (Pollitt, 1984: 87). One of the first tasks of the Conservative Party leader on taking office in 1970 was to find organizational homes for his personal advisers within the Whitehall machinery. By the time Heath became prime minister, a number of his advisers from the Businessmen's Team, along with party professionals from the Conservative Research Department, had moved into Whitehall, either to temporary posts in the civil service or to positions as political advisers to ministers. 'This', it has been suggested, 'gave them the opportunity to pursue the plans that they had prepared in opposition' (Kavanagh, 1987a: 221).

Immediately after the June 1970 election the Businessmen's Team moved into the Civil Service Department. To the extent that the Businessmen's Team was supposed to keep an eye on the implementation of the changes contained in the 1970 White Paper, its institutional location within the CSD was seen as important because that department had jurisdiction over bureaucratic reform policy (Jones, 1970: 19). Originally, the PAR process was supposed to be housed in the CSD, under the authority of the Businessmen's Team (Heclo and Wildavsky, 1981: 277). But the businessmen soon discovered that they could not make PAR work in the CSD because of the opposition of the Treasury. As one senior official argued, 'Putting PAR in the CSD caused the Treasury to be anti. The Treasury wanted to take it over' (reported in Heclo and Wildavsky, 1981: 277). Because PAR was intended to question the use of budgetary resources in the achievement of programme goals, Treasury officials saw it as an extension of their jurisdiction over financial management issues. After a short experience in the CSD, the PAR was moved to the Treasury, thereby reducing the role of the businessmen in the supervision of the White Paper's reforms.

Management consultants and institution building

After having lost their responsibility for co-ordinating the PAR process, the Businessmen's Team refocused their energy on the consolidation of the CSD's management capacities and on the implemention of the Fulton report's key recommendations (Archer, 1971: 8). As seen earlier, the Fulton report criticized the closed character of Whitehall and proposed that there should be a greater interchange of experience between the private sector and government. In 1969, the CSD initiated contact with industrial companies, banks, and management consulting firms with a view to arranging an exchange of staff (CSD, 1970b: 43). Following the election of Heath in 1970, the Confederation of British Industry (CBI), the main association representing business interests in Britain, began to develop, in collaboration with the CSD, a scheme for the interchange of personnel at middle-management level between the public and private sectors (CSD, 1974: 30). Before the 1970 election, Heath's Conservatives had made it clear that, once in power, they would mobilize business expertise to make the civil service more dynamic and efficient. To create the 'Whitehall of tomorrow', one may read in a Conservative pamphlet, we need 'to bring in new recruits . . . from corporate businesses, from small private enterprises, from accountants, from management consultants' (Conservative Central Office, 1970: 31).

It is in this context that the CSD began in 1970 to develop and institutionalize a secondment programme between the civil service and management consulting firms. The secondment programme was meant to introduce more flexible standards of recruitment that would allow the CSD to bring into the civil service more consultants as a way to facilitate the entry of new ways of looking at state management. Management consultants from large consulting firms were sometimes seconded to the CSD for periods of time as long as 15 months, and CSD officials were seconded to the big firms to work on private sector, fee-earning consulting assignments as a way to familiarize themselves with business management practices (Hayzelden, 1972; Matthews and Maxwell, 1974). Following the establishment of the secondment programme, Prime Minister Heath attended a meeting of the Institute of Management Consultants (IMC). He told the IMC that 'management consultants are playing a valuable part in improving the quality of central government management' (CSD, 1972: 5). Heath noted that 'the practice has grown of seconding management consultants to work alongside civil servants' and said that he 'was delighted with the success' of having business experts 'with the experience and qualities we require' in government (ibid.).

In the early 1970s, the CSD also began to organize a series of seminars with consultants designed to help the department build up its competence in management consultancy (CSD, 1970a: 4). In a speech to the annual conference of PA Management Consultants Ltd., the head of the Home Civil Service praised consultants for their help 'in putting at our disposal' their knowledge of private enterprise for improving public management practices (Armstrong, 1970: 79). However, he warned consultants of the limits of managerialism and 'of the differences between the situation in private enterprise and that in the Civil Service . . . [where] we come up against the political factor—the fact that what we do must be subject to democratic control' (1970: 73).

In a talk given to the IMC, one CSD senior official mentioned that the CSD had become 'the central point of reference in Whitehall for the employment of management consultants from the private sector' (Wilding, 1976: 60). Similarly, another CSD representative argued that since its establishment, the CSD had 'developed firm links with the businessmen and outside consultants with whom we frequently work in joint teams' (Archer, 1972: 13).

As indicated in Table 3.1 the construction, within the state, of new management capacities following Fulton went hand in hand with an increase in government spending on external consultants. However, after this period of growth the level of work done for government by management consultants decreased somewhat by the mid-1970s. In a speech given to the IMC, one CSD official said that 'I am very much aware that I am talking to you at a time when the level of Government business for consultants is pretty low. Part of the reason for this is the way in which Government Departments have been developing their own management services skills' (Wilding, 1976: 69).

The fall of rationalism and the 'old' managerialism

Of course, the public expenditure reductions that Heath began to impose to deal with inflation in the wake of the oil embargo was part of the reason why the level of government business for consultants was low in the

TABLE 3.1. UK central government management consulting expenditure

	1964	*1969*	*1972*
Cost	£20,000	£830,000	£4.8 m.
Number of assignments	3	60	300

Note: Data in Table 3.1 exclude assignments from the National Health Service, computer consulting, and work by consultants on secondment from their firms to the civil service. Data concerning management consulting assignments commissioned by government departments come from *O&M Bulletin*. From time to time between 1968 and 1981, *O&M Bulletin* issued samples of management consulting assignments commissioned to private-sector firms by government departments. Before the creation of the CSD in 1968, *O&M Bulletin* was published by the Treasury. In 1973, *O&M Bulletin* was renamed *Management Services in Government*. The *O&M Bulletin* and its successor contain valuable information on the role of consultants in government. The publication of *Management Services in Government* was ended in the early 1980s after the abolition, by the Thatcher government, of the CSD in 1981.

Sources: Archer, J. N. (1972), 'Business Methods in Government', *O&M Bulletin* 27/1: 12; Matthews, R. S., and Maxwell, R. J. (1974), 'Working in Partnership with Management Consultants', *Management Services in Government* 29/1: 27.

mid-1970s (Blackaby, 1978). Indeed, in 1973 the British government was threatened not only by oil shortage but also by a strike by miners (Taylor, 1996). The National Union of Mineworkers (NUM) called a strike to start on 10 February 1974. Asking 'Who Governs Britain?', Prime Minister Heath reacted by calling a general election on 7 February. After the election, a new Labour administration assumed office, to find itself inheriting the reforms of the Heath government. Many of the changes introduced by the 1970 White Paper were regarded by the new administration 'as part of an alien legacy' (Gray and Jenkins, 1985: 106). Deeply suspicious of anything connected with the former Conservative prime minister, Heath, Labour allowed PAR to wither away and defined the role of the CPRS more narrowly (Theakston, 1992: 136).

According to Gray and Jenkins, the White Paper and PAR demonstrated the 'difficulties of institutionalising rational policy analysis in governmental organisations' (1985: 128). They argue that PAR was unable to meet the technical, organizational, and political preconditions for effective policy analysis. It has also been suggested that the White Paper's attempts at strengthening the centre by introducing a new 'rational' approach were 'defeated by the perceived need to defend departmental policies against threats from the centre' (Radcliffe, 1991: 160). The maintenance of the autonomy of departments is said to have undermined a reform aimed at greater policy integration and co-ordination. 'The characteristic departmentalism of British government was maintained at the expense of the broader concept entailed [in the White Paper] approach' (Radcliffe, 1991: 160–1).

The historian of Whitehall, Peter Hennessy, has argued that the Treasury played a key role in resisting the full implementation of some of the ideas that were part of the 1970 White Paper. In the case of the PAR, Hennessy wrote that the 'first step' of senior Treasury officials 'towards smothering it was to remove it from the grasp of Heath's businessmen in the CSD and to draw it into their own citadel in Great George Street from which it never emerged alive' (Hennessy, 1989: 235).

One final element contributing to the decline of support for the White Paper was the crisis in public expenditures that overtook the government of Wilson and Callaghan. The introduction of cash limits in 1976 shifted the attention from long-term strategic planning to more rapid cost cutting (Gray and Jenkins, 1985: 114). This shift is seen by some as illustrating the 'fall of rational decision-making' in British government (Jenkins and Gray, 1990: 56). The decline of rationalism was formalized when the Thatcher government abandoned PAR soon after the 1979 election and abolished the CPRS in 1983 (Gray and Jenkins, 1985: 102).

Thatcherism and the 'Efficiency Strategy'

The full move toward the market-based model of public administration came with the election of a new Conservative government under Margaret Thatcher in 1979.[6] This is not to suggest that the Thatcher government 'gave birth' to the new managerialism. Of course, the Heath years marked a critical period of transition but the shift to wholehearted new managerialism came only after 1979 with Thatcher. This shift owed a great deal to the political support and ideological convictions of Thatcher herself. There is no doubt that she was a tireless patron of the ideas that underlay the reform policies implemented during her tenure as prime minister. But it would be a mistake to assume that policy change could be satisfactorily attributed uniquely to the political determination of Mrs Thatcher. This was an important influence but change would not have gone as far as it did if Thatcher's political programme had not been tied to, and enriched by, the more programmatic ideas provided by experts in management consulting firms. If it is not connected to technical ideas, political conviction alone (and vice versa) does not go very far as an explanation to account for policy change (Weir, 1992: 169). Thatcher's rhetoric celebrated the superiority of the market and championed entrepreneurship, while business consultants and their ideas gave technical credibility to managerialist policies because they came

---

[6] 'Efficiency Strategy' is the umbrella term used to describe the new managerialist programme of bureaucratic reforms implemented by the Thatcher government (Metcalfe and Richards, 1990).

from the private sector. Once in office, the Thatcher government began to change the orientation of bureaucratic reform policy quite dramatically and as we shall see, this change coincided with the creation of new, and more centralized, institutional conduits linking British decision makers and management consultants. During the 1980s, the whole of Whitehall was opened up, ventilated, and dramatically challenged. Bureaucratic reform policy-making agencies became more open to the use of outside management consulting knowledge and this paved the way for the acceptance of the new managerialism as the corner-stone of British public administration.

In October 1979, the Cabinet launched the Scrutiny Programme which was to be placed under the direction of Sir Derek Rayner, Chief Executive of Marks & Spencer (Gray and Jenkins, 1985: 116). Rayner was appointed by Thatcher to advise her on ways of improving managerial efficiency and eliminating waste in central government. He was given *carte blanche* to bring the market disciplines, cost consciousness, and, most important, management techniques of the private sector to government. Rayner was familiar with the corridors of Whitehall, having served as a member of Heath's Businessmen's Team. In implementing his Scrutiny Programme, Rayner was supported by a small unit known as the Efficiency Unit, based in the Prime Minister's Office. The Efficiency Unit had a small staff of career civil servants and private sector management consultants (Metcalfe and Richards, 1990: 9). The appointment of Rayner as head of the Efficiency Unit has been seen by some as 'following the Heath government's precedent of inviting private sector consultants to advise on public sector management' (Zifcak, 1994: 15). The 'precedent' created by Heath consisted in the establishment of the Businessmen's Team. As has been noted, the 'groundwork' for some of Mrs Thatcher's changes in Whitehall, including the use of management consultants as advisers on bureaucratic reform issues, were 'laid in the Heath period' (Theakston and Fry, 1994: 395). This is in part why some have argued that 'Conservative governments have favoured bringing management consultants from the private sector more than Labour governments' (Henkel, 1991a: 74).

The Efficiency Unit, the Policy Unit, and Thatcher's presidential style

From 1979 to 1983, the Prime Minister's Efficiency Unit was directed by Rayner. After the 1983 election, Rayner was replaced as the Prime Minister's adviser on efficiency by Sir Robin Ibbs, at the time an executive director of Imperial Chemical Industries (ICI). The Efficiency Unit was headed by a chief of staff of under-secretary rank. The first, Clive Priestly, was a civil servant and the second, Ian Beesley, left in 1986 to become a senior partner in the management consulting firm Price Waterhouse which, as discussed later, played a major role in the implementation of the Next Steps policy (*Times Higher Education Supplement*, 1986: 3).

One of the key innovations of the Efficiency Strategy was the 'machinery created to give effect to political intentions, notably the Efficiency Unit established within the Prime Minister's Office' and which had direct access to the Prime Minister (Metcalfe and Richards, 1990: viii). The locus of the Efficiency Unit within the Whitehall machinery, where it had high-level political access, was seen as crucial to making the process of reform work and for securing the acceptance, by ministers and civil servants, of the managerialist ideas and policies that were part of the government's Efficiency Strategy (Metcalfe, 1993: 356). The privileged location of the Efficiency Unit, first in the Prime Minister's Office and later in the Cabinet Office, ensured unit advice a direct route to the top. It also made clear that the head of the unit and his team of civil servants and management consultants could call on prime ministerial backing if it was needed, and ensured that bureaucrats and ministers in departments took the Efficiency Unit's work seriously.

In creating the Efficiency Unit in 1979, and particularly in deciding not to locate it in the CSD (which at that moment was still the organization formally responsible for administrative reform in Whitehall), the Thatcher government learned from the past bureaucratic reform experiences of Fulton and of the 1970 White Paper. As discussed earlier, some of the reforms recommended by Fulton and derived from the 1970 White Paper were not fully implemented in part because of bureaucratic resistance. In appointing someone like Rayner with experience in Whitehall managerial reform to direct the Efficiency Unit, and in locating the Unit within the Prime Minister's Office, the Thatcher administration wanted to bypass the bureaucracy— especially the Treasury and the CSD. It wanted to make sure that, unlike the Fulton and Heath's reforms, its management policy agenda would not be blocked by senior departmental officials (Young and Sloman, 1982). The government abolished the CSD in 1981 following a civil service strike. In her early years in office, Prime Minister Thatcher perceived 'the civil service, especially the higher civil service, as an adversary' and saw the CSD as one of the 'relics' left by Labour's interventionist ideology (Fry, 1984: 325). In one meeting, the head of the CSD 'provoked her wrath by disputing the aptness of private sector management principles to the public service' (Campbell and Wilson, 1995: 208). According to Savoie, soon after her election Thatcher became 'exasperated with the officials of the CSD who were constantly defending the department's practices, insisting that government administration was entirely different from business management . . . In short, the CSD did not fit the business-management model' (1994: 201).

Following the abolition of the CSD, responsibility for civil service personnel and pay were then returned to the Treasury and functions related to the organization, management, and efficiency of the civil service, together with personnel matters and policy on training and recruitment, were transferred to a new Management and Personnel Office (MPO) located in the Cabinet Office. In 1987, the MPO was disbanded and its functions went to a new Office of the Minister for the Civil Service, attached to the Cabinet Office (Drewry and Butcher, 1991: 95).

Thatcher not only created the Efficiency Unit and abolished the CSD, but also reintroduced, in 1983, the Number 10 Policy Unit. The unit had originally been created by Labour in 1974 to provide a political, party-oriented, and personal advisory service to the Prime Minister (Donoughue, 1986). In the field of government reform, the Policy Unit is the only legacy of institutional innovation left by the 1974–9 Labour administration, which supported the Whitehall status quo and did not initiate any major plan to change the civil service (Morgan, 1997: 509; Theakston, 1992: 135). The Policy Unit, whose size and influence were said to be in 'expansion' under Thatcher, consisted of individuals with policy expertise drawn from the Conservative Party and of management consultants from big firms such as McKinsey and Coopers & Lybrand (Jones, 1987: 59; Willetts, 1987: 446).

The Efficiency and Policy Units were among the key organizational channels through which management consultants could make their voices heard within the inner circles of policy making. In addition, the fact that private sector consultants employed in the Efficiency and Policy Units worked closely with career public servants seconded from their department to the Prime Minister's Office helped to secure the acceptance by the bureaucracy of the ideas that they promoted. Some of these seconded civil servants were to provide a link between the management consultants working in the units and the bureaucracy. The secondment of civil servants to small organizational entities such as the Prime Minister's Efficiency and Policy Units, stimulated charges of 'politicization' and consequently, a number of seconded officials who became identified with Thatcher's prime ministership were not able to return to the public service at the conclusion of their term in the Prime Minister's Office (Aucoin, 1995: 55).

The creation of the Efficiency and Policy Units—that some have compared to 'the British equivalents of a White House staff' (Campbell and Wilson 1995: 295), has been seen as evidence of the increasing 'presidential' style of the Thatcher administration. Although 'presidentialism' began with Heath, it accelerated under Thatcher's tenure (King, 1985). Like the American presidential system of government, this style of leadership is more centralized and tends to rely more on outsiders for policy advice than on the permanent public service and cabinet colleagues (Foley, 1993; Jones, 1991; Mackenzie, 1987). In relying on outsiders, Thatcher was, to some extent, only continuing a process that began with Fulton which, as we saw earlier, argued that there was a good case for opening up the civil service (RIPA, 1987). In 1983, a report by the Cabinet Office on the British civil service argued, like Fulton 15 years before, that the civil service was too closed and that this was fostering 'parochialism, conservatism and inflexibility' (Cabinet Office, MPO, 1983: 40). The report identified a number of 'disadvantages' linked to the impermeability of the civil service. It argued that it was 'less receptive to new ideas and attitudes or to unconventional approaches' and that there was a 'danger of staleness . . . resistance to change, lack of dynamism and vigour in the closed society at the top of the service'. The report concluded that there were advantages to be gained through 'regular infusion of new blood' by increasing the number of secondments and recruitments from outside (Cabinet Office, MPO, 1983: 40–1).

These recommendations did not fall on deaf ears. The programme of secondments between the bureaucracy and industry, commerce, management consulting firms, and other outside bodies was greatly expanded, 'with anywhere between eight hundred and a thousand secondments in and out of the service throughout the Thatcher years' (Savoie, 1994: 252). The goal behind this was to make the civil service less insular: to expose it to fresh ideas. During the Thatcher period around two-thirds of inward secondments (i.e. into the civil service from outside), were from business, consulting firms, and industrial organizations. Some critics noted that the 'problem is that no clear safeguards exist to guarantee that individuals on short-term secondment will not use the knowledge acquired while working in government to the advantage of their employers' (Baggott, 1995: 95). Whether this has happened or not is an open question. But the growth of secondments certainly strengthened the networks between government and the world of industry and management. This gave to industrialists and consultants 'valuable experience and helped them to develop useful contacts when lobbying on issues affecting their broader interests' (Baggott, 1995: 121).

By the early 1990s, it was suggested that Thatcher's attempts at opening up the civil service had been so successful that this contributed to the 'death' of the Whitehall paradigm, whereby the permanent career bureaucracy had usually acted as the principal source of policy advice to ministers (Campbell and Wilson, 1995). Traditionally, the closed character of the British bureaucracy had often impeded the entry of innovative ideas into the policy process and prevented outside voices from making much political headway (Davidson and Lowe, 1981). But this would no longer be the case. 'The increased infiltration of the civil service by the ideas of people from other walks of life', some argued, 'is likely to make the civil service increasingly pro-active and less resistant to change.' As more 'people with experience of business, the city and industry are appointed as advisers . . . [and] as management consultants are increasingly used to carry out both discrete blocks of work and to work alongside existing staff . . . it will [be] easier for government to implement policies directly with little civil service resistance or distortion' (Greer, 1994: 104).

The Scrutiny Programme

Launched by Rayner soon after his appointment as head of the Efficiency Unit, the Scrutiny Programme had three main objectives: (a) to examine a specific policy or activity, questioning all aspects of work normally taken for granted; (b) to propose solutions to problems and to make recommendations to achieve savings and increase efficiency and effectiveness, and (c) to implement agreed solutions, or to begin their implementation within 12 months of the start of a scrutiny (Greenwood and Wilson, 1989: 123).

In implementing the Scrutiny Programme, the Efficiency Unit learned from previous attempts at reforming the Whitehall bureaucracy. In fact, the experts in the Efficiency Unit sought to reverse the effects of the 1970 White Paper designed by Heath's Businessmen's Team as a way to curtail the autonomy of departments and strengthen the co-ordinative capacity of the centre. Improved management in government was seen by the Efficiency Unit as depending substantially on securing the commitment of the civil service and on obtaining the support of senior officials. 'And this meant working with, rather than against, the grain of departmentalism' (Metcalfe and Richards, 1990: 11). By going with the 'grain of departmentalism' (and not against it as the 1970 White Paper had done) the Scrutiny Programme was designed to secure high-level departmental support. Jealous of their own autonomy, departments 'were allowed a large measure of discretion in deciding how and where to seek savings and effect improvements' (Metcalfe and Richards, 1990: 134). Although the scrutinies took place in the departments and were conducted by departmental personnel sometimes helped by outside management consultants, the total programme was co-ordinated by the Efficiency Unit (Taylor, 1983). The choice of scrutiny topics was the responsibility of the minister in charge of the department, but under the oversight of the Efficiency Unit (House of Commons, 1986).

Prime Minister Thatcher took a keen interest in the scrutinies, 'insisting that she be regularly briefed on their progress' (Savoie, 1994: 120). She asked her ministers to take a direct hand in reviewing the operations and management practices of their department. Many ministers, who preferred to concentrate on politics and policy, were not happy with the 'minister-as-manager' concept that Thatcher advocated. Others, like Michael Heseltine in the Department of Environment (DOE), were strongly committed to the new managerialism. Himself a business manager and former editor of the journal *Management Today*, Heseltine entered Whitehall in 1979 resolved 'to set the private sector as an example for the proper management' of government (Heseltine, 1987: 10). Following his appointment to the DOE, Heseltine recruited a team of outside consultants, a number of them drawn from the big firm Peat Marwick (Hennessy, 1989: 703). When he arrived in the DOE, Heseltine found no adequate management system for giving ministers a clear picture of what was going on in the department (Arnott, 1983). This view was confirmed by a scrutiny conducted by the Efficiency Unit. Based on the result of that scrutiny, Heseltine established in the DOE a system known as Management Information System for Ministers (MINIS), designed to bring together, for the purpose of the minister, information about activities, past performance, and future plans for each part of the department. The system was intended to show how the work of the department was organized and who was responsible for each activity.

The MINIS idea was brought on to the political agenda after having attracted the attention of Prime Minister Thatcher. This happened because MINIS was an idea with a powerful champion, a minister who was a political heavy-weight heading a major department. Ambitious to further his political career, Heseltine knew that Thatcher was encouraging her ministers to take a direct interest in administrative reform and this is why he acted as a champion of the new managerialism. In early 1980, Prime Minister Thatcher asked Heseltine to talk to the Cabinet about MINIS, which subsequently became a 'rallying cry' for managerialist policy innovation in government (Savoie, 1994: 121).

Rayner and members of his Efficiency Unit were strong supporters of Heseltine's system. This enthusiasm was shared by a number of consultants who, based on their experience in the Rayner scrutinies, concluded that there was a need for a comprehensive, MINIS-like, management framework in departments (Gray, Jenkins, Flynn, and Rutherford, 1991: 41). The Efficiency Unit supported this view and in 1981 invited the Management Consultancies Association (MCA) to a Cabinet meeting at Downing Street to press this case at 'the highest possible level' (ibid.). In their presentation, MCA delegates laid out a proposal for a new management system that would help departments to decide priorities, assess effectiveness and see where cuts can be best made. According to Gray, Jenkins, *et al.*, Mrs Thatcher was 'impressed' by the MCA presentation and she strongly supported the type of framework that consultants argued was needed in departments (ibid.). The prime minister's endorsement of the ideas presented in the MCA briefing was translated into policy a few months later when the Financial Management Initiative (FMI) was introduced. As the director of the MCA said, 'from this briefing, were the seeds of the FMI sown'.[7]

The FMI and the mobilization of management consulting knowledge

The White Paper (Cmnd. 8616) of September 1982 specified the three basic principles of the FMI intended to promote in each department an organization and system in which managers at all levels have:

— a clear view of their objectives, and means to assess and, wherever possible, measure outputs and performance in relation to those objectives;

— well-defined responsibility for making the best use of their resources, including a critical scrutiny of output and value-for-money; and

---

[7] Written interview with Brian O'Rorke, Executive Director of the MCA, 15 July 1997.

— the information (particularly about costs), the training and the *access to expert advice* that they need to exercise their responsibilities effectively (italics added, Cmnd. 1982: 8616, para. 13).

The FMI was about financial management and was thus institutionally part of the Treasury's policy territory. But the Treasury was reluctant to decentralize management responsibilities and to give managers in line departments greater discretion in the use of resource (Campbell and Wilson, 1995: 235–41). Reluctance on the part of the Treasury to relax detailed controls over departmental expenditures was very likely to undermine the FMI. This is why the government decided not to give the Treasury sole responsibility for the advancement of the FMI. The Financial Management Unit (FMU)—a small organization like the Efficiency Unit—was established at the centre to lead the initiative. The FMU was a joint creation of the Cabinet Office and the Treasury but it functioned from the Cabinet Office. The FMU was created to provide the 'access to expert advice' that the FMI promised to give to managers, and this expertise came from management consultants who formed the majority of those recruited to work in the FMU. The FMU had full prime ministerial backing and its members had direct access to decision-making centres in Whitehall. The FMU was directed by an under-secretary in the Cabinet Office. The FMU consisted of six civil servants and eight consultants, all from MCA member firms.[8] With the implementation of the FMI, 'the MCA moved swiftly to consolidate its position by developing its network of contacts within the civil service' (Smith and Young, 1996: 142). In the early 1980s, the MCA created within its organization a 'Public Sector Working Party' (PSWP) to develop a more co-ordinated strategy to the promotion of new managerialist approaches and of management consulting to government. According to the MCA, 'the Group dealing with the public sector has established close links with departments employing management consultancy services with the intention not only of establishing a better understanding within Whitehall of the services that we can offer, but of equal importance, ensuring that our membership is aware of the needs and constraints faced by Ministries' (MCA, 1989: 4).

To a large extent, the establishment of the PSWP was spurred by Thatcher's interest in public sector reform which, it was believed, could 'provide a rapidly growing market for management consultants' (Henkel, 1991a: 77). But it must also be seen in the context of the economic recession which, in the early 1980s, led many management consulting firms to focus their attention on the commercial potential of government and other parts of the public sector. As seen in Figure 3.1, in the mid-1980s the PSWP was made of five 'sub-groups', one of which was directly linked to the Cabinet Office.

[8] The consultants were drawn from Arthur Andersen, Coopers & Lybrand, Peat Marwick, and Hay-MSL (Russell, 1984: 146–7).

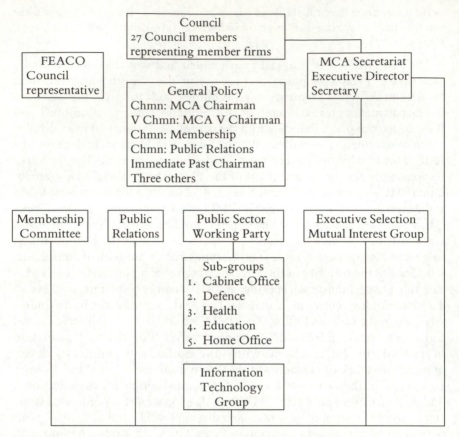

FIGURE 3.1. Organizational chart of the Management Consultancies
Association, 1985

Notes: For confidentiality purposes, I have deleted the names of the consultants who chaired
the various committees and sub-groups. FEACO is the Fédération Européenne des
Associations de Conseils en Organisation.

Source: Management Consultancies Association.

The role of these 'sub-groups' (which still exist today but they are now
called 'mutual interest groups') is to develop channels of communication
with, and to promote consulting to, key actors in policy areas. The MCA
closely co-ordinates the work of these groups, either because some became
during the 1980s the largest consumers of management consulting services
in government (like Health and Defence), or because others (like the
Cabinet Office sub-group) help to make sure, in the words of the MCA
Director, that there is 'a regular dialogue between the MCA and members
of Cabinet and with senior officials' (MCA, 1995: 3).

Following the example of their business association, MCA member firms began in the 1980s to organize various lobbying activities targeted at Whitehall officials and created 'Government Services Division' within their organizational structures. These GSDs are often made up of public officials who have been hired by consulting firms to consolidate links with civil servants and to help sell the firm's ideas. Some of the large consultancies' new GSDs became very active in the promotion of new managerialist ideas and policies. For instance, firms like Peat Marwick (which had consultants working in the FMU) began to organize seminars for civil servants and consultants involved in the process of bureaucratic reform, and published books[9] advocating the adoption of 'a more managerial approach in government which is seeking to learn from (and where appropriate to emulate) some of the culture, attitudes and values of the private sector' (Peat Marwick, 1986: 14).

The National Audit Act 1983 and the institutionalization of VFM ideas

At the heart of the FMI were a host of quantitative techniques and ideas predominantly derived from accountancy and based on the notion of 'value-for-money' (Henkel, 1991a: 12). In the context of the FMI, value for money (VFM) was defined as having three elements: (a) economy: obtaining inputs of the right quality at the lowest possible cost; (b) efficiency: producing the greatest useful output from the given level of inputs; and (c) effectiveness: achieving the objective or objectives of the activity (Likierman, 1988: 97).

With the implementation of the FMI, VFM ideas spread in other institutions of the British central state. In 1983, Parliament adopted the National Audit Act which gave to the National Audit Office (NAO), the body that audits the revenue and expenditure of the government, new responsibilities in the field of VFM. The NAO is headed by the Comptroller & Auditor General (C&AG), an officer of the House of Commons independent of the government. Interestingly, the NAO was given birth—not by a government—but by a private member's Bill, to some extent against the wishes of the Thatcher administration (Garrett, 1986). This is somewhat surprising given the strong managerialist inclination of the Thatcher government. This was, indeed, a government that was constantly preaching VFM in public administration. But this was also a government that did not want to weaken the power of the state. As Andrew Gamble argued, in the political agenda of Mrs Thatcher, the need to maintain a 'strong state' was as important as the need to create a 'free economy' (1988). The government's attitude on the issue of state audit reform was to ensure that the creation of a new parliamentary

---

[9] These publications, all published in the early 1980s, included: *Financial Management in the Public Sector: A Review 1979–1984*; *Management Information and Control in Whitehall*; *Developing the FMI: Changes in Process and Culture*; *Policy Management and Policy Assessment*.

audit agency, that would be responsible for investigating matters of economy, efficiency, and effectiveness, would not affect the powers of the Crown or encroach on the policy prerogatives of the executive.

The political campaign to reform state audit institutions in Britain began in the late 1960s with E. L. Normanton's comparative study of state audit (1966). Normanton found that the British arrangements for central government audit were much weaker and less independent of the executive than those in any other Western country. Normanton noted that the body responsible for auditing the accounts of the government—the Comptroller & Auditor General—was nominated from within government and was closely controlled by the Treasury, a situation which he argued was contrary to the constitutional principle according to which the auditor is independent of—separated from—the body it is responsible for auditing. More than 10 years passed before Parliament took any interest in audit reform. Normanton's criticisms were taken up by Labour MPs in a Fabian pamphlet in the 1970s but it was not until 1981 that a parliamentary committee concluded that new legislation creating a more powerful parliamentary audit agency was needed. Not wishing to expand the powers of Parliament, the government initially resisted reform but changed its mind when an MP introduced a Bill to reform state audit institutions with all-party support, including the support of Conservative MPs who, on this issue, went against the wishes of 'their' government. This shows how, in Britain, the legislature is more independent and how government MPs have more autonomy from party leadership than their counterparts in Canada for instance, where party discipline is much stronger. In Britain independent-minded members can force the party leadership against its wishes to change its policies and 'the government knows that it cannot take its backbenchers for granted' (Franks, 1987: 114).

The National Audit Act 1983 established the C&AG as an officer of the House of Commons; created a National Audit Office and broadened the scope of audit to include most aspects of public management. The C&AG and his office are independent of the executive but they are not independent of the House of Commons, a situation very different from that in Canada where, as will be discussed in the next chapter, the audit office is much more politically autonomous than the C&AG. All the reports on the accounts of the government, including the VFM studies that the C&AG perform, are submitted directly to the MPs who are members of the Public Accounts Committee. This committee then studies the findings made by the C&AG and reports its own observations to the public and the media at the same time as it releases the C&AG study (NAO, 1996: 206). The C&AG is accountable to the Public Accounts Commission, a statutory body created by the 1983 Act and not a parliamentary committee like the Public Accounts Committee. The Commission consists of nine MPs and is involved in the process of appointing and setting the salary of the C&AG.

TABLE 3.2. Expenditure of the UK Comptroller & Auditor General on management consulting services (£'ooo)

Year	Expenditure
1987–8	311
1988–9	352
1989–90	1,067
1990–1	1,042
1991–2	1,952
1992–3	1,755
1993–4	2,300
1994–5	3,242
1995–6	3,619

Source: National Audit Office, 1997: written communication between the author and Sir John Bourn, KCB, Comptroller & Auditor General, 3 April.

Following the adoption of the 1983 Act, the C&AG increased the NAO's use of management consulting services to help his office build and develop its VFM powers (NAO, 1989). As Table 3.2 shows, there has been an almost steady increase in the NAO's use of management consultants. But as we shall see later, because the NAO's reporting powers and financial resources are much more limited than those of its Canadian counterpart, and because the C&AG in Britain is not, as in Canada, hired from the ranks of those pursuing careers in management consulting and accounting, the NAO has not developed close institutional links with consultants, and as a result, it has not become a major institutional platform through which consultants advocate managerialist ideas and policies within the state (Pollitt and Summa, 1997a: 334). Partly because the C&AG in Britain is himself a former senior Whitehall official, the tone of NAO 'reports are still couched in the coded politeness of Whitehall speak rather than employing the more specific and prescriptive terms of a management consultant's report' (Roberts and Pollitt, 1994: 546).

From the FMI to the Next Steps

In 1986, the C&AG audited the performance of the Financial Management Initiative (HC 588, 1986–7). Although the review painted a relatively positive picture of the FMI's development and influence, it nevertheless suggested that more could be done to improve financial management. Following the NAO study, the Thatcher government asked the Efficiency Unit to carry out an evaluation of the FMI and its other efforts to strengthen management practices in Whitehall.[10] The Efficiency Unit study argued that civil servants were now more cost conscious and that the FMI represented an important start at changing the attitudes of the civil service towards management. This happened in part because the implementation of the FMI had created a more decentralized style of budgetary control that broke the structure of departments down into 'cost centres' or 'responsibility centres', with the managers of these centres made more accountable for the management of the costs under their control and for the results they achieve (Zifcak, 1994: ch. 2). With the FMI, the delegation of authority to middle management had started, but it was clear, according to the Efficiency Unit study, that many managers still felt frustrated with what they saw as unnecessary controls. The answer, or the 'Next Steps' to be taken after the FMI, was simple: devolve the cost centres of the FMI still further and turn them into arm's length agencies, thereby giving managers what was seen as real responsibility.

The ideas that went into Next Steps came from a number of sources. First, of course, there was the FMI. The Next Steps is the direct successor of the FMI because it seeks to push further the decentralization of responsibility initiated by the FMI. Secondly, the report from which the Next Steps derived its name was a study entitled *Improving Public Sector Efficiency and Effectiveness: The Next Steps* produced in 1982 by a Conservative MP (Tim Eggar) and a management consultant from McKinsey & Co. (Norman Blackwell) (Arnott, 1983: 76). (In the 1990s Blackwell became John Major's top adviser in the No. 10 Policy Unit.) And third, the Next Steps was closely linked to the 'accountable unit' idea, a concept first developed at General Motors in the USA and advocated by Fulton's Management Consulting Group in 1968 (Drewry and Butcher, 1991: 195; McDonald, 1992: 31). In fact, some even argue that not only the Next Steps, but the entire Efficiency Strategy came from ideas first proposed by the management consultants who worked for Fulton. In an interview with administrative historian G. K. Fry, one senior official who was in government at the time of Fulton, 'ascribed to the Management Consulting Group the authorship of the ideas behind the Efficiency Programme which the Conservative government pursued in government departments after 1979' (Fry, 1991: 432).

Fulton's consultants suggested that certain areas of government work should be designated as separate 'accountable units' and that the managers of these units should be made accountable for results they achieved as compared with predetermined budgets or standards. Such units would be located within a government department under the direction of a minister accountable to

---

[10] Published in 1988, the study in question is entitled *Improving Management in Government: The Next Steps*. It is generally referred to as the Ibbs Report because of the name of the Head of the Efficiency Unit.

Parliament, but with an executive head with a large degree of freedom on personnel and management matters. However, before rising to political prominence in 1988 with the Next Steps policy, the accountable unit idea remained in the shadows, not widely implemented for most of the 1970s and early 1980s. Although the idea of an accountable unit was taken up as part of the 'new style of government' introduced by the Conservative government under Mr Heath in 1970, its application was very limited, with fewer than 10 units established in the mid-1970s (Drewry and Butcher, 1991: 196).

The accountable unit idea, like the Next Steps, raised the problem of achieving the right balance between managerial autonomy and political accountability. How do policy makers make sure that the arm's length unit or agency has enough autonomy to perform its tasks efficiently while ensuring that it remains accountable for its actions to departments, ministers, and the legislature? The difficulties policy makers have in offering a solution to this dilemma provides much of the answer to the question of why almost nothing happened with the accountable unit idea after it was first sponsored by Fulton in 1968 (Flynn, Gray, *et al.*, 1988). But the idea of trying to separate policy (i.e. ministerial) from operational (administrative) functions never totally disappeared from the bureaucratic reform policy agenda because of its political appeal. Ministers in large departments sometimes complain that their reputation or career can be damaged by actions taken by any junior civil servant—with whom the minister may have no contact at all—but for whom she or he is nominally responsible (Campbell and Wilson, 1995: 280). The principle of ministerial responsibility makes the minister 'blamable' for both administration and policy because, in government departments, there is no organizational separation between the two functions. But if policy could be separated from administration, as is done with nationalized industries for instance, the minister would be able to avoid blame for 'administrative' failures that take place at the bottom of the bureaucratic hierarchy. But drawing a line between policy and administration in the case of a government department is more difficult than with a public enterprise, whose activities are to some extent regulated by the market (Horn, 1995). The problem then becomes to develop the mechanisms and techniques that can reproduce the control function played by market forces and that can thus more or less 'replace' the minister as the link by which the units or agencies created to carry out the minister's responsibilities for administration are held accountable by the government and Parliament (Mayston, 1985).

But thirty years ago when Fulton first put the accountable unit idea on the policy agenda, the knowledge and techniques, and especially the refined information systems, required to balance administrative autonomy and political accountability did not exist to make the idea widely implementable (Zifcak, 1994: 168). It is argued that the Next Steps became a major reform because new information technologies and computer-based decision support systems enabled the refinement of the tools needed to make the accountable unit idea more workable than it was in the 1960s (Greer, 1994: 28). Whether technology drove the course of the Next Steps reform programme is debatable. But in the eyes of policy makers the successful prosecution of the Next Steps depended on the presence of appropriate technology and expertise (Butler, 1990).

The government proceeded with the Next Steps by following the same path it had previously used to implement the 1982 Financial Management Initiative (FMI). As in the case of the FMI, a small organization—the Next Steps Unit—with high-level political access was established at the centre of the executive machinery to help develop and implement the policy. As with the FMI which, as we saw earlier, promised 'access to expert advice', measures were taken after the introduction of the Next Steps to ensure that those involved in the creation of Next Steps agencies had access to Management Information Systems (MIS) experts outside government. A Treasury guide on *Seeking help from Management Consultants* was issued for those concerned 'with the use of consultants for such subjects as . . . the development of information systems [and] the setting up of Next Steps agencies' (HM Treasury, 1990: 1). 'Management consultants', the government subsequently recognized, 'have made a significant contribution to the achievement of several important Government objectives—notably . . . the establishment of strong and effective Executive Agencies' (Efficiency Unit, 1994: 3). Price Waterhouse which, since 1986, had the former chief of staff of the Prime Minister's Efficiency Unit as one of its senior partners, was closely involved in the development of the Next Steps (Greer, 1994: 129). In 1989, Price Waterhouse created within its organization an 'Executive Agency Team' which publishes every year *Executive Agencies: Facts and Trends,* a document that evaluates the Next Steps policy and makes recommendations to policy makers on how to improve the performance of agencies. In addition, Price Waterhouse has set up a jury that awards an annual prize for the best managed Next Steps agency (Auditor General of Canada, 1993: C-9).

The politicization of management consulting

For big consultancies like Price Waterhouse and others,[11] the publishing of reports and the holding of seminars on government reform became in the late 1980s an effective marketing tool to promote the firm's public sector experience. Management consultants have traditionally tried to hide behind the cloak of strict client confidentiality. But as Table 3.3 indicates, the public sector became in the 1980s an important source of revenues for management consulting firms and as competition for this increasingly lucrative

---

[11] See Arthur Young, 1990, *The Next Steps: A Review of the Agency Concept*, London. See also the series of lectures on public management reform organized by PA Consulting Group.

TABLE 3.3. Annual UK consultancy income of members of the Management Consultancies Association (£m.)

	1975	1980	1985	1990	1991	1992	1993	1994	1995	1996
Public sector										
Central government	0.2	3	18	90	91	82	93	113	91	82
Nationalized industries	—	1	6	52	17	10	9	28	10	9
Other public bodies	—	2	—	38	27	20	19	30	18	22
Local government	0.1	0.3	11	21	46	23	20	32	20	14
Health Service	—	—	—	17	26	50	66	43	25	17
Total	0.3	6.3	35	218	207	185	207	246	164	144
Private sector	18.7	37.7	108	486	520	510	538	599	786	939
Total income	19	44	143	704	727	695	745	845	950	1,083
Income from central government as % of Total revenue	1.0	6.8	12.6	12.7	12.4	11.8	12.4	13.4	9.5	7.5

Source: Management Consultancies Association, London.

market intensified, consultants and their organizations were intent on more aggressive marketing and lobbying, thereby making their government activities more 'visible' than in the past.

As the government became a more important client, management consultants increasingly sought to get inside knowledge and to obtain information on Whitehall's current and future plan for management reforms. In this search for information, MPs became

important assets in helping to secure valuable Whitehall contacts . . . In 1988 Tim Smith, a Tory MP and consultant to Price Waterhouse, asked no less than eighteen government department parliamentary questions for detailed information on management consulting. The answers disclosed the nature of the contracts, the successful companies, their assignments and the government expenditures involved. (Halloran and Hollingworth, 1994: 198)

As we saw earlier, the Management Consultancies Association (MCA) also sought to gain insight into Whitehall thinking on public sector reform when it established its Public Sector Working Party (now renamed the Public Sector Mutual Interest Group) in the early 1980s. Following its creation, the PSWP began to organize a number of events to facilitate the exchange of ideas between Whitehall officials and consultants. Each year, the MCA runs half-day seminars for civil servants on management reform and on the use of consultants in the public sector. In the past, such seminars were sometimes attended by no fewer than 200 civil servants (MCA, 1995: 3). The

MCA's Public Sector Working Party also holds a series of meetings (four or five a year) attended by member firms and Permanent Secretaries. The purpose of such meetings is to receive an authoritative update on activities within a particular sector of government. As stated in the letters sent by the MCA to the senior officials invited to speak to the PSWP, the goal is to see 'how consultants can act as advisers and partners in helping the Civil Service to face future management challenges'. These meetings are supplemented by a series of small monthly lunches consisting of senior staff from member firms and policy makers. For the MCA, these luncheons 'provide an ideal "off the record" opportunity for wide-ranging discussions on subjects of particular interest to both guests and hosts' (MCA, 1996: 5). In the past, the MCA guests included the head of the Policy Unit, senior Treasury officials, members of the Efficiency Unit, of the Cabinet Office, and representatives of the Department of Trade and Industry (DTI).

The MCA increasingly sought the company of DTI officials for these occasions as the government began to develop its new industrial policy in the mid-1980s. MCA meetings with public officials in the past often dealt with bureaucratic reform policy issues. But this changed with the adoption of the government's new industrial policy in 1987. Management consultants built links with DTI officials and the MCA meetings began to cover both bureaucratic reform and industrial policy issues, thus facilitating the transfer of ideas from one policy sector to the other. After the 1987 election, the government issued a White Paper that relaunched the Department of Trade and Industry as the 'Department for Enterprise'. The DTI was to be at the cutting edge of the 'new enterprise culture' that the government wanted to create. Its role was to reduce state interference and to encourage industry to adopt new attitudes and management practices (Atkinson and Lupton, 1990). The 1988 Next Steps initiative was very much influenced by the same 'new entrepreneurial' thinking that underlay the DTI's White Paper. The Next Steps also sought to cut bureaucratic regulation as a way 'to leave managers free to manage'. And like the government's new approach to industrial growth, the Next Steps mobilized management consulting knowledge to help unleash the entrepreneurial spirit of the civil service. As discussed in Chapter 2, as part of its new industrial policy, the government adopted the Enterprise Initiative, which provided financial support for small businesses seeking management consulting services in key areas such as organizational design, marketing, and quality standards. With the subsidies provided by the Enterprise Initiative, small businesses significantly increased their use of management consulting services. The MCA subsequently revealed that five times more small businesses than in the past were using the services of its members (Hosking, 1987). In his annual report, the MCA Chairman wrote that 'My association welcomed the recent White Paper DTI—The *Department for Enterprise* . . . This should lead to significant benefits for our clients and thus further opportunities for our members.' The

Enterprise Initiative 'is a further recognition of the benefits of consultancy' (MCA, 1987: 3).

Not everyone agreed about the 'benefits' of management consultancy, however. Soon after the introduction of the Enterprise Initiative, the Labour Party's research organization, the Labour Research Department (LRD), released a very critical study on management consultancy, arguing that consultants were being used to bypass trade unions and weaken bargaining power. The LRD study (based on a survey of trade union representatives) said that consultants were politically biased and that in many cases, they were a 'total waste of money' (Labour Research Department, 1988). The study found several instances where the consultants' own lack of expertise resulted in 'chaos' (Naughton, 1988).

This kind of critique had the effect of bringing management consultants under the public spotlight. A political backlash began as civil service unions, the media, and Labour MPs denounced what they saw as the increasing power of management consultants under the Tory regime. In this last section of the chapter I take a brief look at the origins and political consequences of this backlash. This is important because a backlash is a political reaction: it is an indicator that a social group and the ideas that it advocates have become influential (or are perceived as such). To some extent, management consultants became in the 1990s the victims of their own success. As we have seen, throughout the 1980s management consultants were found advising government officials in various organizational units created at the centre to lead the reform process. But it is important to remember that a number of these units were initially established to provide, not bureaucratic, but *political* advisory services to the prime minister. By working in, or by developing close links with, these bodies management consultants lost their apparent neutrality and began to be seen as the Tories' political allies.

The politics of costs and the decline of the new managerialism

As MPs asked more parliamentary questions on the costs of contracting out work to external consultants, newspaper articles began to talk about the 'alarming rising cost of Whitehall consultants', while Labour MPs compared government spending on management consultants to 'outdoor relief for the consulting classes' (Millward, 1990: 4). Parliamentary committees argued in their report that 'the proliferation of the use of management consultants throughout the Civil Service is one of the most remarkable features of the late 1980s and early 1990s' (House of Commons, 1993: 53). As a result of increased pressures and of the Treasury fears that spending on consultancy was perhaps 'out of hand', Prime Minister Major ordered in 1994 an inquiry into the government's use of management consultants, entitled *The Government's Use of External Consultants*. In this one can read that

Over the past ten years the Government has substantially increased its use of external consultants. This has happened for a number of reasons. The initial stimulus came in the mid to late 1980s, primarily from privatisation . . . More recently there has been a further boost from several major changes in Civil Service structure and operations—particularly the creation of Next Steps Agencies. (Efficiency Unit, 1994: 19)

Officially released in August, the study discovered that 'the expenditure by Government on external consultancy grew sharply between 1985 and 1990, increasing nearly fourfold over this period' (Efficiency Unit, 1994: 46). During the conduct of the inquiry, the Efficiency Unit produced a short interim paper setting out its emerging findings. The paper, which was produced for the Cabinet and a copy of which was sent to the MCA, was subsequently leaked to the press and became the subject of very critical parliamentary and press comments. Because of this, the MCA Director argued, 'I fear that now the use of consultants by Government has been moved into the political arena' (MCA, 1995: 3). In his annual report, the Director of the MCA wrote that

1994 was conspicuous for the Cabinet Office Efficiency Unit report on the use of management consultants by the public sector. [The report] was critical of the manner in which the public sector employed members of the industry, and whilst there was little adverse comment about consultants themselves in the report, the media and politicians used the opportunity to attack government and the public sector on their alleged excessive use of consultants. All this was a pity, bearing in mind the number of initiatives launched in the public sector that could not have been undertaken without employing management consultants. Not surprisingly, we received some fall-out from this report and we have launched a major public relations exercise to brief government, the opposition and the media on the valuable role that management consultants play in creating wealth and supporting the economy. This has included meeting with the Chief Secretary of the Treasury, the Head of the Prime Minister's Policy Unit and members of the Shadow Cabinet, and seminars directed at the public sector purchasers. (MCA, 1994: 3)

Following the publication of the Efficiency Unit report, public sector work in 1995 and 1996 began to drop for the first time since the 1980s (see Table 3.3). In fact, what we see, in the aftermath of the Efficiency Unit study on consultants, is more or less the 'return' of the Treasury as the most important player in the field of bureaucratic reform. According to some, this happened when John Major became prime minister. Himself a banker and a former chancellor of the Exchequer, Major has been described as a 'Treasury man' who 'think numbers and cash' (Campbell and Wilson, 1995: 136). During Thatcher's prime ministership, the Treasury was not, of course, relegated to a minor role. But it neither spawned the ideas behind the FMI or the Next Steps nor took sole responsibility for their advancement. The Treasury played 'a secondary role' in these reforms (Wilson and Wright, 1993: 5). Because of its 'control' and fiscally conservative mentality, it was believed that the Treasury would resist the decentralization of financial and managerial responsibilities that both the FMI and the Next Steps implied. Bureaucratic reformers thought that improvements in the performance of complex bureaucratic systems and long-term reductions in costs could only be achieved by the investment of substantial resources in reorganization. The slogan 'spend to save' summed up that idea and suggested that in order to reap longer-term benefits, spending in the short term sometimes needed to be higher (Metcalfe and Richards, 1987: 96). As part of this 'spend to save' strategy, government departments were given more flexibility and authority in the use of financial resources for the recruitment of management consultants. But this, the 1994 study on the use of consultants suggested, was one the key reasons why government spending on consulting services had grown uncontrollably. In 1995, the Treasury imposed spending limits on the use of consultants and the chancellor, Kenneth Clarke, said in a press interview that 'public spending on consultants is excessive and ought to be reduced' (*Accountancy Age*, 1995). The MCA subsequently attacked the chancellor for 'playing politics' and argued that the Major government was wasting too much time 'on the cost debate when the real issue, investment in the future, is neither discussed nor understood' (MCA, 1995: 3). According to the MCA Director, 'fear by ministers that they could be attacked by the Opposition for the use of outside skills, has meant that the essential knowledge exchange between public and private sector is diminishing. No government can afford this if its Civil Service is to catch up, let alone keep level with developments in industry and the private sector as a whole' (MCA, 1996: 4).

Because it was critical of the 'spend to save' mentality that underlay the reform policies implemented during the 1980s, the 'politics of costs' undermined support from the Major government for new managerialist ideas and policies. The 'anti-consultant' attitude that emerged in Whitehall in the aftermath of the Efficiency Unit report was seen by some as a sign that the new managerialism was no longer government policy (Plowden, 1995). Because it had the 'impression that friction exists between Whitehall and our Association' (MCA, 1995: 3), the MCA began in 1995 to intensify its contacts with Labour MPs. 'With an impending general election in the next 15 months we are increasing our contacts with members of opposition parties to ensure that in the event of a change in government, they are aware of the role the industry plays in implementing change' (MCA, 1995: 3).

On 1 May 1997, a new Labour government led by Tony Blair was elected with the strongest parliamentary majority in recent British history. It is still too soon to know if Blair will be as committed to management reform as Thatcher was. But one year after the election, the MCA noted in its annual report the end of the 'dramatic rise in public sector revenues' of the past 15 years (MCA, 1998: 3). Although 'in 1991 over 30% of UK revenues for MCA members came from the public sector, by 1998 that figure has fallen to just 9%'. For the association, this is 'a matter of concern', especially 'if this real decline in government is caused by a pursuit of price at the expense of quality, or lack of general understanding of the contribution made by MCA members to the national economy' (MCA, 1998: 3). It thus appears that consultants may not play as active a role as before in the development of new managerialist policies. This may encourage consultancies to look for new means to ensure that their voice is still heard in the public policy process. For instance, big firms such as Price Waterhouse recently recruited members of the Labour Party and Andersen Consulting has started to give important sums of money to fund the Institute for Public Policy Research, the think tank closest to Labour (Micklethwait and Wooldridge, 1996: 281). The fact, however, that the new leader of the Conservative Party (William Hague) and his party vice-chairman (Archie Norman) are both management consultants from McKinsey & Co. is not very likely to weaken the view shared by some on Labour benches that consultants tend to be Tory supporters. It is not false to argue that 'the era of Conservative government since 1979 has certainly been the age of management consultancy' (Beale, 1994: 13), or that 'the rise of management consultants was one of the distinctive features of the Thatcher years' (Smith and Young, 1996: 137). But it is important to remember that it was not the Tories, but the Labour government who, in the 1960s, first legitimated the participation of business consultants in the process of bureaucratic reform and brought into government the private sector notion of efficiency.

Conclusion

This chapter has argued that the effects of past bureaucratic reform experiences, and the way management consulting interests under Thatcher were institutionalized in the Prime Minister's and Cabinet Offices and had direct access to decision-making centres, provide important clues to the British pattern of support for managerialism. The approach used has been historical, looking for connections among bureaucratic reform policies over time. To understand how managerialism has been institutionalized in the British policy process, let us summarize what these connections were, and how they affected the access of consultants to centres of power where they could advocate new ways of looking at state management that emerged as the basis for redesigning policy.

In Britain, the change from a 'generalist' to a more managerially skilled civil service began with the work of the Fulton Committee. Fulton wanted to replace Oxbridge civil servants with management experts and according to some, his suggestions have been so successful that, nowadays, 'Consultancies have replaced Oxbridge as the nurseries of the powerful . . . In Britain, the consultancy's old-boy list includes the present head of the Confederation of British Industry, the deputy governor of the Bank of

England, the head of the Prime Minister's Policy Unit, and the boss of London Transport' (Micklethwait and Wooldridge, 1996: 45). Whether consulting firms have now become the 'nurseries of the powerful' is an open question, but in the 1960s they were not and when Fulton was created in 1966 it was the first committee to study the administration by using the services of management consultants from the private sector. The creation of Fulton's Management Consultancy Group coincided with the establishment around the 1960s of business and professional associations of management consultants. By using private sector consultants to study the administration rather than the expertise of civil servants as had been done in the past, Fulton made the perspective of bureaucrats less credible. Because they came from outside Whitehall, consultants were seen as being more independent and objective than civil servants. As outsiders, they were seen as being objective and their ideas acquired influence because they conveyed a sense of non-partisanhip and non-controversial technical knowledge.

Fulton thus helped to establish the authority of management consulting knowledge and this process was largely political because, for reasons that had to do with 'class politics', some members of the Fulton Committee distrusted the senior bureaucracy and the Treasury. But because of bureaucratic resistance and the electoral defeat of Labour in 1970, Fulton's recommendations did not have an immediate impact on policy. However, Fulton helped to establish managerialism within the British state by arguing that the government should emulate private-sector management practices as a way to rationalize and strengthen state intervention. That idea, which would later have a very different political appeal for Conservatives, was institutionalized in 1968 when Prime Minister Wilson created the Civil Service Department, which was to be the organization that would help the government to become more businesslike. To build its new management capacities, the CSD recruited consultants from the private sector and this gave them professional and institutional holds on bureaucratic reform policy issues. These holds, however, were not very strong because consultants were not appointed to senior positions and because the CSD was under the control of Treasury officials and career bureaucrats who opposed managerialist ideas.

In terms of the access of management consultants to decision-making centres, the Businessmen's Team represents the most important institutional legacy left by the Heath government. A feature of the Conservative Party under Heath was the use of private sector consultants recruited inside the party's policy-making machinery to advise the leader on bureaucratic reform issues. The Team represented an influential institutional site for the production of managerialist ideas. Members of the Team could also have their ideas come directly to the attention of the Conservative leader and as a result, their views significantly shaped the development of the 1970 White Paper. Of course, the White Paper did not have a significant impact on policy because it failed to overcome 'departmentalism'. However, the practice of using business persons and outside management consultants to advise the Conservative Party leadership on public management issues was thus initiated, and expanded under the 'presidential' or 'prime ministerial' regime of Mrs Thatcher, who established her own Efficiency Unit in 1979. When she created the Efficiency Unit, Mrs. Thatcher built on the precedent established by Heath with his Businessmen's Team. The main difference between the two bodies, however, is that after the 1970 election, the Businessmen's Team was located within the bureaucracy and thus its access to decision-making centres was not as direct as that of the Efficiency Unit. The Businessmen's Team operated inside a government department, the CSD, whereas the Efficiency Unit was originally situated at the heart of the politics-administration nexus, in the Prime Minister's Office.

Organizationally speaking, the Efficiency Unit differed considerably from the machinery on which previous governments had generally relied to co-ordinate their programme of bureaucratic reform. In contrast with what had been done since Fulton, the Thatcher administration did not use the services of the CSD to co-ordinate its programme of bureaucratic reform. Rather, it relied on small organizational entities placed under the direct political control of the prime minister and the Cabinet. Such organizations included the Efficiency Unit and the Management and Personnel Office (MPO), a subdivision of the Cabinet Office created in 1981 as a result of the abolition of the CSD. In dismantling the CSD and in transferring jurisdiction over bureaucratic reform issues to the Cabinet Office, the Thatcher government not only abolished an organization that had previously served to block managerialist ideas from making rapid inroads into policy. It also brought the access point of consultants to the British state closer to the political control of the Cabinet and the prime minister, thereby facilitating the entry of new managerialist ideas into policy. Whereas in the post-Fulton era contacts with management consulting organizations took place at the *bureaucratic* level of the CSD, following its abolition such contacts began to take place at the *political* level of the Cabinet. But if the changes produced by abolition of the CSD made the access of consultants to decision-making centres more direct than in the past, it also brought consultants closer to politics. And as the cost of the state's use of management consulting services became an increasingly politicized issue, government support for new managerialist ideas and policies weakened.

4

Canada: Spreading managerialist ideas through politically independent bodies

We saw in the previo3us chapter that the 'politics of class' and Labour's desire to 'open up' the civil service in the 1960s created openings for the entry of management consultants into the policy process and facilitated the institutionalization of managerialism within the British central state. But in Canada, class politics did not affect the debate about civil service reform as much as in Britain because the Left has never been a strong political force at the federal level and because the federal bureaucracy—partly as a result of American influence on the recruitment system—has never been as élitist and closed as the British civil service. In Canada, there was no resistance from a well-entrenched traditional body of 'intelligent laymen' generalist administrators to the advent of the 'specialist' into government and to the creation of a more 'professional' style of administration (professional in the sense of better trained in modern techniques of management). As Granatstein wrote in his history of the senior civil service, in Canada 'there is no such a thing as a public service dominated by class, family and tradition'. Ottawa's 'mandarinate was not a closed circle. It was remarkably open to new men' (Granatstein, 1982: 1–2). Unlike Britain, in Canada the civil service has never been aristocratic. It was élitist, of course, but it was a meritocratic élite, based on technical expertise rather than on wealth or nobility. Canadian political leaders have historically sought to provide openings in the civil service—less for 'specialists' as in the UK—but more for the appointment of individuals whose identity was organized around region and language (Blackburn, 1969; Porter, 1965).

In trying to understand why, in Canada, the acceptance of managerialist ideas, and the degree to which they were implemented as policies, has been weaker than in Britain—but stronger than in France—this chapter analyses the reforms that preceded the 1989 Public Service 2000 initiative discussed in Chapter 1. This is done to see how the Canadian state's prior experiences with bureaucratic reform affected both the views of policy makers about administrative reorganization and the access of management consultants to decision-making centres. According to the White Paper on the Renewal of the Public Service of Canada which officially launched PS 2000, the reforms that led to the 1989 initiative were: the 1960 Glassco Royal Commission on Government Organization; the post-Glassco financial reforms such as the implementation of the Planning, Programming, and Budgeting System in 1969; the Lambert Royal Commission on Financial Management and Accountability in 1976; the creation of expanded and new institutions such as the Auditor General in 1977 and, the Comptroller General in 1978.

The examination of the institutional and political legacies left by these past policy experiences reveals that since the 1960s, consultants have entered the policy process and disseminated managerialist ideas primarily through 'arm's length' organizations such as royal commissions, the Civil (now the Public) Service Commission, independent study groups, and increasingly since the 1970s through the Office of the Auditor General (OAG). This has happened partly because management policy issues have often been viewed in Canada as technical and non-politicized issues that should be dealt with by organizations that are removed from the politics of passion and interest, and thus located outside formal decision-making settings. In sharp contrast with the British situation where consultants advocated managerialist solutions through small 'political' organizations located at the centre of government, in Canada management consultants have generally pressed their views on bureaucratic reform through 'non-political' bodies that convey a sense of non-partisanhip and that are located outside the executive machinery.

But in the 1960s, Canadian consultants originally followed a path very similar to the one found in the British case. Like their British counterparts in relation to the Civil Service Department, Canadian consultants also built channels of communication with the centre of government following the creation of the Treasury Board Secretariat (TBS) in 1966. The TBS was created on the advice of the Glassco Commission. Glassco also recommended the adoption of programme budgeting which later led to the implementation of PPBS in 1969. One consequence of PPBS was the presentation to Parliament of departmental expenditures in the programme budget form. That change, which coincided with the minority position of the government in the early 1970s and with the appointment of one of the founding fathers of the Canadian Association of Management Consultants (CAMC) to the position of Auditor General, created for the OAG an opportunity to justify an expansion of its mandate in order to adapt its functions to the new PPBS approach. As a result, the OAG was given important new powers in the area of 'value for money' management and subsequently became one of the main access points through which consultants diffused managerialist ideas in the Canadian federal state.

If ideas 'must link up with politics' to influence policy (Gourevitch, 1989: 87), in Canada the fact that consultants have tended to make their voices heard through the OAG—a technocratic body removed from the political arena—has made the 'link up with politics' process much more difficult than in Britain. The institutionalization of management consulting interests in the OAG has meant that their access to decision-making centres in government and their influence over policy have been more limited than in

Britain. In Canada, government support for the managerialist views often pressed by the network of consultants linked to the Auditor General has been weak, not because policy makers in government disagreed with the need for greater flexibility, 'entrepreneurship', 'risk taking', and 'empowerment' that managerialist innovations call for. Support has been weak because managerialism was packaged by the OAG with issues dealing with parliamentary accountability that were not popular with decision makers in government.

In sum, in Canada the struggle over managerialism has been a political contest for parliamentary reform, and in particular about innovations that would create a stronger legislature. Of course, the link between managerialism and the politics of parliamentary reform is not unique to Canada (Stone, 1995). But it has played a much more important role in determining the fate of managerialism in Canada because the Canadian legislature, as a result of federalism and the dynamics of party politics, is comparatively much less independent from, and more politically dominated by, the executive.

'Let the managers manage': The Glassco Commission

In Canada, the roots of managerialism and of its emphasis on the deregulation of bureaucratic controls go back at least to the work of the 1960 Glassco Royal Commission on Government Organization. Glassco's most enduring phrase was: 'let the managers manage'. The Commission was created by the Conservatives in 1960. Canadians elected in 1957 a Conservative government for the first time in almost thirty years. The new prime minister, John Diefenbaker, viewed the federal bureaucracy as unreliable and too close to his Liberal predecessors (Newman, 1963). During the long period of Liberal political hegemony in Ottawa, the line between politics and administration became increasingly blurred (Granatstein, 1982: 264). The practice of recruiting key Liberal ministers from the senior ranks of the civil service became so widespread that 'the question of whether the bureaucrats were Liberals or whether, conversely, the Liberals had themselves become bureaucrats' was, according to Reg Whitaker, 'rather problematic' (1977: 167). Thus when Diefenbaker led the Progressive Conservatives to victory in the 1957 election, the incoming government was filled with mistrust of its senior bureaucracy.

Diefenbaker was 'a populist or a Red Tory, not a neo-conservative of the sort that surfaced in the late seventies' (Bothwell *et al.*, 1981: 198). Diefenbaker wanted to use the power of the state to help the disadvantaged but he felt that the public service was administratively inefficient and had many shortcomings. As he looked for ideas Diefenbaker became highly interested in the work of the Hoover Commission created in the mid-1950s by the United States Congress to inquire into the 'organization of the executive branch of the government'. Diefenbaker 'clearly borrowed from the

American experience when he announced in 1960 the establishment of a royal commission, commonly known as the Glassco Commission, on government reorganization' (Savoie, 1994: 61). In the United States, the task of the Hoover Commission was to study ways that would 'promote economy, efficiency and improved service in the transaction of public business'. In wording almost identical to Hoover's mandate, in Canada Glassco was asked 'to inquire into and report upon the organization and methods of operation' of the government of Canada and to recommend changes that 'would best promote efficiency, economy and improved service in the dispatch of public business' (Canada, 1962a: 8).

In the United States, Hoover relied on private sector consultants and other management experts to conduct its research programme (McKenna, 1996). As Arnold (1988) showed in his comparative history of bureaucratic reform in the United States and Britain, in Washington the tradition has been to attempt large-scale reorganization through *ad hoc* commissions, committees, and task forces. Outside experts were heavily represented on these bodies and the official language and justifications for reforms were apolitical, couched in efficiency terms rather than in policy terms. Following Hoover's example, in Canada Glassco also used the technocratic language of efficiency to justify its recommendations and extensively used the services of external consultants to conduct its inquiry (Johnson, 1963). Glassco has been described as a 'major breakthrough for management consultants in the public service' (Meredith and Martin, 1970: 386). Others viewed it as the 'most prominent assault of the outside management expert on the barricades' of the public service (Hodgetts, 1973: 25).

As the case of the Hoover Commission suggests, bureaucratic reformers in Canada have sometimes looked towards the United States for ideas on how they should organize their public services (Kernaghan and Siegel, 1991: 13). Although Canadian institutions have their origins in the Westminster system of government, the management practices and structures found in the Canadian bureaucracy reveal both British and American influences. But contrary to what is sometimes argued, the American influence on Canadian public administration practices is not merely due to geographical determinism or to the fact that 'Canadian culture and Canadian political life is being swamped by the mass culture of the United States' (Sutherland and Doern, 1985: 29). In the next section, I take a short historical detour and leave for a moment the discussion of the 1960 Glassco Commission to show how the American influence is based on the legacies of past reform. In the early 1900s— at a time when the management consulting industry was non-existent in Canada—consultants from the United States played a key role in the development of the modern merit system in the Canadian bureaucracy. In a short but very informative book, Alasdair Roberts tells the story of how, after the First World War, 'American consultants remade the Canadian Civil Service' and institutionalized scientific management ideas into the Canadian government (1996a).

The American influence and 'Canada's first Glassco'

In *The Biography of an Institution*, a study that looks at the history of personnel management in the Canadian bureaucracy, Hodgetts and his colleagues termed the 1918–19 reforms of the civil service, 'Canada's first Glassco' (1972: 75), partly because both initiatives relied heavily for advice on management consultants from the private sector. In 1918, after having promised to abolish patronage appointments in the civil service, the newly elected government of Prime Minister Robert Borden adopted a number of measures to reform the civil service. For Borden's Union government, civil service reform was a means to improve Canada's contribution to the war in Europe, as many in English Canada believed that corruption and patronage in public administration were undermining the effectiveness of Canada's war effort (Dawson, 1929).

The 1918 Civil Service Act proclaimed the new era of merit in the public service. It introduced the principle of appointment by competitive examination to the entire civil service and gave to the newly reconstituted Civil Service Commission—a body independent of the government and thus outside the reach of politicians—powers to organize and classify the civil service. The principle of classification was the central concern of the merit system of selection. The idea was, first, to analyse the component elements of all civil service positions and then, to devise examinations that would determine which candidates were best qualified to fill specific jobs. The notion of classification was based on scientific management principles which, in the early decades of the twentieth century, became very popular in American cities (especially in Chicago, the government of which was chaotic and corrupted) as municipal officials sought to end political patronage and to create a more efficient administration (Schiesl, 1977).

Following the adoption of the 1918 Act, the Civil Service Commission (CSC) was given the mandate of classifying the civil service. To undertake that task, the CSC decided to use a team of outside management consultants. In the spring of 1918, a team of almost thirty consultants from the Chicago-based accounting firm Arthur Young and Co. moved into the CSC and began to develop the classification system of the Canadian civil service. One of the consultants in the Arthur Young team, E. O. Griffenhagen, was the acknowledged North American expert on scientific management and a leading figure in the development of classification analysis. The CSC justified its choice of an American firm to do this work because 'there was no firm in Canada with trained experts in this particular line' (Hodgetts *et al.*, 1972: 72). The CSC explained its decision by arguing that Arthur Young (the ancestor of Ernst & Young, one of the Big Five accounting firms that now dominate the world consulting market) had been 'established for twenty-five years and had an experienced staff of civil service specialists' (quoted in Hodgetts *et al.*, 1972: 67). After nine months of work, the management consultants and the CSC delivered their new classification plan,

known as the 'Book of Classification', to Parliament in June 1919. The new
plan was not well received by the civil service, partly because of its complexity (the 'Book' ran to almost seven hundred pages and described 1,729
classifications) and because many civil servants disagreed with the way their
own positions (and therefore salaries) had been classified (Hodgetts *et al.*,
1972: 70). But the government nevertheless went ahead with its reform and
the CSC subsequently spent several years implementing and transforming
the Arthur Young classification scheme into a complex and heavy-handed
system of rules and regulations.

The 'old' managerialism and the emergence of rationalism

The Civil Service Commission—which through the years had become the
lead agency in the management area—was the main villain emerging from
the pages of the Glassco report issued in 1962. Glassco accused the CSC of
being responsible for the growth of red tape and unnecessary bureaucratic
controls that took place in the federal government following the adoption
of the merit system. Glassco strongly supported the merit principle but
said that the merit system (i.e. the collection of centralized and uniformly
applied rules, regulations, and procedures) needed to change. The system
was made of 'many absurd procedures', Glassco argued (Canada, 1962a: 262).
It had become 'too elaborate and complicated' (p. 292). It was leading to
'waste' and its procedures were 'costly and time-consuming' (p. 255).

Glassco not only slammed the CSC's approach to personnel management,
but also was strongly critical of the government's old budgeting system
which, it argued, was out of date and inefficient. Glassco came forward with
a series of sweeping proposals designed to create a new and more decentralized approach to government management. The Commission envisaged
a system of 'checks and balances' (p. 61) whereby departments were to be
given increased responsibility for the management of their operations and
where a new central agency (an expanded Treasury Board) would be established to provide a framework of guidance. Within this new framework,
detailed administrative controls would be reduced and complemented
by performance evaluation as the main vehicle for accountability (Johnson,
1992: 9). Glassco's new approach to management was based on the belief
that differences between private and public organizations should not prevent
the incorporation of the best practices and principles of private business
management into government (Johnson, 1963: McLeod, 1963). Although
it recognized that 'between government and business there are, of course,
significant differences' the Glassco Commission argued that despite these
'apparent differences both kinds of organization share the same objective of
maximum productivity. The immediate aim of the techniques of management developed for industry is to attain the organization's goals with the
greatest possible economy of effort. Consequently, most of the techniques

of management developed for business can be adapted to government' (Canada, 1962*a*: 46–7).

According to some, the Commission's tendency to attenuate the essential differences between public and private sector management was related to the fact that many of the experts employed in the Commission's research staff were 'drawn from management consulting firms whose experience lay mainly in the field of private rather than public administration' (Hodgetts, 1973: 257). The research staff of the Commission was divided into 21 project teams. Each project team produced a study investigating various areas of government organization and management, and each of these was published as part of the Commission's final report. Almost 80 per cent of the Glassco budget ($2.2 million) was spent on research services (Canada, 1962*b*: 126; Tunnoch, 1964). At least six of the Glassco Commission's project teams were under the direction of senior partners in some of Canada's largest and most important accounting and management consulting firms.[1] According to one estimate, 'well over half' of the research staff of some 170 specialists engaged by the Commission were associated with accounting and management consulting firms and most of the remainder were drawn from executive positions in the private sector (Hodgetts, 1973: 25).

Glassco as a formative event in the development of management consultancy

When Glassco was formed in 1960 there existed no association of management consultants in Canada. Until after the Second World War, management consultancy was largely undeveloped in Canada and to compensate for this situation the federal government sometimes used the services of American consultants, as happened during the 1918–19 civil service reforms. As we saw in Chapter 2, the early involvement of the accounting profession was a distinguishing feature of the development of management consulting in Canada. Many large accounting firms such as Price Waterhouse and Peat Marwick began to sell management consulting services in the 1950s, but inside the firm, the consulting activities were not (and are still not) organizationally separated from the accounting and auditing practices. As a result, management consultancy was not in Canada seen as an occupation distinct from accountancy. But, for the first time, Glassco brought a large number of

---

[1] The study on Financial Management was directed by a partner from Peat Marwick; the study on Paperwork and Systems Management was directed by a senior consultant from Urwick Currie Ltd.; the study on Purchasing and Supply was directed by a partner from the accounting firm McDonald Currie & Co.; the study on Printing and Publishing was directed by a senior consultant from the international firm PA Management Consulting Ltd.; the study on The Make or Buy Problem was directed by a senior accountant and partner from Price Waterhouse; and the study on the Canadian Broadcasting Corporation was directed by a representative of Peat Marwick.

people doing consulting work together and, in doing so, contributed to the fostering of a sense of common professional identity among them. The Canadian Association of Management Consultants (CAMC) was created one year after the publication of the Glassco report. It was founded following a meeting held in 1962 by a group that consisted of the heads of the six major accounting firms in Canada. At least half of these firms were at that time heavily involved with the Glassco Commission, having lent their most senior experts to work for or to direct some of the Commission's 21 project teams. Ted Hodgetts argued that Glassco was 'by far the most impressive demonstration of the influence' of what he called—in a term illustrating the domination of accountants in consulting in Canada—the 'management expert-cum-accountant' (Hodgetts, 1973: 25). According to a document describing the history of the CAMC,

The [Glassco] Commission's impact on Canadian consulting was profound . . . It was probably the most important development that took place in the early 1960s. The practice of using external consultants was given a significant boost by the Royal Commission on Government Organization . . . The list of specialists working for the Commission often resembled directories of Canadian management consulting . . . The Glassco Commission gave virtually every management consulting firm an opportunity to work in Ottawa and be schooled in the machinery and mechanisms of the management of the federal government. (Mellett, 1988: 22)

Glassco not only helped consultants to gain first-hand knowledge of the workings of government. But, like other royal commissions created throughout the post-war years in Canada, by using the services of management consultants Glassco also provided a definition of 'who has a legitimate right to speak on the matter at hand' and thus helped to legitimize their role in the bureaucratic reform policy process (Jenson, 1994: 45). The final product of the work of the Glassco Commission consisted of more than twenty studies printed in five volumes, containing about 300 recommendations. The most important proposals for reforms made by the Glassco Commission were in the area of financial management and included the reorganization of the Treasury Board and the replacement of the government's line-budgeting approach by a programme and performance-based budget system (White and Strick, 1970: 90). Glassco suggested that all the management functions (other than staffing) performed by the Civil Service Commission be removed from its jurisdiction and handed to a reconstituted Treasury Board Secretariat that would be placed under the direct control of the Cabinet and be responsible for the general management of the civil service. Since the early 1900s, responsibility for the administration of the bureaucracy was under the control of the CSC and this meant that most management issues were kept at 'arm's length' from ministers because the CSC was (and its successor is still) a politically independent body located outside the executive. This institutional arrangement reflected the scientific management belief in the separation of administration from politics that the federal state inherited from the 1918–19 reforms which sought to end patronage by removing most civil service matters from the direct control of politicians (Roberts, 1996a).

The Bureau of Government Organization

Prime Minister Diefenbaker enthusiastically endorsed the findings of Glassco and immediately established, within the Privy Council Office (PCO), a Bureau of Government Organization to review the Commission's report and to select those recommendations that appeared readily applicable and desirable. The Bureau was intended to act as a 'ginger group' to ensure that the recommendations would not fall by the wayside (Savoie, 1994: 64). 'Uneasily housed, under somewhat indirect supervision, and with slender resources, the Bureau', according to Hodgetts, 'nevertheless played the invaluable role of instigator, gadfly and facilitator. At least, it ensured that all the major recommendations of the commission were canvassed and, where agreements were secured, that action on them was initiated' (1973: 260).

The Bureau was placed under the political direction of a minister without portfolio in the Diefenbaker Cabinet (Senator W. McCutcheon) and some of its members were drawn from the group of management consultants who had been employed by the Glassco Commission. For instance, one senior adviser to the Bureau of Government Organization was Mr Donald Yeomans from the management consultancy Urwick Currie Ltd. Yeomans had been loaned by his firm to the Glassco Commission staff in 1961, to serve as director of the Organization Research Group (Institute of Public Administration, 1970: 1). Through the Bureau, consultants who had been involved in Glassco were thus given direct access to decision-making centres in the PCO. A majority of the Commission's recommendations on financial management were subsequently adopted by the new Liberal government, which announced its support for Glassco soon after its election in 1963 (White and Strick, 1970: 93).

Following the election of the Pearson government, the Bureau of Government Organization was moved from the PCO to the Department of Finance and Yeomans was appointed Assistant Secretary to the Treasury Board. In the Treasury Board Secretariat—which went through an important process of institution building after having inherited most of the management responsibilities previously hold by the CSC—Yeomans was responsible for the Management Improvement Branch, created following a recommendation of the Glassco Commission to encourage the use within the public service of modern management techniques (Hodgetts, 1973: 306). The new Management Improvement Branch took over the functions of the Bureau of Government Organization[2] and became responsible for

---

[2] After the 1963 election, the Bureau of Government Organization was gradually abolished and its staff dispersed to other departments or absorbed into the staff of the Treasury Board (Hodgetts, 1973: 261).

evaluating and promoting the implementation of the recommendations of the Glassco Commission (White and Strick, 1970: 108). The recommendation to create a Management Improvement Branch had been formulated by the Glassco Commission's Research Group on Paperwork and Systems Management, which was under the direction of a senior consultant from Urwick Currie Ltd.,[3] the same management consulting firm that had previously loaned the services of Yeomans to the government (Canada, 1962a: 190). In the course of its study, the Research Group on Paperwork and Systems Management observed that 'the newer administrative techniques developed by large-scale industrial and commercial enterprises have been less than adequately utilized throughout the government' (Canada, 1962a: 220). To compensate for this situation, the Research Group proposed to establish a division (the Management Improvement Branch) that would set policy in the area of management advisory services. The Research Group also suggested that in its early years, the Management Improvement Branch would 'need to draw upon resources outside the government, such as universities and consultants' (Canada, 1962a: 223).

According to Bruce Doern, Mr Yeomans was part of the 'influx' of personnel—'some from the Glassco Commission itself and some from consulting firms brought in to implement the Glassco recommendations'—which 'produced a cadre of officials' that was 'primarily centred in the Treasury Board' (1971: 87; see also Mansbridge, 1979: 530). Another case of co-optation was that of J. J. Carson who, after having worked as a management consultant for Glassco, joined the TBS and was subsequently appointed Chair of the CSC in 1965. In the CSC, Carson oversaw the formation of the Bureau of Management Consulting (BMC) established in 1967 to provide a range of management services to the departments and agencies of the government. The BMC superseded the Management Analysis Division that the CSC created in the 1940s to help spread 'management consciousness' in government (CSC, 1947: 12). But as we have seen, after Glassco the TBS proceeded to establish the Management Improvement Branch which was designed to establish overall policy in the area of management consulting services. Following Glassco, some officials expressed concern about the diffusion of management consulting effort in the federal government. The transfer of responsibility for management policy from the CSC to the TBS created organizational confusion and raised the question of 'whether it would be better to situate management consulting services in the CSC or the Treasury Board' (Hodgetts *et al.*, 1972: 335). As one official wrote in 1966, 'the most important thing in this area [e.g. management consultancy] is to eliminate the wastefulness of parallel development, of duplication, of purposeless rivalry, and of confusion' (S. H. Mansbridge, quoted in Hodgetts *et al.*, 1972: 335).

---

[3] Urwick Currie was bought by Price Waterhouse in 1984.

Because of bureaucratic politics and of disagreements between the CSC and the Treasury Board, 'nothing was done about the dispersal of the various management services throughout the civil service' (Hodgetts *et al.*, 1972: 336). The situation subsequently became even more complicated when in 1968 a major government reorganization provided for the transfer of the BMC to the newly formed Department of Supply and Services (DSS). In its report, Glassco had called for a body like the DSS to handle the provision of common services for the government. For private-sector consultants, the overlap of responsibility between the DSS and the TBS in the management consulting field was always a source of problems because it meant that they could not concentrate their effort at building channels of communication with the state on only one ministry or agency, as was the case, for instance, in Britain following the creation of the Civil Service Department. Accordingly, following Glassco, the Canadian Association of Management Consultants (CAMC) began to duplicate their public relations activities and to make 'periodic representations to officials of government departments and agencies in the Treasury Board and the Department of Supply and Services' (Mellett, 1988: 22). But this soon changed when the Planning, Programming, and Budgeting System (PPBS), adopted in 1969, opened a new institutional route through which consultants could press their views within the federal state.

The search for a framework of central direction

If the management reforms implemented following the Glassco Commission decentralized authority to departments and agencies, the late 1960s and early 1970s witnessed the first attempts to implement the control side of the equation. Some seven years later, the Treasury Board Secretariat (TBS) started to initiate the kind of broad framework of central direction and accountability that Glassco had advocated in its report in 1962. As indicated earlier, the Glassco Commission envisioned a 'checks and balances' system where the TBS would provide a framework of central guidance within which detailed controls would be reduced and complemented by performance evaluation as the main vehicle for accountability. The implementation by the government of PPBS in 1969 was intended to set in motion the kind of central framework suggested by Glassco.

The PPB system and Trudeau's paradigm of 'rational management'

Glassco did not speak of PPBS. But it urged the government to replace its line budgeting approach by a programme and performance-based budget system and this recommendation later paved the way for the introduction of the Planning, Programming, and Budgeting System (PPBS) (Doern, 1971: 87). The programme budgeting idea came from the Hoover Commission in the United States and was first advocated in Canada in a report produced for the Glassco Commission by management consultants from Peat Marwick.[4]

In 1965 President Johnson ordered all US government agencies to adopt PPBS. The functioning of PPBS has been described well elsewhere and it suffices to say here that its purpose was to highlight the real goal of spending (Wildavsky, 1979). Expenditure requests were to be presented in terms of the objectives of spending rather than in terms of input cost and particular functions. This was intended to raise the sights of politicians from the details of money spent on furniture to the big issues of the relative amounts spent on different functions of government. In the United States, PPBS was meant to strengthen the power of the executive (Knott and Miller, 1987). Many thought that it would remove politics (i.e. Congress) from the budgetary process by providing the executive with clear and rational answers that Congress would be compelled to embrace (Yates, 1982). The Canadian government soon heard about PPBS in the United States 'and liked what it heard' (Savoie, 1994: 72). As the then-secretary to the Treasury Board wrote, PPBS in Ottawa was considered to be such a powerful technique that many believed it was meant 'to substitute science for politics in the decision-making process' (Johnson, 1971: 16). As in the United States, politics in Canada has historically had a 'bad name', often synonymous with corruption, patronage, and factionalism (Stewart, 1986; Laycock, 1990). This is why scientific management's promise of separating politics from administration 'caught on' as it did in Canadian state institutions after the First World War. Moreover, the belief that politics involves conflict and division in a federal country like Canada that already feels fragile and fragmented by regions, provinces, language, and ethnicity helps to delegitimize politics whenever it can be plausibly argued that there exist rationalist-scientific techniques that can potentially solve a given social problem. During the 1960s, the view that politics was divisive became more widespread in Canada with the intensification of provincial–federal conflicts and the the growth of nationalism in Quebec (McRoberts, 1988).

The election of Pierre E. Trudeau, who became prime minister in 1968 to fight what he saw as the 'irrationalities' of nationalism, spurred the search for rationalism and the use of technocratic means for resolving issues. As Peter Aucoin convincingly argued in an influential article, Trudeau's 'rational management' style meant that he was much enamoured of the 'scientific' approach to politics (Aucoin, 1986). Trudeau's non-ideological and apolitical

---

[4] The Glassco Commission's recommendations on programme budgeting are contained in 'Report 2: Financial Management'. The Project Group responsible for the research and drafting of the report on financial management was under the direction of James C. Thompson, a chartered accountant and partner in the accounting and management consulting firm Peat Marwick. Associated with Mr Thompson on the Project Group were 11 project officers, all drawn from Peat Marwick (Canada, 1962a: 84).

approach to governance merged well with the philosophy of PPBS (Doern, 1971). In 1969, the government issued a guide to departments and agencies on how to implement PPBS. The guide explained that PPBS was intended to introduce an 'analytic approach to government decision-making' (Government of Canada, 1969: 6). At the time PPBS was introduced, major changes were made to the machinery of government. Besides the creation of the TBS mentioned earlier, the Cabinet committee system was restructured and a Priorities and Planning committee was established. Changes in Cabinet committees were accompanied by a significant expansion of the Privy Council Office to facilitate policy co-ordination.

The PPBS approach produced changes not only at the centre of government, but also in the way the estimates were compiled and presented to Parliament. One of the results of PPBS was the presentation for the first time in February 1970 of departmental expenditures in the programme budget format in the Estimates Blue Book. This format created an opportunity for the Office of the Auditor General to justify an expansion in its mandate, with important consequences for the access of consultants to decision-making centres and the institutionalization of managerialist ideas.

Feeding the information requirements of the PPBS

A major element of the PPBS is its application of cost-benefit analysis to departmental programmes and activities (Hinrichs and Taylor, 1969). In the information system envisioned by the 1969 PPBS guide, cost-benefit analysis represented one of the main feedback mechanisms through which departments were to generate the data required by the TBS to measure attainment of programme objectives. Thus, an important aspect of PPBS was to establish within departments workable measurement devices and techniques whereby programme performance could be evaluated. With PPBS, the aim of the Treasury Board was to make performance measurement an integral part of the budgetary process and to provide an empirical basis upon which to conduct programme reviews. To do so the Treasury Board issued a number of guidelines on performance measurement, including the manual on *Operational Perfomance Measurement* (1974); a booklet entitled *A Manager's Guide to Performance Measurement* (1976); and the *Cost-Benefit Analysis Guide* (1976). These various measurement devices were all 'designed primarily to close the information gap in PPBS' (Yeomans, 1975: 27).

Within the bureaucracy, the implementation of PPBS meant that each department and agency had to establish in its organization a unit—called a 'Program Analysis Unit'—composed of a small staff of experts whose sole responsibility was to perform the 'analytic work' (i.e. cost-benefit analysis and performance measurement) associated with programme budgeting (Government of Canada, 1969: 50). The creation of these units enhanced the government's capacity in the management policy field and this eventually reduced the government's use of private sector consultants, which had significantly increased after the Glassco report. According to the Canadian Association of Management Consultants (CAMC),

by the end of the 1960s, public sector work constituted the largest part of the billing of most firms. In the wake of the Glassco Commission, government had provided a steady source of billings for CAMC members. As a result, relations with the public sector had not been the association's greatest concern . . . At the time, business from the public sector was good and appeared to be increasing. Therefore, government received inconsistent levels of attention from CAMC. (Mellett, 1988: 22–3)

But in the CAMC's view, the 'situation began to change for the worse' in the early 1970s when government assignments started to drop following the implementation of PPBS (Mellett, 1988: 23). Paradoxically, part of the reason for this decline was the way the federal state had been developing its own management capacities following Glassco. Some consultants in the CAMC saw this change as a positive sign. CAMC firms, they argued, had become too dependent on the federal public sector and they saw reduction in the government's use of consulting services as something that would help CAMC member firms to move 'out of a position of vulnerability' (ibid.). But others in the CAMC thought differently and saw this as 'a very negative trend, which indicated a declining presence in Ottawa' (ibid.). To counter this situation, the president of the CAMC argued that the association needed to become 'a real force at the federal level' (ibid.). 'CAMC as an institution has never been that influential if you're honest about it', he said. 'While there were sporadic meetings with government officials at the ministerial level, it was not a sustained, well-organized program with adequate follow-up' (ibid.). In the early 1970s, as the CAMC began to mobilize the support of its members to develop what consultants called 'a persistent program directed at Ottawa' (ibid.), one of its founding fathers, James J. Macdonell, took leave of the association to become Auditor General of Canada.

The Auditor General's study on financial management and control

In 1974, in his annual report to Parliament, the new Auditor General and former president of the Canadian Association of Management Consultants launched a government-wide investigation called the Financial Management and Control Study (FMCS). The initiation of the FMCS by the Office of the Auditor General was made possible by the expectations created by PPBS introduced in 1969. Traditionally, the 'audit entity' (i.e. the organizational parameters within which the scrutiny takes place) consisted of concrete elements such as budget categories or parliamentary votes. However, with the implementation of PPBS the audit entity became much broader, often including whole government programmes and departments. State auditors have accordingly assumed duties of a wider scope than their traditional financial audit work and since the 1960s they have conducted broad-scope scrutinies that include almost every aspect of public management (Chan and Jones, 1988).

Thus, in launching the FMCS in the early 1970s, the OAG justified the qualitative change in the audit function of his Office by the new approach to expenditure management of the 1960s, the adoption of PPBS, and the decentralization of financial control following upon the Glassco Commission's report. The objective of the Auditor General's two-year FMCS was to see if the government was adequately meeting the information needs that the PPB system required for the proper functioning of the framework of guidance that the Treasury Board established to balance the decentralization of authority that took place following Glassco (Auditor General of Canada, 1974: 67–8). According to the OAG, the FMCS 'turned out to be the most comprehensive independent examination of the government's financial management and control systems since the Royal Commission on Government Organization (Glassco) reported in 1962' (Auditor General of Canada, 1975: 3).

The OAG's comparison of its 1974 FMC study with the Glassco Commission is relevant in more than one way. Not only were the two studies 'independent', in the sense of both having been conducted by bodies autonomous of the direction and control of the political executive, but the OAG, like the Glassco Commission, also made important use of individuals drawn from large accounting and management consulting firms. In transforming the function of his Office from the traditional financial audit to the audit of the government's 'management systems', Auditor Macdonell started to bring in a large number of management consulting experts. The outside help for the FMCS came from 34 partners and managers associated with 16 of Canada's most important accounting and management consulting firms such as Arthur Andersen; Coopers & Lybrand; Deloitte, Haskins & Sells; Ernst & Ernst; Peat Marwick; Price Waterhouse; and Touche & Ross (Auditor General of Canada, 1974: 69–70; 1975: 3). Robert B. Dale-Harris from Coopers & Lybrand headed the OAG's study on Financial Management and Control. Based on the findings of this group, the Auditor General expressed serious concerns about the adequacy of departmental systems and procedures for financial management and control in his 1975 and 1976 reports. In 1975, the OAG stated in its annual report to Parliament that 'The present state of the financial management and control systems of departments and agencies of the Government of Canada is significantly below acceptable standards of quality and effectiveness' (Auditor General of Canada, 1975: 4).

The results of the second year of the special FMC study were apparently worse than the first. In its 1976 annual report, the OAG rocked the government to its foundations when he claimed that he was 'deeply concerned that Parliament—and indeed the Government—has lost, or is close to losing, effective control of the public purse' (Auditor General of Canada, 1976: 9). The Auditor argued that he had been 'inescapably' led to this opinion by the full results of the two-year FMC study.[5] That study, the OAG argued, had come to the conclusion that the government's financial management system was 'grossly inadequate' (Auditor General of Canada, 1976: 9). According to the OAG, the inadequacy of the government's financial management control system was due to the fact that certain key recommendations on management control made by Glassco in 1962 had not been implemented and were misunderstood. Although the Glassco recommendations concerning the decentralization of financial authorities had been fully implemented, the concurrent and equally important counter-balancing controls had not been instituted. This meant that 'control over public funds would appear to have been deteriorating for at least the last 15 years' (Auditor General of Canada, 1976: 11).

To rectify the situation, the OAG prescribed major changes to the machinery of government. The Auditor recommended the creation of a new central agency, the Office of the Comptroller General (OCG), which would be responsible for helping departments produce the data necessary to close the PPBS information gap (Auditor General of Canada, 1976: 14). The Comptroller General's mandate would include government-wide responsibility for the evaluation and measurement of the effectiveness, economy, and efficiency of government programmes. The recommendation that the government establish a single agency that would be responsible for providing unified central direction and leadership to departments in all matters relating to financial management and control had already been made by the OAG in its 1975 report (recommendation 10.40). Accordingly, in March 1976 the Treasury Board president announced the establishment of a Financial Administration Branch within the Treasury Board under the authority of a deputy secretary (House of Commons [Canada], 1976: 1230). But later, in the course of his appearance before the Public Accounts Committee, the Auditor General argued that the establishment of the Financial Administration Branch was not enough; what was needed was an agency separated from the Treasury Board and placed under the authority of a new officer reporting directly to the president of the Treasury Board. But the Treasury Board president originally resisted that idea. He argued that this would confuse the chain of command within his organization and that 'he did not want two deputy ministers reporting to him' (Jean Chrétien

---

[5] As the Auditor stated in his 1976 report, 'My over-all conclusion and opinion is based on the breadth and depth of the Financial Management and Control study that my Office, with the very substantial support of the Canadian public accounting profession, conducted throughout the government during the last two years. More than 100,000 professional hours have been devoted to the study by my staff and by more than 50 partners and staff members of leading public accounting firms' (Auditor General of Canada, 1976: 10).

quoted in Savoie, 1990: 110). But again in its 1976 annual report, the OAG reformulated its recommendation about a separate Office of the Comptroller General, this time arguing that this change was urgent because the government was in the course of 'losing control of the public purse'.

There was an immediate and vociferous public demand from the House of Commons that the Trudeau administration do something immediately to correct the problem identified by the OAG and its network of consultants (Hartle, 1979: 369). The government offered a three-faceted response to the OAG. First, the government appointed in 1976 the Royal Commission on Financial Management and Accountability (Canada, 1979). Secondly, in August 1977, Parliament adopted Canada's first Auditor General Act, which considerably extended the responsibilities of the OAG by including in its mandate the powers to undertake 'value for money' auditing. Thirdly, in June 1978, the government amended the Financial Administration Act to create the Office of the Comptroller General, which was given the responsibility for the development of government-wide procedures to ensure that efficiency and effectiveness were measured by departments and agencies. Each element of the government's response to the 1976 OAG's report are discussed separately in the following sections.

The Royal Commission on Financial Management and Accountability

The Royal Commission on Financial Management and Accountability was created in November 1976. Also known as the Lambert Commission (its chair was Mr Allan Lambert, president of the Toronto Dominion Bank), the Royal Commission had a mandate to examine the structure, systems, and procedures whereby financial management and control were exercised and administrators held accountable for their administration (Canada, 1979).

The Lambert Commission's final report produced 165 recommendations contained in a 586-page document which was made public in 1979. In organizing its research agenda, the Lambert Commission did not adopt the broad strategy of the Glassco Commission. Besides a small permanent staff, the Lambert Commission also had a group of six special advisers who could communicate their ideas directly to the commissioners. One member of the group was Mr Donald Yeomans, who had previously worked as a management consultant on the Glassco Commission before being appointed to the Treasury Board in 1965. Another member was Robert B. Dale-Harris from Coopers & Lybrand (Canada, 1979: 2–3). As indicated earlier, Dale-Harris was the consultant who had headed the OAG's two-year Financial Management and Control Study (FMCS), the findings of which, according to Macdonell, had 'inescapably' forced him to declare that the government's financial management system was 'grossly inadequate'.

Packaging administrative with parliamentary reforms

The OAG's reports had an important impact on the definition of both the mandate of the Lambert Commission and the problems that it was asked to investigate. The Commission's terms of reference stated that 'Reports from the Auditor General have caused the government serious concern that the state of financial administration in the Government of Canada is not now adequate to ensure full and certain control over and accountability for public funds' (Canada, 1979: v).

In deciding in its 1976 report to define the problem as one of 'control' of the public purse by Parliament and government, the OAG created a situation where most of the recommended reforms would also have implications for the accountability relationships existing between bureaucrats, ministers, and the legislature in a parliamentary system of government (Johnson, 1992: 15). In parliamentary states based on the Westminster model, the accountability relationships of senior officials to ministers and of ministers to Parliament are essentially what make 'control' possible (Judge, 1993). As a result, the Lambert Commission made recommendations to reform both the bureaucracy and the House of Commons. The Commission called for a strong emphasis on management rather than policy and made suggestions to reform parliamentary committees and to hold senior officials more accountable for their actions. Lambert suggested that parliamentary committees be greatly strengthened and be given a staff budget in order for MPs to undertake in-depth studies of the impact of government programmes. Lambert also recommended that deputy ministers be held 'directly accountable to Parliament for matters of daily administration that fall under [their] responsibility' (Canada, 1979: 43). The deputy head should be designated Chief Administrative Officer of the department and be liable to appear before the House of Commons' Public Accounts Committee (PAC) to render an account of his or her administration.[6]

In recommending such sweeping deputy ministerial accountability to Parliament, Lambert said that it did not intend to weaken ministerial responsibility. Lambert argued that ministerial responsibility had to be reconciled with the growing complexity of modern government which meant, in the commissioners' view, that ministers have less time to oversee the management of departmental affairs (Canada, 1979: 42). Lambert believed that its ideas for direct administrative accountability would reinforce the convention of ministerial responsibility, in the sense that the minister's accountability for the overall administration of the department would

---

[6] The notion of Chief Administrative Officer suggested by Lambert was an attempt to adapt into Canadian political institutions the British Accounting Officer convention (Franks, 1997). In Britain, the Permanent Secretary, or deputy minister, is also the Accounting Officer of his or her department and he or she is held directly accountable for financial matters to the House of Commons' Public Accounts Committee (PAC). The Accounting Officer is the person who signs the accounts for a department, defends them before the PAC, and is held directly responsible for the faults the committee finds in them.

become clearer through the recognition that certain spheres of departmental operations were, *de facto*, under the deputy's control. Lambert's recommendation implied that lines would have to be drawn between the *political* responsibility and the *administrative* responsibility of ministers and deputy ministers respectively. Here we see resurfacing, again, the old policy-administration dichotomy which has been part of the Canadian institutional landscape since the early 1900s and which assumes that there is an unbridgeable qualititative difference between politics and management.

The question of direct administrative accountability

Although they have never been formally implemented, Lambert's ideas for direct administrative accountability represent its most enduring legacy in recent discussions about administrative reforms in Canada. In making recommendations on bureaucratic change as part of a policy package that also included parliamentary reforms, Lambert ensured that subsequent attempts at reforming the federal administration would almost always be linked with questions dealing with parliamentary reforms. As mentioned earlier, Lambert was led to look at questions dealing with parliamentary accountability because of the way the OAG initially framed the problem in its 1976 report as one of 'control' by Parliament and government of the public purse. And as a result, the OAG, along with backbenchers in the House of Commons, has been one of the most fervent partisans of Lambert's recommendations on direct administrative accountability.

The way bureaucratic reform policy was packaged by Lambert significantly affected the process of alliance formation by generating opposition from the government, but support from MPs for the idea of direct administrative accountability. For actors located in the legislative branch of the state, Lambert's ideas on accountability were politically attractive because they would have given them a more important role in scrutinizing the executive. The legislature is much less independent of the government in Canada than in other parliamentary systems based on the Westminster model (Aucoin, 1995: 228). Party discipline at the national level is extremely strong largely because of federalism and the nature of the party system. Most interpretations of party politics in Canada describe the party system as a 'brokerage' system (Brodie and Jenson, 1988; Gagnon and Tanguay, 1989; Smith, 1981; Thorburn, 1991). This view describes parties not as groups differentiated by principled stands, but rather as brokers of ideas that pick and choose among contending ideological principles to suit their electoral purposes. Parties are willing to adopt any ideas they think have a wide appeal, to maximize their support across the various groups that make up Canada, a country where there are persistent and 'deep' linguistic, religious, and regional cleavages. Parties do not have clear and consistent political views and they do not only appeal to one social group because to do so would be to court electoral suicide or inflame social tensions in the country. Rather, they adopt vaguely defined programmes as a way to reconcile the various social groups that make up the fragmented Canadian electorate.

Patronage, rather than ideology, has played a crucial role in cementing the organizational base of federal parties in Canada (Simpson, 1988). And in the absence of shared ideological principles that would unite party members around a common political goal, party discipline has provided— within the parliamentary wing of parties—the 'glue' that political leaders believe necessary to maintain unity and avoid divisions along regional or linguistic lines (Aucoin, 1985). This means that MPs and backbenchers who are part of the governing majority are closely controlled by the party leadership and thus do not have much room to play an independent policy role and to be critical of government actions (Franks, 1987: 110–15). This is why Lambert's ideas on parliamentary and administrative reforms were so well received by MPs. If adopted, they would have significanly enhanced MPs' influence in the public policy process. But the government opposed these ideas, viewing their implementation as likely to remove whole areas of public administration from the minister's sphere of intervention. None the less, ideas of direct administrative accountability did not disappear in 1979 with the Lambert Commission. The reason that they did not do so was that the interests attached to them (the OAG, MPs, the Public Accounts Committee) had sufficient institutional power to maintain them on the public agenda. But in associating managerialist policy proposals with issues dealing with parliamentary accountability, the Lambert report did not mobilize strong governmental backing for its recommendations.

Overall, the Lambert report has had very little influence on government operations. By the time the Commission's report was made public, a number of events had taken place which distracted attention from its recommendations. First, there was a change of government. In May 1979, two months after the publication of the Lambert report, the Trudeau government was defeated by Joe Clark's Conservatives. In addition, some of the most important reasons that had justified the creation of the Lambert Commission had already evaporated when its final report was made public. In April 1977 the government announced its decision to create the Office of the Comptroller General (OCG) along the lines first suggested by the Auditor General. And finally, while the Lambert Commission was conducting its inquiry, the government had adopted in 1977 the new Auditor General Act which, as discussed below, was seen as another tool that would help to rectify 'waste or maladministration' in government (Canada, 1975: 108).

The Auditor General Act 1977

The position of Auditor General is occupied by an appointed official who makes reports to the legislature. To carry out its functions appropriately, it is believed that the Office of the Auditor General must have what private-sector auditors call 'independence', that is, the auditor must not be under the direct control of the organization being audited—in this case the executive branch of the government. One element of this independence is ensured by the fact that the Auditor is an officer of Parliament. The Auditor's powers to report directly to the House of Commons, his or her method of appointment, and the fact that he or she has protection from arbitrary dismissal from office by the government: are all aspects intended to ensure the OAG's independence of the control and direction of the political executive.

The Auditor General Act was promulgated in August 1977. However, the idea of having a law to deal specifically with the OAG started during the late 1960s and early 1970s, when the responsibilities and relationships of the Auditor General became the source of considerable controversy. Before the adoption of the Act in 1977, a number of draft Acts had been proposed. In the early 1970s, the Treasury Board was in the course of drafting a proposed Auditor General Act, and it is in this context that James J. Macdonell, head of Price Waterhouse's management consulting division and co-founder of the Canadian Association of Management Consultants, was appointed Auditor General by the government in the spring of 1973. A few months before the retirement of Macdonell's predecessor (Maxwell Henderson), the president of the Treasury Board had established a committee, consisting of the heads of five major accounting firms, to identify suitable candidates for the position of Auditor General.[7] One member of the search committee was Gordon Coperthwaite, head of the Toronto-based accounting and management consulting firm Peat Marwick. Like Macdonell, Coperthwaite was also a co-founder of the Canadian Association of Management Consultants and a past president of the CAMC in 1967–8 (Mellett, 1988: 51). In February 1973, Coperthwaite communicated with Macdonell to let him know that his name was on the top of the shortlist of qualified candidates. A few days later, the Treasury Board president officially announced the appointment of Macdonell.

In mid-April, Macdonell met with the Treasury Board president (Charles Drury) to discuss with him the responsibilities he was about to take on. One item on the Treasury Board president's agenda was the proposed Auditor General of Canada Act, drafted in the last months of Auditor Henderson's

---

[7] In Canada, the Auditor is appointed by Parliament on the nomination of the prime minister. However, to help ensure the highest quality appointment, there is a tradition that, in making this nomination, the prime minister will rely on the advice of a committee of senior representatives from leading accounting and consulting firms. Once appointed, the Auditor serves a fixed term of 10 years, or until he or she reaches 65 years of age. One way to ensure the independence of the Auditor from the executive is that he or she can only be dismissed for inappropriate behaviour after a majority vote of the House of Commons and Senate and the concurrence of the governor general.

tenure, and pronounced satisfactory by him before his retirement and now ready to be presented to Parliament (Sinclair, 1979: 104). The Treasury Board president wanted to know if Macdonell would object to the early launching of the draft Act. Macdonell did indeed object. The Bill contained a number of clauses which awarded to the OAG control over the recruitment and classification of his personnel. These were the powers that Auditor Henderson had asked for, and they were the ones that the new legislation would give to his successor. But Macdonell believed that the new Act should also address the issue of the scope of the investigating and reporting powers of his Office. The draft legislation was thus shelved.

In October 1973, appearing before the House of Commons Committee on Public Accounts, Macdonell announced that he had just created an independent review committee that would inquire into the OAG's responsibilities and recommend needed legal and administrative changes (Canada, 1975: 3). One of the responsibilities Auditor Macdonell believed it was 'crucial' to include in the mandate of his Office was 'value for money' (VFM) auditing, or the power to report on whether public funds were spent economically, efficiently, and effectively (Sinclair, 1979: 115). While Macdonell was attempting to give new life to the OAG, the Trudeau government was in a minority position. During the years 1972–4, Canadian parliamentary government was more 'legislature centred' than 'executive centred' and this created an opportunity for the legislature and the organizations attached to it to play a stronger role in influencing government policy. Between 1972 and 1974, the balance of political power was in favour of the legislature, that is, in favour of the same body to which the Auditor General is linked—and this significantly shaped the unfolding of the events that are discussed next.

The Wilson report and value-for-money auditing

The Independent Committee for the Review of the Office of the Auditor General of Canada consisted of three members (two accountants and one lawyer), appointed by Macdonell. The Committee's chairman was J. R. M. Wilson, a retired partner of Clarkson Gordon & Co.[8] The Wilson Committee issued its report in March 1975. Among its 47 recommendations, the one about which the OAG was most enthusiastic and the one which it believed would generate 'the most heated debate', was recommendation No. 3, on 'value for money' (Sinclair, 1979: 119). The Wilson Committee recommended that the role of the OAG be substantially expanded to allow the Auditor to

---

[8] Clarkson Gordon was originally an accounting firm based in Canada. One of its directors, G. P. Clarkson, was among the founders of the Canadian Association of Management Consultants in 1963, and was the Association's first president, in 1963–4 (Mellett, 1988: 51). Clarkson Gordon and its management consulting practice, Woods Gordon, have, from the mid-1980s, been known as Ernst & Young, as a result of the mega-mergers that produced the Big Five firms that now dominate the world's consulting market (ISTC, 1991a: 8).

report to Parliament cases where 'money has been expended other than for purposes for which it was appropriated by Parliament or value for money has not been obtained for any expenditure or expenditures' (Canada, 1975: 36).

As the Commissioners pointed out, 'the Auditor General has for some years now been interested in assessing value for money' (Canada, 1975: 33). First developed in the private sector, the VFM concept, which later became known as 'comprehensive auditing', examines whether the money is expended economically and efficiently, and whether the programme on which it is expended is effective in meeting its goals (CCAF, 1985). The Commission contended that the first two components, economy and efficiency, 'are susceptible to reasonably objective definition and measurement' (Canada, 1975: 33). The application of the concept of effectiveness, however, was more problematic. Effectiveness is the extent to which a programme achieves its objectives and is often a matter of value judgement rather than objective measurement. The Committee admitted that the concept of effectiveness raised methodological problems of measurement, in that many government programmes 'defy quantification. For instance, how can one translate the purposes of the Department of External Affairs into quantitative terms that permit objective measurement of performance?' (Canada, 1975: 34). Yet in spite of these problems, the Committee argued that 'significant progress' had been made in the social sciences in the development of 'methods of measuring effectiveness' (Canada, 1975: 35). The fact that the systematic measurement of the effectiveness of a programme 'presents problems of identification and evaluation should not be taken as an excuse to question the Auditor General's right of reporting on obvious case of ineffectiveness' (ibid.). It 'is important that the new legislation be broad enough', wrote the Committee in recommending a new legal status for the OAG, 'to ensure that the Auditor has the right to report . . . on the evaluation of the effectiveness of programs' (ibid.). Although it was recognized that it is 'true that there is a strong element of personal judgement involved in [effectiveness] reporting' and that some future holder of the office may be tempted to overstep the boundaries of his powers, the commissioners believed that this represented only a 'very slight' risk (Canada, 1975: 36). They concluded that, 'even if the risk become reality, it would be better that the Auditor General exercise greater latitude than was intended, than [that] any Member of Parliament or private citizen should feel that he was unable to speak freely about the facts he had discovered in the performance of his duties' (ibid.).

The question of evaluating effectiveness

In the spring of 1975, the recommendation of the Wilson Committee that the OAG be given the powers to report on value for money was greeted with 'great reserve' by ministers and senior civil servants, particularly the proposal dealing with the evaluation of the effectiveness of programmes (Johnson, 1992: 11). The government was unenthusiastic about the Wilson Committee's recommendation of evaluating programme effectiveness because it believed that evaluation of effectiveness was largely a political function that should be performed by the executive and the parliamentary opposition. The government was not willing to allow the OAG to investigate the effectiveness of its programmes because this would have almost amounted to open pronouncement on policy. It was thus argued that the VFM recommendation would have to be modified if it were to prove acceptable to the government (Hartle, 1975). However, the government's original resistance to the question of evaluating effectiveness became politically more difficult to sustain when the OAG published, just a few months after the Wilson Committee's report, its 1975 annual report where, as mentioned earlier, it was argued that the government's management control system was 'grossly inadequate'.

That statement, added to the suggestion made the next year by the Auditor General that the government 'was close to losing control of the public purse' created, in the words of the parliamentary opposition, 'a crisis situation' in the federal bureaucracy that required rapid and drastic actions (House of Commons, 1976: 1232). In periods of crisis, state structures often become more malleable and crisis also supplies opportunities for new ideas to influence the direction of policy (Goldstein, 1989). As a result, the ministers and senior bureaucrats opposed to the VFM idea found their objections swept away. The media and the parliamentary opposition presented the government argument, that evaluation of effectiveness involved judgements on policy, as self-serving resistance to managerial improvement (Sutherland, 1981: 193). This situation eventually turned the tide in favour of the OAG. Following a period of negotiation between the Treasury Board and the Auditor General, the government agreed to allow the Auditor General—not to undertake evaluations of effectiveness himself—but as will be discussed later, to report on the systems established by the Comptroller General to measure programme effectiveness.

The institutionalization of links with accounting and consulting firms

A few months before the adoption of the Auditor General Act in 1977, in anticipation of his new expanded responsibilities, Macdonell launched a Study on Procedures in Cost Effectiveness (SPICE) intended to help the OAG develop the methodologies and techniques needed for auditing economy and efficiency and for evaluating programme effectiveness. The SPICE had three objectives: (a) to compile information on the 'state of the art' of management control systems in the public sector, in terms of economy, efficiency, and effectiveness; (b) to assess and report on existing procedures for planning, measuring, and controlling activities in Canada's public service (in the interest of economy, efficiency, and effectiveness); and (c) to recommend to the OAG how this new mandate should be exercised in the future (Auditor General of Canada, 1977: 249).

Management consultants were a major source for the ideas that went into the development of the OAG's approach to VFM auditing. Macdonell appointed two management consultants as directors of the SPICE process: Kenneth Belbeck, president of the management consulting firm Stevenson & Kellog Ltd.,[9] and his associate Ronald Robinson (Auditor General of Canada, 1977: 249). Belbeck was not unknown to Auditor Macdonell. Like Macdonell, Belbeck was also a founding member of the Canadian Association of Management Consultants. Belbeck succeeded Macdonell as President of the CAMC in 1966 (Mellett, 1988: 51). Working in the SPICE process under the direction of Belbeck and his associate were 'approximately 60 senior professionals' recruited from 'leading accounting and management consulting firms across Canada' (Auditor General of Canada, 1977: 249). The intent of the SPICE was very similar to that of the 1974–6 Financial and Management Control Study (FMCS) described earlier. Again, the purpose was to scrutinize and describe management control systems in government which monitor or measure economy, efficiency, and effectiveness. The information would help the OAG develop the knowledge and technical strategies for its new responsibilities. And again, like the two-year FMCS, the SPICE process was also under the direction of management consultants from large accounting firms. Most of the consultants involved in the FMCS and the SPICE were recruited and lent by their firms to the OAG under the Executive Interchange Program of the Public Service Commission (PSC). In 1974, the Auditor General negotiated with John Carson, chairman of the PSC, the application, on a large scale, of the Executive Interchange Program (EIP) to his Office.[10] In negotiating the application of the EIP, Macdonell argued that his Office had personnel problems and was operating at 25 per cent below its authorized establishment of professional staff (Auditor General of Canada, 1974: 69). It has been reported that the PSC chairman was 'a little startled' when he was told that Auditor Macdonell was contemplating using the EIP on a large scale for the loan of 40 to 50 top-level consultants, considerably more than the total number of executive exchanges in the entire government during the three years since the programme's initiation (Sinclair, 1979: 130). Carson accepted Macdonell's requirements, and in early 1974 the Auditor General received assurances from the chairman of the PSC that the EIP could be applied 'on a significant scale'

[9] Stevenson & Kellog is now part of the Peat Marwick organization (ISTC, 1991: 8).

[10] The EIP was an exchange programme which the PSC had launched in 1971 to encourage a cross-pollination of managerial talent between the federal government and the private sector. It was seen as a 'means of developing a better understanding of the problems as well as the areas of interest common to industry business and government' (Auditor General of Canada, 1974: Appendix III, 100).

to his Office (Auditor General of Canada, 1974: 69). Some argued that Carson and Macdonell had no difficulties reaching an agreement over the EIP because, 'with their common management consulting background, the two men soon discovered that their ideas moved along parallel wavelengths' (Sinclair, 1979: 129). We saw earlier that before being appointed chairman of the Civil (now Public) Service Commission in 1965, Carson was a management consultant who worked for the Glassco Commission.

According to the OAG, 'the melding of the professional resources of the Audit Office and private sector audit and consulting firms proved so effective and successful' in the conduct of government-wide studies that it 'has become an integral part of our operations' (Auditor General of Canada, 1979: 32). Starting in the mid-1970s, Macdonell began to institutionalize, at the top of the hierarchy of his Office, the practice of receiving advice from members of Canada's major accounting and management consulting firms. In doing so, the Auditor General was to some extent following the recommendations of the Wilson Commission which had encouraged the Audit Office to develop 'close and cooperative relationships' with professional organizations outside the federal government (Canada, 1975: 79). In May 1976, for instance, the Auditor created the Independent Advisory Committee on Financial Management and Control Standards. The Independent Advisory Committee was originally composed of the partners of the same accounting and management consulting firms as had, according to the Auditor General, been 'intimately involved' in his study on Financial Management and Control between 1974 and 1976 (Auditor General of Canada, 1976: 11). Macdonell invited the partners of these firms to become the Independent Advisory Committee, because he believed that 'in this way, their valuable counsel, based on their wealth of knowledge and experience in financial management and control systems and practices in both the public and private sectors, will continue to be available to me and my senior officers' (Auditor General of Canada, 1976: 11).

The OAG's Independent Advisory Committee consisted in 1976 of a majority of firms associated with what was known then as the Big Eight group (now the Big Five).[11] The organizational chart of the OAG (Figure 4.1) shows the Independent Advisory Committee on Financial Management and Control Standards at the top, linked directly to the Auditor himself (Auditor General of Canada, 1978b: 243). As the diagram indicates, two further independent advisory committees were created in the mid-1970s: the Committee on Government Accounting and Audit Standards and the Committee on Computer Audit Standards. These two committees also consisted of a majority of

---

[11] It was composed of two partners from Coopers & Lybrand; one partner from Touche Ross; one partner from Peat Marwick; one partner from Woods Gordon; and one partner from Price Waterhouse (Auditor General of Canada, 1976: 11).

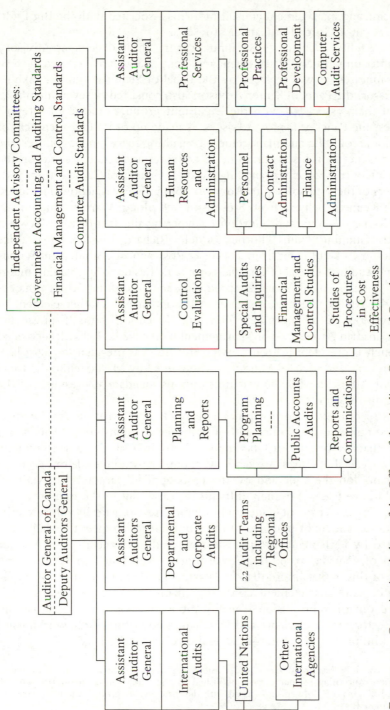

FIGURE 4.1. Organizational chart of the Office of the Auditor General of Canada, 1978

Source: Office of the Auditor General of Canada, *Annual Report*, 1978, pp. 242–3. Reproduced with permission.

accounting and management consulting firms associated with the Big Eight group (Auditor General of Canada, 1978b: 245).

In the Auditor General's 1980 annual report, the Independent Advisory Committee on Financial Management and Control Standards, created in 1976, had disappeared. It was replaced by the Panel of Senior Advisors. Like its predecessor, the Panel of Senior Advisors also consisted of seven members, most of them associated with the Big Eight group.[12] As the 1980 report indicates, the Panel of Senior Advisors 'is made up of leading members of the major accounting and management consulting firms' and it counsels the Auditor General on his programme of activities and strategies and on the application of comprehensive auditing (Auditor General of Canada, 1980: 364). Members of the Panel of Senior Advisors appointed by Macdonell included in 1980: Kenneth Belbeck from Stevenson & Kellogg; Warren Chippindale from Coopers & Lybrand; Gordon Cowperthwaite from Peat Marwick; Kenneth Gunning from Thorne Riddell; Richard Mineau from Price Waterhouse; Robert Rennie from Touche & Ross; and Jack Smith from Woods Gordon (Auditor General of Canada, 1979: 224). Besides being leading members of some of Canada's largest accounting and consulting firms, a majority of the Auditor's Panel of Senior Advisors shared another element in common: four out of seven have been, like Macdonell himself, presidents of the Canadian Association of Management Consultants. Belbeck succeeded Macdonell as president in 1966; Cowperthwaite was president in 1967; Jack Smith in 1974; and Richard Mineau was appointed by Macdonell to the Panel of Senior Advisors while he was finishing his mandate as president of the CAMC in 1978–79 (Mellett, 1988: 51).

In his 1979 annual report, Macdonell proudly noted that the combination of the resources of his Office and of management consulting firms was a feature that 'is believed to be unique both in Canada and elsewhere' (Auditor General of Canada, 1979: 32). Without the use of outside management consultants 'on the scale and on the basis applied', argued the Auditor, it would have been 'extremely difficult' to carry out in the mid-1970s the 'far-reaching government-wide studies which have drastically reformed the organization and audit practices of the Audit Office to meet the challenges presented by Parliament through the new Auditor General Act' (Auditor General of Canada, 1979: 32). According to Macdonell, one result and benefit of this is that 'more than 500 partners and staff members of public accounting and management consulting firms from across Canada have rounded out their professional qualifications and competence by gaining public sector audit experience and first-hand knowledge of the workings of public administration' (Auditor General of Canada, 1979: 33).

---

[12] The Panel of Senior Advisors still exists today and according to the most recent information concerning its membership published by the Audit Office, in 1991 it was still composed of a majority of firms associated with the then Big Six group (Auditor General of Canada, 1991: E-2).

TABLE 4.1. Expenditure of the Office of the Auditor General of Canada on consulting and accounting services ($Can.'ooo)

	Management consulting*	Accounting*	Total Professional services
1971	4,926	0	35,811
1972	4,997	0	43,259
1973	5,000	0	48,149
1974	290,778	132,333	469,481
1975	242,515	269,093	577,804
1976	2,473,773		2,896,934
1977	6,969,951		7,821,820
1978	7,643,119		8,640,284
1979	7,444,720		8,812,966
1980	6,543,449		8,263,727
1981	7,198,539		9,036,211

* From 1976 the classifications 'Management Consulting' and 'Accounting' were amalgamated in the Public Accounts.

Source: Public Accounts of Canada.

The Auditor General claimed that to build the value-for-money auditing capacity of his Office, it was 'more economic, efficient and effective' to rely on the professional resources of accounting and consulting firms than on a 'permanent bureaucracy' (ibid.). Permanent bureaucracies are generally known for not facilitating the entry of innovative ideas into policy because they are governed by rigid guidelines that emphasize conformity to established civil service norms (Hall, 1983). But an organization like the OAG, where the Executive Interchange Program introduced more flexible standards for recruitment to allow the Auditor General to bring in outside consultants, provides a much more hospitable setting for the emergence of innovative ideas within state institutions (Weir, 1989: 59).

According to the author of the history of the OAG, 'Macdonell's advisory boards and successive contingents of Executive Interchange recruits add up to a network of supporters which encompasses virtually everybody who is anybody in Canada's accounting and consulting professions' (Sinclair, 1979: 201). Among the 'more than 500' accountants and consultants involved during the second half of the 1970s in the reform of the organization and practices of the OAG, some were loaned to the Auditor under the Interchange Program or employed through 'short-term professional service contracts' (Auditor General of Canada, 1979: 8–9). The frequent use of service contracts during that period led to a major increase in the portion of the OAG's budget spent on external professional services. As Table 4.1 shows, the OAG's expenditure on professional services increased from $35,000 in

1971 to $9 million in 1981. The most important increase in expenditure on professional services took place in 1976 and 1977, when the OAG was given its new VFM powers.

The Auditor General's reporting powers

The part of the Auditor General Act of 1977 which pertains to the VFM concept states that the Auditor shall call attention to cases where: 'money has been expended without due regard to economy or efficiency; or satisfactory procedures have not been established to measure and report the effectiveness of programs, where such procedures could appropriately and reasonably be implemented' (Auditor General Act 1977, section 7(2)(d) and (e)).

In calling attention to cases where the mechanisms used by the government to measure programme effectiveness do not work appropriately, section 7(3) of the 1977 Act empowers the Auditor to submit his report directly to the House of Commons. Unlike its counterpart in Britain, the Canadian OAG does not report to one specific body made of a small number of politicians, such as the Public Accounts Committee (PAC), but rather directly to the entire House of Commons and through the House, to the media and public in general. This institutional arrangement is believed to enhance the political independence of the OAG. In Britain, it was noted in Chapter 3, the OAG's counterpart, the Comptroller & Auditor General (CA&G), reports directly to the PAC, and then the PAC examines the audit findings and reports its own conclusions to the public and the press at the same time that it releases the audit report. The PAC's members get media and public attention in return for their work, which can help their chances of re-election and legitimizes their role *vis-à-vis* the public (Sutherland, 1993). In contrast, in Canada it is the Auditor General, and not the MPs who are members of the PAC, who gets media and public attention. In Canada, the public sees only the Auditor General as he tables his report in the House of Commons, gives press conferences, answers journalists' questions, and then dominates the papers and the news on television for a few days. This indicates that the OAG in Canada functions with much more 'independence' of the Parliament it is supposed to serve than its counterparts in other Westminster systems (Pollitt and Summa, 1997b).

The publicity and all the media attention that the Auditor General gets from the tabling of his report create a powerful political leverage for the OAG and greatly enhance its capacity to diffuse ideas about how government should be managed. The media coverage of its annual report also means that the OAG is able to bypass the government by addressing its message directly to the public. Moreover, as 'Parliament's servant', the OAG also often tends to present itself as the servant of all Canadian taxpayers. In the eyes of the public, the institutional separation of the OAG from the executive is a key legitimizing factor which helps to strengthen the belief in the political objectivity of its observations regarding government management. This helps make the OAG a high-profile public actor in discussions pertaining to state management and bureaucratic reform and it can also sometimes give to the OAG the power to impose its policy ideas on the government. For the government, being against the ideas suggested by the OAG, or critical of its recommendations, is almost like being against 'Parliament's servant' and, indirectly, against the 'servant' of all Canadian taxpayers. In the face of the OAG politicians and bureaucrats are always in a defensive position, guilty until proven innocent. As Donald Savoie once noted, the 'Auditor General is feared in government if only because of the publicity given the annual report' (1990: 35). In the end, however, it is this fear, or defensiveness, that makes the government sceptical about strongly supporting the management ideas that the OAG's network of consultants advocate through the Auditor General's reports.

The Office of the Comptroller General

The creation of the Office of the Comptroller General (OCG) in June 1978 represents the last element in the government's three-faceted response to the allegations made by the Auditor General in 1976 that Parliament was losing 'control of the public purse'. That statement had a major impact: it initiated a process that led to fundamental changes in the government's management system. It created the perception (whether warranted or not) of failure in the government's management system. The perception of failed policy represented an important pre-condition for change in the government's management policies. It produced a period of policy de-legitimation that then led to the opening of a political space or opportunity, which in turn created an interest in change among policy makers and the public. However, for change in policy to occur, new ideas or some alternative policy strategy had to be available. In the present case, value-for-money (VFM) ideas and other related managerialist concepts imported from business management were available and had been sponsored for some years by the OAG and its network of management consulting experts. And once they became embedded in the Auditor General Act 1977, VFM ideas were perpetuated and institutionalized into new government organizations such as the Office of the Comptroller General.

It was seen earlier that in March 1976, in response to the recommendation from the OAG's Financial and Management Control Study, the government had already implemented its own version of the OCG by creating the Financial Administration Branch within the Treasury Board. The government originally resisted the Auditor General's recommendation concerning the creation of an OCG but as events unfolded, the government's position changed. The implementation of the Auditor General Act 1977 paved the way for an OCG whose role would be different from that originally envisioned in the Financial Administration Branch. As a result of the OAG's 1976 statements about the 'control of the public purse', pressure on the Treasury Board president mounted. Many government MPs reported in caucus that their constituents were more concerned with the issue of financial control than with the newly elected sovereignist government in Quebec (Savoie, 1990: 111). The Treasury Board president initiated a series of one-to-one meetings with the Auditor General to discuss the OCG idea. Then, the Treasury Board president sought approval for the idea from the Cabinet's Priorities & Planning committee. It met considerable resistance from senior bureaucrats, especially those in the Treasury Board who believed that many of the responsibilities that were to be given to the new OCG would overlap with their own. However, the Treasury Board president reported to the cabinet that he had struck a deal with the Auditor General. Unless he could deliver it, the government would be subjected to a new round of criticism from the media, the opposition, and the Auditor General himself. On the basis of those arguments, and with the support of the Prime Minister, the Treasury Board president was finally able to get his proposal through. Notwithstanding the support from the Cabinet, there was still strong opposition to the creation of the new office in the Ottawa bureaucracy. Indeed, it took the government nearly one year to appoint the first Comptroller General, and many outside government believed that bureaucrats 'were deliberately dragging their feet in the hope that the idea would eventually die' (Savoie, 1990: 113).

The institutional link between the OAG and the OCG

In allowing the OAG to report directly to the House of Commons on the procedures established by the government to measure programme effectiveness, the terms of the Auditor General 1977 Act assumed that such procedures did in fact exist. If such procedures were believed to be non-existent or not 'appropriate' by the Auditor, then a body had to be responsible for developing them wherever the Auditor would judge they could 'reasonably be implemented'. The terms of the Auditor General Act thus opened the door for the creation of the Office of the Comptroller General (OCG). The OCG was intended to be the organization that would establish the procedures that would allow the Auditor to fulfil the VFM mandate conferred upon his Office by the 1977 Act. There is a situation of mutual bureaucratic support and legitimation between the OAG and the OCG. The OAG's VFM mandate 'operates symbiotically with the responsibility of the OCG to ensure that effectiveness evaluation is conducted' (Sutherland, 1980: 621). It is through the OCG that the OAG, a body independent of the executive and attached to the legislature, can apply its power to the bureaucracy. The relationship between the two bodies basically works in the following manner.

TABLE 4.2. Contracting expenditure of the Canadian federal government on management consulting and professional services ($Can.'ooo)

	1973	1984	1993	*Average annual growth rate (%)* 1973–84	1984–93
Management consulting	6,129	56,454	189,209	22.3	14.4
Total contracted professional and special services	383,780	2,933,857	5,205,600	20.2	6.6

Note: To compare the evolution over time of public spending on management consulting services and other professional services, the data have been divided into two periods defined according to the availability and comparability of information otained from the Public Accounts of Canada and the Treasury Board Secretariat. The first period covers most of the 1970s and the second most of the 1980s.

Source: Treasury Board Secretariat, 1994, *Contracting for services: an overview*. Ottawa, 11 April.

First, the OAG reports to the legislature that procedures to ensure the evaluation of programme effectiveness are not in place; according to the Auditor General Act 1977, the OAG can recommend which procedures should be adopted and where they should 'appropriately and reasonably be implemented'; the OCG then puts in place the recommended procedures and, as indicated in the 1977 Act, if these procedures are not judged to be 'satisfactory' by the OAG, the Auditor, in the following year, formulates critical observations about the state of government management in its annual report to the legislature. Armed with its new VFM powers, the OAG has thus been in a position to exercise—through the OCG—continuous pressures on the bureaucracy in order for government departments to put in place the systems or techniques that can measure or evaluate the effectiveness of public programmes. In the face of such pressures, and to avoid being publicly blamed in the OAG annual report and thus put their minister in political 'hot water', government departments have developed and implemented the various techniques designed to measure programme effectiveness. In doing so, they have increasingly come to rely on the services of private-sector management consultants (as is shown by the figures in Table 4.2).

Through its link with the OCG the OAG acquired a more dominant voice in the bureaucratic reform policy sector. Following the implementation of the Auditor General Act 1977 and the creation of the OCG in 1978, jurisdiction over management issues in Canada to some extent became a policy domain, not *legally* but *politically*, shared by the OCG and the OAG, and thus *divided* between the executive and the legislature. As a result, the management policy sector became more fragmented, and as the American example teaches us, when jurisdiction over policy is divided, building support for policy is also more difficult (Jones, 1994). This is, to some extent, what happened in Canada in the late 1970s and the legacies of fragmentation produced by the 'division of labour' between the OAG and OCG regarding management policy issues subsequently made it more difficult for the government to give strong support to new managerialist ideas and policies. This situation contrasts sharply with that of Britain where, as we saw in Chapter 3, there is a single position of Comptroller & Auditor General (C&AG), whose responsibilities are not separated between the government and the legislature, as happens in Canada.

Building programme evaluation capacities

The position of Comptroller General was created in 1978 by Bill C-10, an Act to Amend the Financial Administration Act, to oversee the quality and integrity of financial administration systems and related practices and procedures in use throughout the federal public service. The Office of the Comptroller General was also responsible for developing and maintaining policies, procedures, and practices necessary to evaluate and report upon the efficiency and effectiveness of government programmes (Rogers, 1978). The first Comptroller General of Canada, Harry Rogers, vice-president of Xerox Canada, was recruited to government from the private sector. The second, Michael Rayner came from Price Waterhouse and was a former Deputy Auditor General in the OAG.

One of the main policies through which the OCG began discharging its responsibilities for evaluation was the Treasury Board Policy Circular 1977-47, 'Evaluation of Programs by Departments and Agencies'. The period from 1978 to 1981 was one of intense institution building, when the OCG attempted to give substance to the 1977 Circular (Rogers, 1980). The development of the programme evaluation function by the OCG in the early 1980s involved extensive consultation with senior department officials, as well as outside management consultants (Segsworth, 1990). Within the OCG, the Program Evaluation Branch (PEB) was responsible for promoting VFM ideas and for helping departments to establish appropriate policy and frameworks for the evaluation of programme effectiveness. The PEB was also responsible for training evaluators in the use of government-wide evaluation concepts, vocabulary, and techniques of analysis (McQueen, 1992). To promote professional development, the PEB organized a series of seminars on programme evaluation. One such seminar dealt with 'Working with Consultants in Evaluation' and focused on the evaluation manager's interaction with management consultants (Comptroller General, 1983). The PEB also worked hard to create new constituencies in support of VFM ideas and programme evaluation policies. One initiative of the PEB was the 'Program Evaluation Newsletter', a quarterly publication linking public managers, academics, and private-sector management consultants, and whose goal was to create, attached to the OCG, a 'program evaluation community' (Comptroller General, 1981). It is also in this context that the Canadian Evaluation Society (CES) was created in 1981, its main objective being the development of training in programme evaluation (Love, 1991; House, 1993). The CES was founded by government departments, the OAG, the OCG, academic institutions, and management consulting firms (Mayne and Hudson, 1992: 16). The CES also published a biannual journal, the *Canadian Journal of Program Evaluation*, whose editorial board was originally directed by senior officials from the OAG and composed of academics and consultants from Price Waterhouse.

By the autumn of 1981, the 1977 circular on evaluation (as reinterpreted by the Program Evaluation Branch) was outlined in and put into operation through two publications: *Guide on the Program Evaluation Function* ('the *Guide*') and *Principles for the Evaluation of Programs by Federal Departments and Agencies* ('the *Principles*'). According to the *Guide* and the *Principles*, deputy heads of departments and agencies have overall responsibility for the organization and functioning of programme evaluation within their areas of jurisdiction. To assist deputy heads, the policy requires that evaluation units be established in all departments. In a section on the use of management consultants, the 1981 *Guide* encourages evaluation units to supplement their resources 'through the use of outside consultants'. According to the *Guide*, 'consultants can be an effective additional means of bringing expertise, experience and credibility to the evaluation process' (Program Evaluation Branch, 1981: 56–7). The OCG subsequently established more or less regular contacts with management consulting organizations. Harry Rogers delivered an address to the Management Consulting Institute in 1979 and later met with representatives of the CAMC to discuss a number of issues related to public-sector reform (Mellett, 1988: 40; Rogers, 1979).

The CAMC and its 'Ottawa Committee'

The demand for knowledge of programme evaluation inside government was not the only factor explaining the development of closer links between consultants and the OCG in the early 1980s. Of course, this *rapprochement* was greatly facilitated when in the mid-1980s, Michael Rayner, partner-in-charge of the Ottawa office of Price Waterhouse, was appointed Comptroller General. As he wrote after his appointment, the programme evaluation market of the federal government was booming in the 1980s 'and lots of consultants are making a living out of this work. Before my current job, I was a partner in one of those consulting firms so I know both perspectives' (Rayner, 1986: 3).

The state's growing use of management consulting services in the 1980s was also, to a large extent, a supply-driven process. In the late 1970s, as many business entrepreneurs reduced their use of consulting services (because of slow economic growth), management consulting firms and their associations began to turn their attention to the commercial potential of the public sector. In the 1970s the world economy went into a recession and for the first time the sustained and steady growth that the Canadian management consulting industry had known since the 1960s came to a halt. Most firms experienced declines in the growth of assignments and revenues. In trying to counter this trend, consultants sought to revitalize their business organization, the CAMC. Following a 1976 study (known as the Currie report) on the successes and failures of the CAMC since its establishment in the 1960s, member firms decided to enhance the role of their association and urged it to take a more active commercial public relations role. In the late 1970s the CAMC intensified its public relations function as a way to raise the visibility of the management consulting industry in Canada. The CAMC engaged a firm of public relations consultants to spread the CAMC message and to implement a public relations programme that included seminars, conferences, and a CAMC newsletter (Mellett, 1988: 35).

As part of its new and more aggressive PR strategy, the CAMC decided to develop a more co-ordinated approach to the promotion of consulting to the federal government. The CAMC formed in 1976 its Committee on Federal Government Relations, known as the 'Ottawa Committee'. The Ottawa Committee was composed of a representative from each CAMC firm with an Ottawa office. Its primary objective was 'to improve the image and marketing effectiveness of CAMC member firms with respect to federal government consulting' (Mellett, 1988: 39).

Although their work in the Audit Office since the 1970s had allowed them to become more knowledgeable about government management, and to acquire what they saw as a 'good profile' in the bureaucracy, consultants believed that they had 'a very low profile (if any) at the political or ministerial level' (Mellett, 1988: 40). If they wanted to have more impact, the 1977 CAMC president argued, consultants had to go beyond the bureaucratic level and 'attempt to influence policy at a higher, political level' (Mellett, 1988: 39). Thus, in 1978 the Ottawa Committee established political contacts with the Conservative Shadow Cabinet. Following the election of the short-lived Conservative government in 1979, a meeting was arranged between the CAMC and Treasury Board president Sinclair Stevens who, at that time, was preparing his privatization policy. In a letter to the Treasury Board president the CAMC explained how its members could help in:

such matters as the return of certain Government operations to the private sector; improved financial management in Government; cost containment studies and productivity improvement reviews; as well as work in the area of financial management systems development. All member firms stand ready to assist the Government and its departments in whatever way seems most appropriate. (Mellett, 1988: 40)

At the meeting with the Treasury Board, the CAMC raised concerns about the Bureau of Management Consulting, the government's internal consulting division which, as mentioned earlier, was created in 1960s following the Glassco Commission. The BMC had been a long-standing concern of the CAMC. For private-sector consultants the BMC was not only an institution that blocked or at least limited their access to the federal government consulting market. It was also a competititor. After its transfer to the Department of Supply and Services, the BMC began in the 1970s to sell its services on a fee basis both within and outside the federal government. The CAMC was strongly opposed to the BMC's bidding on private-sector consulting contracts, seeing the BMC as an unfair competitor subsidized by government money (Mellett, 1988: 40).

While the CAMC was making contacts with the Conservatives in 1978 and 1979 its president, Richard Mineau from Price Waterhouse, was appointed to the Panel of Senior Advisors, the committee made up of a majority of the Big Five firms which advised the Auditor General on his programme of activities and strategies. We saw earlier that J. J. Macdonell largely played the role of a 'policy entrepreneur' when, in the early 1970s, he began his quest to obtain from the government the power to report on value for money. By significantly expanding the powers of his Office in the 1970s Macdonell subsequently made it possible for several hundreds of management consultants to gain inside knowledge of the government machinery, thereby helping to further the growth of a profession that he had helped to establish in the 1960s. During Macdonell's mandate we see a close interaction between institution-building processes inside the state and the organizational development of management consultancy.

But Macdonell's term as Auditor General ended in 1980 and it was up to his successor, Kenneth Dye, to interpret the scope of the mandate that he believed the Auditor General Act 1977 had conferred upon the OAG. Dye essentially argued that the OAG's mandate included what he once described as 'negative' and 'positive' aspects (Auditor General of Canada, 1987: 1). He argued that his new VFM powers included the right to subject policy advice to audit. To make sure that policies are not made—in the language of the Auditor General Act—'without due regard' for economy, efficiency, and effectiveness, the Auditor contended that the 1977 Act included the review of policy advice from officials to ministers. And if the OAG was to be able to assess the quality of advice given by bureaucrats to ministers, senior officials had 'to come out of the closet', in the words of the Auditor General, and become accountable to the House of Commons Public Accounts Committee that reviews the OAG's reports (House of Commons, 1982: 59). Ministers have insisted on the confidentiality of the advice rendered to them by public servants. Ministers and their senior officials are not willing to have the content of politically sensitive advice made public and criticized (Johnson, 1992: 27). The idea of making available to the OAG and to Parliament—and thus to the Opposition—the content of the advice given to ministers by bureaucrats has been strongly resisted and, as Osbaldeston found in his study of the accountability of deputy ministers, is not popular among ministers and senior officials (1989).

But trying to make officials 'come out of the closet' to hold them accountable in the House of Commons was only one part of the OAG's mandate which, the Auditor General argued, also included a more positive aspect consisting of informing Parliament of the 'excellent management procedures' that civil servants could use in government (Auditor General of Canada, 1987: 1). For instance, in 1983 the OAG published a study on 'Productive Management' which urged the government to decentralize its administrative practices and reduce the burden of regulations and procedures on departmental managers. The OAG's ideas on productive management did not go unnoticed. In their election campaign in 1984, the Conservatives enthusiastically embraced the managerialist language of 'productive management' sponsored by the OAG. Productive management was enunciated by the Conservatives a 'top political priority' and, as Peter Aucoin found, the Conservatives' campaign proposals on 'productive management drew heavily on the 1983 report of the Auditor General wherein was found an entire chapter devoted to "Constraints to Productive Management in the Public Service"' (Aucoin, 1988*b*: 344).

From Nielson to PS 2000: The new managerialism in the Mulroney era

The new leader of the Progressive Conservative Party, Brian Mulroney, was committed to increasing the efficiency of government by making the public sector behave more like the private sector (Gollner and Salée, 1988). In taking up the OAG's 'productive management' cause, the Conservatives promised to 'shift from reliance on regulations, controls and detailed procedures towards greater reliance on managers' competence and their achievements of results. Our goal is to simplify government and to "let the managers manage"' (Progressive Conservative Party of Canada, 1984: 1). The Tories also promised to review all the government programmes left by the Trudeau administration from the Auditor General's much prized perspective of 'value for money' (Aucoin, 1988*b*: 344).

One day after the Conservatives' victory in 1984, Prime Minister Mulroney created the Ministerial Task Force on Program Review with the mandate of evaluating the effectiveness of existing programmes and the efficiency with which they were functioning. The Task Force was an *ad hoc* Cabinet committee consisting of four ministers, chaired by Deputy Prime Minister Erik Nielsen. Nielsen established a 12-member private sector advisory committee whose role was 'to inject new ideas into the management of the Government of Canada' (Canada, 1985: 2). Because he distrusted the bureaucracy that he inherited from his Liberal predecessors, the Mulroney government preferred to solicit input into policy development from outside the regular bureaucratic systems of the federal government (Aucoin, 1986). The private sector advisory committee of the Nielsen Task Force was chaired by a senior partner from Coopers & Lybrand and also included Ted Netten of Price Waterhouse and president of the CAMC. For the CAMC, this was an indication that its 'stature in Ottawa was improving' (Mellett, 1988: 41). The CAMC president credited his 'association's "pro-active initiatives" toward the Conservatives while they were in opposition with having helped gain representation on the Task Force' (ibid.). CAMC directors considered

the Nielsen representation to have been one of the Association's most significant achievements in recent years. It marked the first time the federal government had singled out CAMC, and the management consulting profession in general, for direct input into policy formation. It also provided an opportunity for the association to make a significant intellectual contribution, while at the same time to generate valuable exposure with national decision-makers. (ibid.)

The Nielsen Task Force reviewed 989 programmes reflecting annual expenditures of more than $Can.92 billion (Canada, 1986). But its proposals did not have an important impact on policy. This happened because three months after the tabling of the Task Force reports, Nielsen left the Cabinet over the mishandling of a political scandal. With Nielsen gone, no other minister came forward to champion the Task Force ideas in Cabinet. Many bureaucrats in government also strongly opposed the Task Force recommendations. Senior civil servants in the Ottawa bureaucracy disliked the Nielsen exercise because they believed that 'the private sector people [on the Task Force] were walking around with a slashing mentality' (reported in Savoie, 1990: 135). Of course, this 'cut and slash' mentality was very much in vogue during the first term of the Mulroney government. But the anti-government rhetoric of Mulroney soon led its administration into political troubles. Low morale, information leaks, public sector strikes, and civil servants openly engaged in partisan activities to defeat Tory candidates during election times, all provided evidence of the increasingly tense relations between the government and its employees (Blais, Blake, and Dion, 1997). After having had some second thoughts about the excesses of bashing the bureaucracy, Mulroney launched, at the beginning of his second mandate, Public Service 2000. As discussed in Chapter 1, PS 2000 sought to increase morale and self-esteem in the civil service. PS 2000 was an internally generated initiative led by senior public servants. The Conservatives did not ask outside business experts and consultants for direct policy input into the development of PS 2000. This happened partly because, after

Nielsen, 'the Mulroney government proved reluctant to involve the private sector again' in public sector reform (Savoie, 1990: 146).

The abolition of the CAMC

But even if Mulroney had wanted to involve the CAMC in PS 2000 as it had done with the Nielsen Task Force in 1984, this would have been impossible. While policy makers in government were developing PS 2000, the CAMC put an end to its existence in 1990 by merging with the Institute of Certified Management Consultants of Canada, the consulting industry's professional body. The new organization retained the name Institute of Certified Management Consultants of Canada. As we saw in Chapter 2, the ICMCC is a federation of seven regional and provincial institutes and its role is to promote the professional development of management consulting in Canada.

Why did the CAMC decide to abolish itself? The reasons are unclear but it seems that the 'forces of federalism' played a certain role—in the sense that the association became increasingly divided along regional or provincial lines. As Canadian scholars of interest group politics have shown, federalism is a cross-cutting force that creates tensions by imposing a territorially based form of collective action on the pursuit of functionally defined interests (Pross, 1992). Originally, the CAMC was based in Toronto, Montreal, and Ottawa. In the late 1970s, the association attempted to expand its regional base and began to create 'regional committees' to speak for the consulting industry in their region (Mellett, 1988: 44–5). As some of these regional committees became better organized, they initiated major projects on government relations and focused more on establishing contact with policy makers at the provincial level, thus making the existence of a 'national' organization less relevant than in the past (Mellett, 1988: 45). In Canada, federalism and the presence of powerful provincial governments—all of which are potential consumers of consulting services—have made it more difficult for the management consulting industry to concentrate its resources and lobbying activities on only one major level of government, as would more likely be the case in a unitary regime.

By becoming in 1990 a purely professional organization, the CAMC committed political 'hara-kiri' and abandoned its lobbying activities at the governmental level. The CAMC was a business association whose role was to promote the commercial interests of its members. The CAMC essentially defended the *private* interests of its members while the ICMCC, like any other professional organization, seeks to protect the *public* interest by making sure that clients who use the services of those who are recognized as Certified Management Consultants have a recourse when things go wrong. As a professional body the ICMCC seeks to convey a sense of non-partisanhip removed from the political arena. With the abolition of the CAMC in 1990 management consultants lost the only 'collective' organization they had, as an industry, to lobby government. Of course, throughout the 1980s many of the large firms that were members of the CAMC developed their own lobbying capacities by creating a 'Government Services Division' (GSD) within their organization. It may well also be that CAMC member firms have, individually, been more successful than the CAMC as a whole in establishing effective channels of communication with policy makers in government—which could be another factor explaining the CAMC's abolition in 1990.

The 'Ottawa Committee' of the CAMC was apparently not very influential in decision-making circles. In 1982 the CAMC produced an internal policy document, 'Strategy for the Government of Canada', which assessed the association's position in Ottawa. Although the CAMC's programme of relations with the federal government had become more substantive since the establishment in 1976 of the Ottawa Committee, the paper said that 'the results at both the administrative and political level were very limited' (Mellett, 1988: 40). To increase the visibility of the CAMC in Ottawa, the document recommended the development of 'a series of soirées for senior public servants, such as deputy and associate deputy ministers' (ibid.). In 1983, the CAMC introduced the soirées, to be known as 'Senior Management Forums'. In the words of the CAMC president, these forums were intended 'to sell the consulting industry to government' (ibid.). The forums brought together CAMC representatives and senior government officials to discuss common concerns, and hear a guest speaker from the business sector. The first forum took place in February 1983 and it featured the president of IBM as guest speaker. Several other forums were held following the election of the Conservatives in 1984 (Mellett, 1988: 41).

Besides public sector management, another policy area where CAMC displayed an active stance toward government was the submission of a major study on free trade in 1986. After his election in 1984, Mulroney began to consider the idea of freer trade with the United States. What consultants called 'the American invasion' was a major and long-standing concern of the CAMC. The CAMC created in 1979 a 'Committee on US Consultants' to study the extent of work done by American consultants in Canada (ibid.). The Committee found that US immigration officials were much slower than their Canadian counterparts in issuing work permits. According to the CAMC, this uneven application of rules created disadvantages for Canadian consultants. One study found that, in 1984, 40 American consulting firms did a total of $Can.30 million business in Canada. By comparison, 12 CAMC firms conducted only $Can.3 million of work in the United States (Mellett, 1988: 43). The CAMC strongly supported the free trade initiative —and thus the Mulroney government—because consultants believed that the creation of a free trade zone would remove differences in the administration of immigration laws that limited the access of Canadian firms to the

American management consulting market. As is well known, free trade became the key issue in the 1988 federal election. With the free trade initiative, the Mulroney government sought to 'free up' the economy through the elimination of trade barriers—a 'deregulation logic' that the government subsequently extended to the management policy sector with the introduction of PS 2000, which also sought to cut red tape so that managers could focus more on results than on rules, procedures, and processes.

The politics of parliamentary reform

With its PS 2000 initiative, the Mulroney government clearly signalled its support for the new paradigm of managerialism. Indeed, when it was launched in 1990, PS 2000 generated a lot of enthusiasm among members of the senior civil service (Tellier, 1990). All the talk about 'empowerment' was generally well received by senior bureaucrats because the managerialist language of PS 2000 announced a new era where public servants would be given more responsibilities and would no longer be held back and constrained by a control-oriented management approach. But even before the Liberals came to power in 1993, government support for the new managerialism and positive references to PS 2000 had diminished considerably. Paradoxically, the tremendous thrust toward managerialism that characterized most of the 1970s, and which gained new impetus when the business-oriented Conservatives took power in 1984, stalled soon after the introduction of PS 2000. In the early 1990s, a 'control lobby' of parliamentary bodies including the OAG and the Public Accounts Committee (PAC) began to put pressures on the government, arguing that PS 2000 had not provided an adequate accountability system (Roberts, 1996a). In the words of the PAC's Chairman, 'Public Service 2000 fails to provide an accountability system for public employees and does not indicate how Parliament and members of Parliament would exercise control over public employees' innovative ideas on behalf of Canadians. In fact, the two major elements still lacking in PS 2000 are an efficient accountability system and parliamentary control mechanisms' (House of Commons, 1992b: 5).

Parliamentarians and the OAG contended that with its focus on 'risk-taking' and on the need for public servants to be more innovative and 'entrepreneurial', PS 2000 could end up giving too much discretion to bureaucrats and this, they believed, could not be reconciled with traditional requirements for parliamentary control. In testimony before the PAC, the Auditor General explained what he saw as the incompatibility of increased management flexibility with parliamentary accountability. He said that his office 'was pushing to make sure there is the right balance between delegation and accountability . . . We will be the conscience of Public Service 2000 and we will make it known to this committee and to Parliament in general if we feel the delegation that's taken place is not accompanied by adequate accountability' (House of Commons, 1992a: 10).

Of course, the 'adequate accountability' system the Auditor General had in mind was the direct administrative accountability concept that the OAG and its parliamentary allies had been actively sponsoring since the 1979 Lambert report. According to this concept, the convention of ministerial responsibility is outdated and no longer valid in an era of 'big government' where the volume of demands on politicians' time tends to encourage the devolution of responsibilities to professional staff. Consequently, the argument goes on, it is not realistic to expect that the 'overloaded' minister can know everything that is going on in his/her department. In this context, the doctrine of ministerial responsibility is seen as undermining the potential for genuine accountability on the part of those who should be accountable: the senior bureaucrats in charge of the department. The concept of ministerial responsibility, to use the words of the Auditor General, 'only serves to cloud the real accountability of those who are in charge of day-to-day operations' (Auditor General of Canada, 1985: para. 1.53).

The 1984 election and the injection of much new blood in the House of Commons gave new life to the OAG's attack on ministerial responsibility and renewed the impetus for parliamentary reform. In 1984 the Conservatives won 211 seats in the House of Commons, the largest majority in Canadian history. Although Prime Minister Mulroney gave ministerial portfolio to about forty members of his parliamentary majority—the largest Cabinet ever seen in Canada—there still remained a very large number of Conservative backbenchers, full of expectations and ambitions, anxious to play a more important role in Parliament as a way to gain visibility in the hope of, one day, catching the eyes of the Prime Minister's Office. Soon after the election, a new special committee on parliamentary reform was set up under the chairmanship of James McGrath, MP. Issued in 1985, the McGrath report sought to reinforce the clout of backbenchers in Parliament. Much of the McGrath committee's work focused on freeing up the private member from party discipline (Canadian Study of Parliament Group, 1992). McGrath saw, as one of the only ways to enhance the influence of MPs, the loosening of party discipline. The unusual strength of party discipline in Canada—which is stronger there than in any other parliamentary system of government (Campbell and Wilson, 1995: 161)—ensures that the question of parliamentary reform is almost always on the political agenda because each new generation of MPs who enter Parliament after a general election soon feels dissatisfied with its limited influence and initiates projects to make the Canadian Parliament more like the American Congress, where party discipline is weaker and where elected officials have a more important impact on policy (Mallory, 1979).

The McGrath recommendations were not fully implemented because they failed to see that the change from a tight to a looser form of discipline would involve a substantial shift of power from parties to individual MPs (Franks, 1987: 136–42). But they did enhance the autonomy of parliamentary committees by giving them the power to launch inquiries into public issues. In making its proposals, the McGrath report used themes taken from the 1979 Lambert report and much of its thinking on the need to give to parliamentary committees the power to hold public servants accountable in the House of Commons came from the OAG. McGrath proposed a 'new doctrine of deputy ministerial responsibility' that would include 'the obligation to testify before parliamentary committees on matters of administration. Under this system, the testimony of deputy ministers before committees would be an everyday occurence' (House of Commons, 1985: 20).

Thus, much of the discussion about accountability that took place following the PS 2000 initiative must be seen in the context of the post-McGrath reforms which created expectations on the part of MPs that they could play a more influential role in the public policy process. It was in this context that the government eventually allowed a committee of the House of Commons to put into practice the idea of direct administrative accountability and to review the advice given by bureaucrats to ministers over a controversial immigration policy decision. This resulted in a complete public relations disaster. Senior officials were publicly blamed by backbenchers for apparently having been too 'entrepreneurial' while the government was accused of not adhering to Westminster practice and accepting responsibility for gaffes and misjudgements (Sutherland, 1991). Consequently, support for PS 2000 inside government quickly evaporated and 'by 1992, the bloom was off the PS 2000 rose' (Swimmer *et al.*, 1994: 172). For policy makers, the new managerialist rhetoric of PS 2000 sent a mixed message: they were encouraged to become more 'entrepreneurial' and to take risks in making decisions, but in return for the new management flexibilities they were given, they had to account directly to Parliament, a political forum that also includes the opposition whose role is to make the government and its collaborators 'look bad'.

Conclusion

To understand the potential of managerialist ideas and policies to attract government support, I have used the concept of 'policy legacy', which suggests that policy actors may reject or support policies depending on their past experiences with similar measures or with policies that appear similar. The way managerialist ideas have in the past been associated with a series of measures more or less imposed on the government by the OAG offers important insights to permit an understanding of why government support for managerialist policies has been relatively weak in Canada. Of course, PS 2000 itself is not a policy that the OAG has 'forced' on to the government, but it is informed by managerialist principles similar to those advocated in the past by the Auditor General.[13] PS 2000 was preceded, in the 1970s, by reforms that the government often implemented unwillingly, as a response to the OAG's famous comment on the 'loss of control of the public purse'. As Peter A. Hall wrote, the concept of policy legacy implies 'that states will be predisposed toward policies with which they already have some favourable experience' (1989: 11). With this insight in mind, it can be argued that if in the 1980s the Canadian state did not strongly support the managerialist ideas on which PS 2000 was based, this was because it did not have a 'favourable experience' with the 1970s reforms which were based on similar ideas and which—as the government once said—were adopted only to address the 'criticisms of the Auditor General' (Canada, 1990: 30).

This chapter has also shown that since the mid-1970s, the OAG has become a key public actor in the bureaucratic reform policy process and one of the main access points or platforms through which management consulting interests have promoted managerialist ideas within the Canadian state. One consequence of this is that the access of consultants to decision-making centres, and the opportunities for their ideas to mobilize political support from the government and to strongly influence policy, are rather limited—because the OAG is organizationally separated from the executive and independent of its control and direction. From the government's point of view at least, the OAG is a body that belongs to the opposition and any suggestions coming from the Audit Office tend to be viewed with suspicion.[14] As a body attached to the House of Commons, the OAG is also linked to interests (those of MPs, parliamentary committees, and the opposition) that advocate changes in the balance of power between the executive and the legislature. Thus, the managerialist solutions for reforming the administration that consultants sponsor through the OAG's public reports are packaged by the Auditor General with ideas unpopular with the government because they seek to restructure accountability relationships.

It has been suggested that the OAG's position towards managerialism is one of 'ambivalence' (Roberts, 1996b: 492). The evidence presented in this

---

[13] The 1993 Annual Report of the Auditor General to the House of Commons indicates that 'because PS 2000 appeared to be based on principles that we have promoted . . . the Office supported the initiative from the outset' (Auditor General of Canada, 1993: 161).

[14] In theory, the OAG is a body, independent of the government, that belongs to the legislature. But in parliamentary systems where one party alone forms the government, there is no political separation between the executive and the legislature because the government is the legislature to the extent that it controls a majority of seats in the House of Commons (Norton, 1990). The real separation is not between the executive and the legislature but between the government and the opposition and, in this context, any organization that is not owned by the government therefore belongs to the opposition. The impression, from the government perspective at least, that the OAG 'belongs to the opposition' is even stronger when it is noted that the Public Accounts Committee (PAC), which is the only institutional link of the Auditor to the House of Commons, is also the only parliamentary committee to be chaired by a member of the opposition and not by a member of the ruling party.

chapter supports this view and shows that the OAG is, indeed, a 'schizoid' institution because it serves two apparently conflicting communities of interests: those of legislators and management consultants. On the one hand, the managerialist ideas that consultants advocate through the OAG are critical of bureaucratic controls and of the cost imposed by traditional accountability regimes. But, on the other hand, as a body that also serves parliamentarians, the OAG is regularly calling for stronger parliamantary controls as a way to counterbalance managerial decentralization. But the effect of such calls, in the end, is to stifle managerialist innovations because they are seen by decision makers as threatening the policy prerogatives of the executive, or the balance of power between the government and the legislature.

5

France: Reforming from within, or statism and managerialism

Introduction

In contrast to Britain and Canada, the French state began to incorporate management consulting knowledge within its structures not in the 1960s but much later, following the adoption of the 1989 policy on the Renewal of the Civil Service. The Renewal initiative launched by Prime Minister Rocard gave a high priority to: (a) human resource management, through training sessions, professional and geographical mobility, and career path renewal; (b) *responsabilisation* or accountability, through the creation of centres de responsabilité (CDR) and the use of *projets de service* or administrative statements describing targets and resources in each service; (c) programme evaluation, through the creation of the Comité interministériel de l'évaluation, the Conseil scientifique de l'évaluation, and the Fond nationale de l'évaluation; and (d) service delivery, through the Charte des services publics designed to improve relations between the bureaucracy and the citizen-user.

Many of the techniques and ideas required to implement the measures introduced by the 1989 Renewal policy were associated with the new managerialism (Postif, 1997). They included the use of decentralized budgetary techniques, programme evaluation, techniques for setting standards and raising the quality of public services, and the move from hierarchy to contract in the relationships between various administrative units (through the *projet de service* and the creation of CDR). During the first year of the Renewal policy, management consultants from the private sector played an important role in helping French bureaucrats implement these new techniques. But as we shall see, senior officials in the central bureaucracy did not welcome the ideas promoted by consultants because they viewed them as too much based on business management experience. As a result, the French government decided in 1990 to create its own internal management consulting service.

In building within its administration a management consulting capacity, the French state was doing almost thirty years later what the British and Canadian governments had done in the 1960s on the advice of the Fulton Committee and Glassco Commission. We saw in the two previous chapters that the construction of intragovernmental management consulting capacities in Britain and Canada during the 'rationalist 1960s' coincided with the entry

of accountants into the management consulting field and with the emergence
and development of business and professional associations of management
consultants. In Britain, internal management consulting capacities were established in the Civil Service Department (CSD) in 1968 and in Canada in the
new Treasury Board Secretariat (TBS) in 1966. In building their expertise,
these new institutions established channels of communication with management consulting organizations and co-opted consultants from the private
sector into the state apparatus, thereby giving them an institutional and professional hold on bureaucratic reform policy issues. The legacies left by the
creation of management consulting capacities within the British and Canadian
states in the 1960s powerfully shaped further developments in the area of
bureaucratic reform and the acceptance of managerialist ideas and policies
in the two countries.

It was possible for the British and Canadian states to incorporate consulting knowledge within their structures much earlier than France could
do so because in these two countries, management consultancy is organizationally better developed, as a result of its historical and institutional links
with accountancy. Consequently, British and Canadian policy makers were
much more likely than their French counterparts to entertain managerialist
policies, either because they had internal management consulting capacities
for implementing such policies, or because they were able to rely on a large
and well-developed consulting industry outside the state sector. By comparison, because management consulting is not as strongly developed in France,
public officials have sometimes viewed it as an esoteric field of activity of
limited use to their efforts to improve the administration of the state (Bruston,
1993). In France, research suggests that management consulting 'suscite encore
pas mal de scepticisme quant à son utilité sociale et économique' (Sauviat,
1991: 4). Clearly, if ideas are advocated by those whose expertise in the field
is seen as being limited, there is little chance that they can be influential and
become an important component of policy. In other words, the social status
of the idea's bearer significantly influences whether it is used by decision
makers in government as the basis for policy.

Although managerialist ideas are clearly present in France, they have not
been incorporated into policy as readily as they have been in British and
Canadian reforms (Pollitt and Summa, 1997a). As noted in Chapter 1, the
use of market criteria for allocating public resources by allowing private
sector involvement in the delivery of public services, and the perception
of public service recipients as 'clients' rather than citizens, were absent from
the 1989 French policy. By contrast, countries like Britain have placed the
introduction of market elements at the heart of their reforms. Such elements
include the 'market testing' initiative introduced by the 1991, White Paper
Competing for Quality. Examples in Canada derived from PS 2000 include,
for instance, the creation of Special Operating Agencies (SOAs) designed
to improve the delivery and cost effectiveness of government services 'by

applying private sector management techniques' (Canada, 1990: 24). The managerialist conviction that there are no major differences between business management and public administration is clear in the Canadian approach. 'The Public Service', claims the PS 2000 White Paper, is 'like any other enterprise and must be efficient and well-managed' (Canada, 1990: 14).

The case of France shows that even if French bureaucratic reform discourse contains a fair share of new managerialist or new public management ideas, there is, in reality, not only no one dominant or 'global' pattern of adaptation but different reform trajectories (Hood, 1995; Peters and Savoie, 1998). In France, managerialist ideas have been less influential because they are coupled with bureaucratic reform policy ideas that emphasize the distinctive *public* dimension of state administration (Chevallier, 1996; Trosa, 1995a). To the extent that in France new managerialist ideas are present and sustained in the political sphere, they have been advocated more as a critique of the corporatism of the corps system—partly responsible for what Crozier called in an influential book *The Stalled Society* (1973)—than as an attack on the legitimacy of the state (which is more how they have been used in Britain and, to a lesser extent, in Canada). Accordingly, the French policy of administrative modernization has been described by some as an attempt to articulate 'a distinctive neo-statist set of values [with] the introduction of business-type managerialism' (Clark, 1998: 107). In the same way, others have argued that the 1989 Renewal policy represents 'a blend of managerialism and statist interpretation of public administration reform' (Rouban, 1993b: 410). Accordingly, the principal task in this chapter is to explain why managerialist ideas were less influential in France, and why they were 'blended' with statist ideas.

Blending statist with managerialist ideas

Étatisme or statism is the term used by students of French politics and society to talk about the predominantly interventionist role of the state in the economy (Gueslin, 1992). Of course, in recent years there has been a change from a *dirigiste* or state-directed economy, to a more market-oriented one. Europeanization, deregulation, privatization have all reduced the power of the state over the economy; and decentralization has diminished the power of Paris over the periphery (Schmidt, 1996).

But statism is still useful as an ideal type for comparing France with other nations and for characterizing a polity in which the state is seen as strong and autonomous (Flynn, 1995). In the statist pattern of policy making, government officials take a leadership role in policy making and have primary control over structuring the relationship between state and society, meaning that they are for the most part able to dictate the pattern of interest representation and to resist (if they wish to do so) the pressures of societal interests (Nordlinger, 1981; Skocpol, 1979). In statist polities, state structures tend to be centralized, with governments afforded strategic advantages through particular institutional arrangements and organizational processes, generally a powerful executive backed by a majority party and/or a strong bureaucracy, which tends to be legitimized by history and reinforced by culture (Rosanvallon, 1990). In sharp contrast with the situation in pluralist polities, in a statist context the government has the power and authority to take unilateral action without prior consultation with those most interested in the policy (Hayward, 1986).

Statism in post-war France is best exemplified by the establishment of an extensive system of national industrial planning (Cohen, 1977). After the Liberation, the planning system was designed to help reconstruct a war-ravaged economy, modernize infrastructures, and rationalize industrial production through the gradual replacement of small firms by larger and publicly owned enterprises (Kuisel, 1981; Shonfield, 1965). Because the private sector, made up of small and medium-sized family firms, was historically timid and lacking in entrepreneurialism, state-owned enterprises (SOEs) took on an ever-increasing importance as innovators and engines for the economy (Zahariadis, 1995). The creation of SOEs, as well as the design of their management structures and processes, played an important role in stimulating the growth of the French consulting industry (Sauviat, 1991: 26). As we saw in Chapter 2, a number of 'home-grown' French consultancies which are now major players in the market emerged after the war and were born in the heyday of planning and *dirigisme*. Whether this automatically makes French consultancies more 'statist' is uncertain. But these consulting firms partly owe their existence to the state and to the statist frame of mind that animated the post-war expansion of the industrial public sector around which many of them grew in the 1950s and 1960s (Henry, 1994).

Of course, statism in France has deeper historical roots and it emerged well before the creation of the planning system in the 1940s. Institutionally, the ideology of statism is embedded in the existence of a strong, independent administrative bureaucracy, which has a tradition going back at least as far as Napoleon, and is imbued with a sense of the state (Suleiman, 1974). Observers characterized France as a 'République des fonctionnaires' to describe the power and autonomy of bureaucratic agencies (Pfister, 1988). The bureaucracy is peopled by an élite corps of highly skilled, technically trained civil servants whose *esprit de corps*, or corporate self-consciouness, is reinforced by their membership in the prestigious *grands corps* of civil servants and their attendance at the same state élite educational institutions (Bourdieu, 1989). According to Luc Rouban, many of these institutions, because they focus on training people for state service, until the 1990s, 'paid little attention to public management teaching' (1997: 142). As he argues, 'the very idea of "management", with its Anglo-American sound, has never seduced higher civil servants' (Rouban, 1997: 142).

Anti-Americanism, as Richard Kuisel showed in his book on *Seducing the French: The Dilemma of Americanization*, has become—at least since de Gaulle —a relatively important part of French national identity (1993). The United States is the birthplace of modern management, and, beginning with the disciples of Frederick Taylor in the early 1900s, followed by the 'missionaries' of the Marshall Plan in the 1950s, there have been, through the years, a number of more or less successful attempts at introducing American management methods in French industry (Boltanski, 1990; Kipping, 1997). Americans established some of the first consulting firms in France and—as they did in several other countries—played an important role in the diffusion of American management ideas and techniques (Kipping, 1996). For instance, in the late 1960s, Jean-Jacques Servan-Schreiber, in *The American Challenge*, highlighted the role of US consultancies in spreading an 'American-style management' in France and throughout Europe (1968: 38).

Thus, although this is not a study of French culture and its reaction to US global domination in the post-war period, it is worth drawing attention to the point that both attraction and resistance characterize French attitudes toward 'management'—an idea that is seen as an American invention (Djelic, 1998). For France, America is both a model and a menace. Essentially, the dilemma for France is to find a way to possess American prosperity and industrial power, while preserving French values and traditions—which include what Dyson calls the 'state tradition' (1980). This ambivalence is reflected in the fact that the French approach to administrative reform is said to be a mix of both managerialist and statist ideas. It is a way to make the state more 'modern' (as the French notion of administrative modernization suggests) by marrying business management with traditional republican ideals of public service and social solidarity.

France as a contrasting case

Unlike the British and Canadian cases which received extensive discussion in the two preceding chapters, the contrasting or control case of France is here discussed in less detail because it is used strictly for the purpose of helping to validate the main argument about the links between: (a) the organizational development of management consulting; (b) the legacies left by past reforms in terms of facilitating or impeding the access of management consultants to decision-making centres; and (c) the influence of managerialist ideas on bureaucratic reform policy. The French case shows that the influence of managerialist ideas on bureaucratic reform policy is less important when the organizational development of management consulting is weaker; and when past administrative changes left legacies that limited the access of management consultants to the inner circles of policy making within the central state.

One of the consequences of the legacies left by the creation in 1945 of the École nationale d'administration (ÉNA) has been to provide state officials with the knowledge, capacity, and means that they believe are necessary for policy making in the area of bureaucratic reform. As a French consultant once said, there is a strong impression that 'in terms of administrative expertise it is difficult to compete with [ÉNA graduates]' (quoted in Lamarque, 1996: 132). In Britain and Canada there is no institution comparable to the ÉNA. Unlike their British and Canadian counterparts, French officials charged with responsibility for policy making in the area of bureaucratic reform policy have not looked outside the state for management expertise, thereby not only limiting the possibilities for consultants to bring business management ideas to the attention of bureaucratic reformers but also depriving the consulting industry of an important market (the central administration) that could have helped to stimulate its growth and development.

The French approach to bureaucratic reform is one where the impulse for change has traditionally come from inside the central administration. In this sense, the pattern of policy making in the bureaucratic reform policy sector is profoundly statist. One aspect of statism has to do with the extent to which policy making is centralized. When, in a policy sector such as bureaucratic reform, public officials have at their disposal, within the state, the expertise and instruments they think they need to make policy, their 'points of contact with other societal institutions are minimized, and the initiatives for policy are consequently more likely to come from within the state itself' (Hall, 1986: 165).

But interestingly, the study of public management reform in France also highlights what can be called the 'paradox of statism'. The allegedly 'strong' French state with its 'heroic' policy style seems to be quite 'weak' in the sense that the changes in structures and processes brought about by public management reforms have been much less significant than in other countries. The presence of an élite corps recruited from the same educational institutions— one of the key sources of cohesion and state strength in the Fifth Republic —can under certain circumstances also lead to state weakness (Suleiman, 1987). An examination of the role of consultants in recent attempts to make the administration of government more managerialist reveals that the corporatism or *esprit de corps* that characterizes the senior bureaucracy can also be a drag on change and limit policy innovation. In a widely read article, Peter A. Hall argued that there is a close relationship between policy innovation and state structures (1983). The *grands corps* system is one such structure that can play a critical role in impeding or facilitating the entry of innovative ideas into policy. When senior officials come from the same élite educational institutions—when they form a 'closed caste system' as Ezra Suleiman once suggested (1995: 178)—and when the prospects for advancement are governed by practices that emphasize conformity and a respect for hierarchy and traditions, bureaucrats are more likely to display attachment to standard procedures and established policy positions than a willingness to strike out in innovative policy directions.

In Britain academics coined the term 'consultocracy' to describe how the entry of managerialist ideas into policy went hand in hand with the growing presence of consultants in policy-developing circles. But at the risk of over-simplifying, the evidence reviewed in the rest of this chapter suggests that in France, the *Énarchie* (e.g. the fact that ÉNA graduates form a good proportion of the French ruling élite) is in part responsible for having blocked the rise of a 'consultocracy' and delayed the influence of managerialism on policy.

It has been said that the case of France is one of 'managérialisme à rebours avec dix ans de retard sur les autres pays occidentaux' (Rouban, 1993*a*: 207). Managerialist ideas entered into the formulation of policy later in France, in the late 1980s, at the same time that consultants from the private sector began to play a more important role in the process of administrative reform. This started after the passing of the framework Law on Decentralization in 1982, which opened the doors of the newly empowered devolved levels of administration to management consultants, and facilitated the entry of managerialist ideas into local government policy. Following the decentralization, local officials increasingly sought the services and expertise of consultants to help them develop the practices and systems needed for managing and co-ordinating the new administrative powers that they inherited from the central state. In turn, the increasing use of their services by local governments stimulated the organizational development of management consulting. In the mid-1980s, consultants established channels of communication with local officials through which they began to sponsor Total Quality Management (TQM) ideas. These ideas were first translated into policy (in the form of quality circles) at the local level, and later spread to the centre. This happened when the right-wing coalition led by Chirac introduced its quality policy in 1987 on the advice of consultants who had previously been actively involved in the dissemination of TQM ideas in local governments. However, the TQM ideas imported from the private sector by consultants did not take hold in the central administration to the same extent that they had done in local governments. By the end of the 1980s, the TQM policy was considered a failure, because the business management solutions advocated by consultants were not sufficiently adapted to the requirements of the central administration. It was as a reaction to the legacy left by the TQM failure that the government decided to build its own management consulting capacity in 1990.

The legacies of post-war reforms

The legacies of the post-war reforms in France did not make the central administration more open to advice from outside consultants and this played a crucial role in impeding the emergence of managerialist ideas within the French bureaucracy. During the period of the Liberation, far-reaching administrative reforms were believed to be urgently needed in France to rebuild the legitimacy of the administration, especially the top administration, a portion of which had been discredited by collaboration during the Vichy regime (Paxton, 1972). The most important reform was the creation in 1945 of the ÉNA, whose role is to select and train the nation's top administrators (Owen, 1990). In France the administrative élite (as opposed to the technical élite recruited from the École Polytechnique) is almost entirely recruited from the ÉNA (Suleiman, 1978; Boltanski, 1987). The ÉNA serves three main purposes: first, it conducts the initial recruitment of potential top civil servants; secondly, through its own testing, examining, and ranking procedures it selects the members of the different corps and thus singles out those who are destined for high-flying careers; and thirdly, it provides an initiation into various aspects of administrative life and a measure of work experience and training (Kessler, 1986).

In France, civil servants are organized into categories defined by the educational qualification required for entry. Each of these categories is made up of different corps. Nowadays, there are some 1,800 different corps (Clark, 1998: 99). A corps consists of officials who are subject to the same specific terms and conditions (*statut*) within the general framework of civil service law, which guarantees security of employment (Quermonne, 1991). The most prominent corps are the so-called *grands corps* (Kessler, 1986). All the *grands corps* were established 150 years ago (Osborne, 1983). Although there is no strict definition of the *grands corps*, it is generally recognized that there are three administrative *grands corps* (the *Conseil d'État*; the *Cour des comptes*; and the *Inspection des finances*) and two technical *grands corps* (the *Mines* and *Ponts et Chaussées* engineers). The three administrative *grands corps* are primarily concerned with controlling and checking the work of other civil servants.

As a broad generalization, the technical *grands corps* dominate decision making in the industrial public sector, in policy domains such as energy, transport, and telecommunications. In these domains, the new managerialist approach is said to be more developed because 'it fits well in the professional culture of civil servants coming from the ranks of technical *grands corps*' (Rouban, 1997: 142). Unlike their technical *confrères*, the administrative *grands corps* tend to occupy top positions in the Finance Department and in the central decision-making milieu—those officials who staff the interministerial committees at the political core of government (Grémion, 1982). The administrative *grands corps* are almost all recruited from the ÉNA and the technical *grands corps* from the École Polytechnique (Stevens, 1992: 125–6).

The ÉNA has gained a high reputation in its rather brief existence and its students, nicknamed *Énarques*, have now 'colonised' many key positions at the top of various ministries (Bodiguel, 1978; Wright, 1990). According to some, this is hindering the introduction of new management ideas and techniques in government because the ÉNA's 'quasi monopoly of access to top administrative posts does not permit the recruitment of businessmen experienced in dealing with problems of organization and management' (Ashford, 1982: 95).

Pantouflage: A one-way street in the circulation of ideas

ÉNA graduates occupy important positions not only in government but in the private sector as well. Although it was not intended to train managers for private enterprise (this is the function of the Écoles des Hautes Études Commerciales—HÉC) studies have shown that French employers often prefer former ÉNA students to their HÉC counterparts (Barsoux and Lawrence, 1990: 40). One consequence of the process of economic and industrial planning initiated by the state after the Second World War is that the competence, in relation to economic and industrial matters, of the members of the administrative *grands corps* recruited from the ÉNA has generally been broadly accepted (Armstrong, 1973). Because of the state's involvement in economic affairs, senior civil servants are believed to possess an intimate knowledge of the rules and regulations and thus, clearly have something to offer most private employers. As a result, the practice of *pantouflage*, by which state officials moved back and forth from the administration to posts in nationalized companies or in the private sector, has become increasingly common during the Fifth Republic (Birnbaum, 1978). For instance, in 1973 it was estimated that 43 per cent of the heads of the hundred largest corporations (public and private) had at one time been senior civil servants (Birnbaum, 1977: 141). As noted, this helps to consolidate the ideology of statism in the private sector because the practice of *pantouflage* is a way of 'ensuring that the state maintains its hold through the colonization of French business by state-trained former civil servants' (Schmidt, 1996: 445). Thus in France, unlike Britain and Canada, it is not so much that private managers come to work in the administration to help improve the efficiency of government as that the *Énarques* and members of the *grands corps* move on to key positions in business. As the president of one of the largest management consulting firms in France (Eurequip) noted, rather sarcastically,

Dans la plupart des pays démocratiques occidentaux, il est courant que des responsables du secteur privé fassent un passage dans l'Administration publique pour la faire bénéficier de leurs compétences pendant quelques années. Ils savent que durant cette période leur rémunération sera moins importante mais, outre la satisfaction d'apporter leur contribution à l'intérêt général, ils pensent y acquérir une meilleure compréhension des grands mécanismes administratifs, une vision plus systémique de la société dans laquelle ils vivent. De son côté, l'Administration qui, par nature, n'est que gestionnaire et peu habituée à la pratique du management, bénéficie, à l'occasion de la venue de ces responsables du secteur privé, d'un véritable transfert de compétences managériales. Est-ce à cause de son histoire et d'un sentiment de supériorité qu'auraient eu longtemps ses hauts fonctionnaires par rapport au monde des affaires, toujours est-il que l'Administration française fait exception et que sur la passerelle qui unit le public et le privé, on circule essentiellement dans un seul sens: de hauts fonctionnaires viennent 'pantoufler' au somment des organigrammes du secteur privé. (Sérieyx, 1993: 141)

As B. Guy Peters wrote, 'implementing the ideas of managerialism is one of several ways to think about developing closer links between the public and private sectors' and increasing 'interchange between public and private managers' (1997: 260). We saw in the previous two chapters that the institutional arrangements governing recruitment to administrative posts, that bring 'outsiders' into state institutions, were crucial in determining the penetration of managerialist ideas in the bureaucracy. In the British and Canadian cases respectively, the introduction of the secondment programme between the Civil Service Department and large management consulting firms in the early 1970s; and the use by the Office of the Auditor General of the Executive Interchange Program in 1974 provided these two organizations with flexible standards of recruitment that facilitated the entry of outside consultants and the diffusion of managerialist ideas within state institutions. Of course, in France the existence of ministerial *cabinets* (the minister's private office charged with important political and administrative functions) give ministers the flexibility to recruit their personal staff. Although a minister may in theory nominate to his or her *cabinet* someone from outside the administration this almost never happens. Those who are selected are usually 'insiders' (senior civil servants). This is why many observers talk about the 'politicization' of the senior civil service (Lacam, 1994; Mény, 1987; Stevens, 1978). Whether one focuses on politicization or *fonctionnarisation* (the fact that many ministers are former civil servants), the point is that the close relationship between politics and administration at the top of the state machinery does nothing to facilitate the introduction of anti-statist reforms that would have the effect of 'deprivileging' the civil service, as happened in Britain, for instance (Hood, 1999).

The mobility between private and public sectors that became more significant in Britain and Canada in the 1970s simply does not exist in France. What does exist is a one-way channel: from the public to the private sector, and almost never the other way. According to Suleiman, 'civil servants look with great disfavor upon the appointment of a "foreigner" to an administrative post' (1974: 140). Interestingly, in a comparison with Britain, Suleiman noted that while the Fulton Committee strongly emphasized the need to bring 'outsiders' into the civil service, 'in France, such a practice is unlikely to occur. [French] higher officials argue that a man [sic] from the outside could not win the confidence of his subordinates' (Suleiman, 1974: 141).

Besides the creation of the ÉNA, another important post-war reform was the establishment of the Ministère de la Fonction publique et de la Réforme administrative (MFPRA). Among the three countries compared in this book,

France is the only one to have had for a long and sustained period of time a minister (generally of state) presiding over a government structure specifically dedicated to administrative reform (Massot, 1979: 201). The MFPRA, and the Direction générale de l'administation et de la fonction publique placed under its authority in 1945, were established to design, plan, and co-ordinate the post-war reforms of the civil service (Grémion, 1979; Pinet, 1993). The MFPRA's responsibilities include: (a) questions relating to staff management (recruitment, promotion, training, and remuneration); (b) supervision of ÉNA; and (c) actions to promote, stimulate, and co-ordinate the modernization of administration and management methods, and the diffusion of innovative management practices.

The first minister appointed to direct the MFPRA was Maurice Thorez, leader of the Communist Party and a member of General de Gaulle's second coalition government in 1945 (Legendre, 1968). In creating a specialized organization to deal on a permanent basis with issues exclusively related to administrative reform, the French government tried to emulate the model of its Planning Commission, created in 1946 and first directed by Jean Monnet. As has been reported, 'L'idée d'une réforme administrative organisée et planifiée s'est répandue à la Libération en même temps que celle du plan Monnet' (Lanza, 1968: 47). The idea underlying the creation of the MFPRA was to put at the disposal of policy makers the knowledge and instruments needed for developing bureaucratic reform policies from within, as a way to facilitate their acceptance by civil servants. The intent was 'd'associer les fonctionnaires à la réforme' (Burdeau, 1989: 350). This was especially important since the Confédération générale du travail (CGT), the largest and most powerful union in France after the war—with a significant number of its members drawn from the public sector—was a close political ally of the Communist leader and minister responsible for administrative reform (Lorwin, 1954; Ross, 1982).

The Rationalisation des Choix Budgétaires

The statist approach to administrative modernization inherited from the post-war reforms was well reflected in the *Rationalisation des Choix Budgétaires* (RCB), the French version of PPBS adopted in 1968. The introduction of the RCB in France was made possible by the example of PPBS in the United States and by the French experience with the National Planning System (Bréaud, 1970; Ducros, 1976; Huet and Bravo, 1973). Originally, the Planning System had three main functions. It was intended to be: (a) a five-year macro-economic forecast of the national accounts of the country; (b) a programme of major public investments; and (c) a forum for discussions on past and proposed policies for government officials, trade unionists, and industrialists (Estrin and Holmes, 1983). Initially, it was hoped that the introduction of RCB would result in a greater co-ordination between the annual budgetary process and the preparation of the National Plan (Green, 1980: 111). The idea was to use the RCB as a way to tie the short-term annual budget to the five-year National Plan.

The implementation of RCB was co-ordinated by a central group under the chairmanship of the Secretary of State for the Budget (Lévy-Lambert and Guillaume, 1971). An 'RCB Mission' consisting of civil servants was established in the Finance Ministry to overcome the resistance that was anticipated from the spending departments (Hayward, 1973: 188). Because of the RCB's link with the National Planning System, the 'RCB Mission' was also loosely tied to the Planning Commission, the agency responsible for the preparation of the Plan (Ashford, 1977).

The primary source of ideas for the RCB came from a group of upper-middle grade civil servants, many from the Finance Ministry, who went to the United States in the mid-1960s to study programme budgeting (Ashford, 1977: 148). As noted, 'RCB had an essentially administrative origin' and 'the original impulse came from public administrators' rather than from the private sector (Bréaud and Gergorin, 1973: 117). As one director general in the Finance Ministry argued, in developing the RCB, it had been 'essential to act from within' because 'any attempt at a graft from the outside [would have] inevitably provoked fatal rejection symptoms on the part of the administrative body' (Huet, 1970: 284).

This situation differs sharply from the cases of Britain and Canada where the ideas that went into the Canadian and British versions of PPBS originally came from management consultants who visited the United States and who were part of the Glassco Commission and of Heath's Businessmen's Team. Of course, like their French counterparts, British and Canadian civil servants also visited the United States in the 1960s to study PPBS practices, but it was management consultants who acted as agents of diffusion of PPBS ideas. In France, the closed character of the institutions that have jurisdiction over bureaucratic reform policy issues, and the fact that in the early 1960s management consulting was an almost nascent industry, made it difficult for PPBS ideas to enter the French state on the 'shoulders' of consultants as they did in Britain and Canada. Moreover, the fact that in France PPBS ideas were intended to be linked to the National Plan meant that those involved in sponsoring these ideas needed to have some knowledge of the planning system. Senior bureaucrats from the Finance Ministry, which is responsible for the execution of the plan, were more likely to possess that knowledge than consultants from the private sector.

Programme budgeting and the Cour des comptes

Like Canada, but unlike Britain, France adopted the RCB in the late 1960s, soon after the introduction of PPBS in the United States by President Johnson in 1965. France and Canada adopted their versions of PPBS before the

American experiment with programme budgeting was reported to have failed and was officially abandoned in the mid-1970s (Savoie, 1994: 78). Britain adopted its version of PPBS in 1971 at a time where there was already some disillusionment with PPBS in the United States. As a result, the British version of PPBS was not as comprehensive as the RCB in France or programme budgeting in Canada (Heclo and Wildavsky, 1981: 272).

In Canada and France, one change resulting from the adoption of PPBS and RCB was the presentation to the legislature of departmental expenditures in programme budget form (Kessler and Tixit, 1973). But in France, the RCB and the presentation of government expenditures in the programme budget form to the National Assembly did not lead, as in Canada, to programme evaluation and to an expansion in the mandate of the *Cour des comptes* (Ducros, 1976). The *Cour des comptes* is the French state's supreme audit body. Members of the court are judges. They stand aloof from both legislative and executive branches of government (Descheemaeker, 1992). The French *Cour des comptes*, although reporting to Parliament, is not institutionally linked to the legislature as are the corresponding bodies in Britain and Canada. Because political control (the legislature) and external audit institutions (the *Cour des comptes*) are dissociated, the construction of political alliance between the two is difficult. In contrast to the Canadian situation, it would not be possible for the court to promote management reforms that would expand its powers by presenting them as necessary to strengthen the oversight role of Parliament. In France, it is believed that the 'absence of an institutionalized articulation' between the Parliament and the *Cour des comptes* has constituted 'perhaps the main obstacle' to establishing managerialist policies dealing with value-for-money analyses (Quermonne and Rouban, 1986: 400). Similarly, others have suggested that this has been 'a retarding factor' in the development of managerialism in France (Derlien, 1990: 158). Another element of this situation is the fact that the court's working methods are primarily rooted in public law and financial auditing. The use of these methods means that the court primarily 'investigates the legality of decisions and actions, thus moving the focus away from the effectiveness of programs' (Derlien, 1990: 159). The control of the court is thus limited to working within the rules of public law and traditional financial accounting 'which are not suitable for evaluating management according to a value-for-money strategy' (Dreyfus, 1990: 145).

The development and impact of the RCB

In developing the technical knowledge needed to develop the RCB, the French state did not rely on outside resources, and the fact that it did not also played a critical role in impeding the entry of managerialist ideas into the administrative system. The 'RCB developed without tight links with universities or private research institutions' (Bréaud and Gergorin, 1973: 117). To help civil servants to become more familiar with the management methods needed to implement the RCB, the French government created in the early 1970s the Centre de formation supérieur au management and the Centre d'études supérieures du management public (Pinet, 1993: 435). Their creation provided a centre of gravity and institutional support for the production of management ideas that take into account the statist dimensions of French public administration (Chevallier, 1996).

Ten years after the start of the RCB experiment, results fell far short of expectations (Chevallier and Loschak, 1982). Departmental managers distrusted the RCB and rejected it because they saw it as an attempt to reinforce the power of a few groups of top civil servants located at the centre of the bureaucratic machinery (Ashford, 1982: 75). In 1983, the RCB policy was officially abandoned (Perret, 1994: 106). Following the RCB experiment, the government more or less retreated from attempts to implement centralized, rationalist, and top-down schemes designed to push through across-the-board management reform.[1] One important indication of that retreat from 'rationalism' was the decline of the process of central economic planning to which, as indicated earlier, the RCB experiment was closely tied (Hall, 1986: 185).

After President de Gaulle's departure, attempts at improving the internal management practices of the administration were to some extent displaced by the implementation of policies aimed at 'humanising the style of the civil service' (Clark, 1984b: 68). The 1970s were marked by a growing desire on the part of government to improve relations between the administration and the public.[2] After the Gaullist period, which was characterized by a powerful *dirigiste* ideology and an interventionist administration extending into the most diverse areas of social life, it appeared essential to give citizens new means of communicating with the state (Dreyfus, 1990: 148). Thus, in 1973 the government created the *Médiateur de la République* (ombudsman) whose mandate is to investigate complaints from members of the public about administrative malfunctioning (Clark, 1984a). Annual reports from the *Médiateur* to the president were important factors in the introduction, during the late 1970s, of further reforms which have enhanced the ability of the public to scrutinize administrative actions. In 1978 and 1979 two laws on administrative transparency were adopted. These laws specified that citizens had the

[1] During the 1970s and early 1980s, the French government 'did not introduce any general reforming measures' in relation to the management of the public service. 'This failure to make major and general changes probably has much to do with the failure of RCB—the French equivalent of PPBS' (Fortin, 1988: 102).

[2] According to one observer, the recent history of administrative reform in France can be divided into two broad periods: the first one before the 1970s, when 'l'effort a principalement porté sur la recherche d'une meilleure efficacité des services; et dans une seconde période (à partir de 1970) où la préoccupation dominante, sinon exclusive, a concerné l'amélioration des relations entre l'administration et les usagers' (Bellon, 1983: 506).

right to know what computerized information was held about them, and that they also had a right to see all official documents, except those specifically exempt (Lasserre, Lenoir, and Stirn, 1987). But more important for the purposes of our analysis is the 1982 Law on Decentralization which, not unlike the various reforms that preceded it in the 1970s, sought to make the central administration more accessible to the citizens by devolving powers to the local level of government. As discussed below, the 1982 decentralization reforms played a critical role in facilitating the entry of management consultants and the institutionalization of managerialist ideas into local governments.

The decentralization reforms of 1982

When the Socialists came to power in 1981, there was widespread agreement among the Left that the administration of the French state needed to be democratized. Democratization was to be made possible by a number of means, including changing the procedure for recruitment into the state bureaucracy and decentralization of power from Paris to local authorities.

While in opposition in the 1960s and 1970s, the Left regularly denounced the undemocratic and unrepresentative nature of the system for recruiting and training the bureaucratic élite. Mitterrand was well known for his hostility to the élitist nature of the ÉNA and to the *grands corps* structure (Suleiman, 1995: 163). Indicative of his desire to transform the mechanisms through which the state élite perpetuates itself was the President's appointment of a Communist as minister of the civil service in 1981. A few months later, the minister, Anicet Le Pors, presented to Parliament a project aimed at widening the recruitment of higher civil servants. The principal innovation of the reform was to allow trade union leaders, local elected officials, grassroots activists, and members of various associations to enter the senior bureaucracy as a way of altering the bourgeois character of the group that managed the affairs of the nation. The hope was to transform the senior administration from an élitist institution into one that reflected the social diversity of French society. But most observers agree that the reform did not prove very successful, and was promptly abolished by the Chirac government in 1986 (Birnbaum, 1985). Tinkering with access to the ÉNA without changing the structure of the corps system did not affect the French higher civil service which, according to a former ÉNA director, still 'resemble[s] the aristocracy of the ancien régime' (quoted in Suleiman, 1995: 165).

The other, and more successful, Socialist project for democratizing the state, the policy of decentralization, was to be, in Mitterrand's words, the 'grande affaire du septennat'. The Law on the Rights and Liberties for Municipalities, Departments and Regions was adopted by the National

Assembly on 2 March 1982.[3] This was basically an enabling Bill; over the next four years a further 22 laws and 170 government decrees completed the decentralization programme (Mazey, 1990: 158). The goal of the following discussion is not to describe and analyse in detail the 1982 decentralization initiative, which is a very complex policy consisting of several administrative, fiscal, legal, and political dimensions. Rather, the intent is to identify those aspects that undermined the traditional statist approach to bureaucratic reform and made possible the entry of consultants and the penetration of managerialist ideas into local administrations. The following section provides some background information on a number of key relevant aspects of the 1982 decentralization.

The transfer of executive powers and administrative functions

The declared goals of the decentralization reforms were threefold: (a) to devolve state responsibilities to local authorities; (b) to transfer powers at each level (*départements*, regions, communes) from the administrative to the locally elected officials; and (c) to increase opportunities for local participation (*Cahiers français*, 1992). The most significant symbolic aspect implemented by the March 1982 law on decentralization was the transfer of executive power from the prefects—the legendary symbol of central state authority in the periphery—to the presidents of the elected councils of local governments. This transfer signalled the abolition of the prefects' *pouvoir de tutelle* (i.e. power to impose all forms of a priori administrative and financial control) over the administrative acts and budgets of local authority. The *tutelle* has been replaced by an a posteriori legal and financial system of review and control over the actions of local governments (Schmidt, 1987).

The transfer of executive powers completed, the second item on the decentralization agenda was the transfer of administrative functions and authority. The list of functions transferred from the centre to local governments included regional economic planning, industrial development, professional education, the delivery of health and social services, transportation (for the complete list, see Schmidt, 1991: 122–5). Along with the transfer of

---

[3] In France, the local government system is organized around three units: the communes (municipalities), the *départements* (counties), and the regions. The communes and the *départements* have existed for more than two hundred years. They have long been recognized as units of local democracy with their own powers, subjected, however, to the a priori control of the prefects, the central state representative in the periphery. The regions are more recent. They were created after the Second World War as bureaucratic units to facilitate the planning process and to act as the intermediate level between Paris and the *départements*. The regions were given legal recognition and the power to elect their own representatives only with the 1982 decentralization (Bernard, 1983). For the purposes of simplifying the following discussion, these three levels of authority are referred to as 'local governments', because in terms of the issues that are most relevant to our analysis (the transfer of executive powers and civil service reform), they were all more or less equally affected by the 1982 decentralization (Schmidt, 1991: ch. 4).

new administrative duties came the transfer of personnel from the central civil service to the local civil service. To facilitate this process, the government adopted a national code for local civil servants designed to boost the low status of local officials.

Prior to the 1982 decentralization, local civil servants were under the formal authority of the prefect, and thereby under the control of the central government in Paris (Ridley and Blondel, 1969: 93–6). Formally, they were part of the central or national civil service and regulated by the *Statut général des fonctionnaires*, the civil service code adopted in 1946 whose application is the responsibility of the *Ministère de la Fonction publique et de la Réforme admininistrative*. However, civil servants working in the periphery never had the prestige nor the career opportunities of their counterparts in the central administration, whose main task is to provide policy advice to ministers (Grémion, 1982). On the whole, in comparison with civil servants in central administration, they were poorly trained, poorly paid and treated, with little opportunity for upward mobility (Mazey, 1990: 158).

The new local civil service code was to remedy this situation by making local civil service as attractive as the central service. The Socialist government wanted thereby to provide local officials with the experienced personnel from the central administration to enable them to exercise their new powers effectively (Schmidt, 1991: 130). However, the new code met strong opposition, in particular from local elected officials. Although the law establishing the new code was passed in 1984, promulgation of the rules allowing the government to implement the code was delayed for two years. They were adopted on the very day of the Socialist defeat in the March 1986 legislative elections. Local elected officials were against the establishment of a national code for local civil servants. They believed that this would represent a form of 'recentralization' by the state that would curtail their powers significantly in personnel matters, by acting as a check on their ability to select whomever they considered best qualified for a given position. This resistance helps explain the delay in implementing the reform. During the first period of 'cohabitation' in 1986–8, the Chirac government modified the reform by effectively giving control over local public service to local elected officials. Local governments were given much greater flexibility in the rules governing recruitment and gained complete freedom in relation to the internal organization of their bureaucracies (Schmidt, 1991: 115). These new powers subsequently played a critical role in facilitating the entry of management consultants and the penetration of managerialist ideas into local government. In contrast to the previous situation, where the rules governing recruitment were rigid, emphasizing uniformity and imposed from the centre, the new flexible standards of recruitment allowed local elected officials to bring in external consultants, and this provided a more hospitable setting than before for the emergence of managerialist ideas in local administration.

The decentralization reforms also gave local government some new financial resources directly, through the transfer of state taxes, and guaranteed others through a system of block grants (Richard, 1988). The financial capacity of local government thus became much more important than in the past. Total local government expenditures almost doubled in six years, from 300 billion francs in 1981 to 600 billion in 1990. As a result, in the 1980s French consultants began to turn their attention to the commercial potential of the local public sector (Abiker, 1996: 4).

The penetration of managerialist ideas into local administration

In her study of the political and administrative history of decentralization, Vivien Schmidt argued that one important political consequence of the 1982 decentralization was that it deprived local elected officials of the 'rhetoric of centralization' (1991: 342). With this 'rhetoric', local politicians had been able, in the past, to present themselves to the public as the defenders of local interests against the intrusion of the centre, and they could avoid taking responsibility for their actions. Deprived of this rhetoric, Schmidt suggests, local elected officials created a new line of argument that focused on the financial limits of decentralization. In the first few years of decentralization, the discourse in the periphery suggested that the state had not compensated local administrations adequately for their newly transferred powers. As a result, local politicians argued that they were left with the unpopular alternatives of raising taxes or cutting public services. Central state officials rebutted this view by arguing that local governments in fact had sufficient resources. In this context, Schmidt argues, local officials increasingly turned in the mid-1980s to the 'rhetoric of good management' whereby they experimented with new administrative techniques, hired management consultants, and tried to 'adopt new managerial attitudes and run local government as they would a business' (Schmidt, 1991: 372). Nowadays, much of local officials' discussion focuses on mastering their expenditures, 'all with an eye on the bottom line, as well as on seeking advice from consultants and getting management audits of their performance from outside experts' (Schmidt, 1991: 373).

The development of this new managerialist thinking on the local government scene coincided with the increasing use of private sector consulting services by local officials from the mid-1980s. An article in *Le Monde*, based on interviews with management consultants, indicated that 'La décentralisation a ouvert aux consultants le marché des collectivités locales' (Chirot, 1993: 17). The cartoon reproduced in Figure 5.1, which accompanied the article, shows two management consultants as angels standing above the entrance to a town hall.

Some of the most important players on the local government scene include firms such as Bossard, CEGOS, Ernst & Young, and Price Waterhouse

FIGURE 5.1. The entry of consultants into local governments

Source: Cartoon by J.-C. Mézieres accompanying article by F. Chirot, 'Les élus se font conseiller. Les consultants ont convaincu les collectivités locales de leur utilité', *Le Monde*, 11 October 1993, p. 17. Reproduced with permission.

(Chirot, 1993: 17). According to two senior managers in Price Waterhouse's Paris office, 'An increasing number of large local authorities are employing auditing and consulting firms to advise them on specific areas of their own activity or the activities of their companies or other related bodies which they control' (Paquier and Towhill, 1991: 13). In the 1980s French consultancies like Bossard and CEGOS created 'Local Collectivities Divisions' within their internal structure and these divisions employ around 30 management consultants each (Abiker, 1996: 22). Former bureaucrats, especially those from the largest local authorities, have been, since the late 1980s, hired by consulting firms to develop networks of contacts with local civil servants and to help sell the firms' many and varied services (Abiker, 1996: 21).

The use of consulting services by local authorities became so important in the late 1980s that local officials and consulting firms began to organize annual conferences entitled 'Collectivités locales, du bon usage des consultants', intended to share experiences and best practices in the area of local government consulting (Chirot, 1993: 17). Similarly, in the late 1980s and early 1990s, a number of publications intended for local government officials began to publish numerous articles (written by consultants) on how to build successful partnerships with management consultants.[4] The publication of such articles not only allowed consultants to spread the managerialist gospel in local government. It also provided consultants—described as 'ideas peddlers to elected politicians' by *Le Monde*—with a marketing device that was useful for raising the awareness of potential clients to the services sold by their firms (De Chenay, 1991: 13). In addition, when they appeared in more 'learned' journals, such articles helped to establish the authority and validity of the knowledge that consultants claim to have to improve the efficiency of local government management. According to one study on the role of consultants in local governments, 'la publication d'articles remplit une fonction symbolique autorisant le consultant, représentant d'intérêts privés, à prendre la parole sur des questions d'intérêt général' (Abiker, 1996: 89).

Local governments increased their use of private sector consulting services from the mid-1980s for at least three reasons. First, because the decentralization gave them the flexibility to recruit whomever they wanted and the powers to reorganize the management of their administration without first seeking the approval of the centre. Secondly, they had greater financial resources at their disposal after 1982. A third reason local governments not only increased their use of consulting services, but also began to develop more regular links with management consultants, had to do with their new responsibilities over industrial development. As indicated earlier, this was one of the main powers transferred from the centre to the periphery. Local governments' powers over industrial development include the promotion of local business and job creation, expansion, and innovation (Schmidt, 1991: 128). In the 'innovation' category, local governments and the central state jointly initiated in 1984 a policy designed to provide financial support to small and medium-sized industrial enterprises (SMEs) to encourage them to call on outside management consulting expertise to improve their efficiency. This programme, setting up *Fonds régionaux d'aide aux conseils* (FRAC), or Regional Funds for Aid to Firms Calling on Consultancy Services, was briefly discussed earlier in Chapter 2. As indicated there, the FRAC was one component of the operation *Développement du professionalisme des consultants*, launched by the Department of Industry in the mid-1980s. It was created in 1984 with the dual objective of stimulating the development of management consulting, and of making SMES more efficient and competitive by encouraging them to use outside consulting expertise more often.

---

[4] *Le Quotidien du maire*, 30 June 1990: 'Le cabinet Deloitte & Touche explique ses méthodes aux collectivités'; *La Gazette*, 20 April 1992: 'Études, conseils, audit: comment travailler avec les consultants?'; *Vie publique*, December 1993–January 1994: 'Consultants, mode d'emploi'.

With the creation of the FRAC, local government officials came into increasing contact with consultants through the examination of the applications for FRAC aid submitted by the SMEs. Each application is accompanied by a detailed proposal presented by the consulting firm that the SME intends to use if awarded an FRAC grant. In 1993, 3,060 applications for FRAC aid were approved, for a total amount of 173 million francs distributed among the consulting firms involved in FRAC operations (OECD, 1995a: 124).

The emergence of the total quality management movement

When it was established in 1984, the FRAC was supposed to help SMEs to call on consultants to implement initiatives in the area of quality management (OECD, 1995b: 121). Generally, more than 40 per cent of the money spent for FRAC aid goes to projects in the area of quality management (OECD, 1995a: 124). In the early 1980s, there emerged in France an important movement promoting Total Quality Management (TQM) and the implemention of quality circles in private sector organizations (Chevalier, 1991). Promoting this movement was the Association française des cercles de qualité (AFCERQ), an organization created in 1981 by management consultants and staff managers in large companies. In 1983, about 360 companies were members of the AFCERQ, whose mission was to promote TQM ideas and to help companies develop quality circles (Juran and Gryna, 1988: 35). The interest in TQM in France was such that 1981 was named the *Année de la qualité* by the government (Collignon and Wissler, 1988: 1). During that period, some of the largest French-based management consulting firms were very active in diffusing TQM ideas by publishing books designed to help managers to introduce quality circles in their companies.[5]

In the public sector, local governments were the first to experiment with TQM ideas (Pochard, 1995: 49). The introduction of TQM ideas into local government was said to be an almost 'natural' consequence of the decentralization which sought to improve the quality and responsiveness of public services by making their delivery closer to the citizen-user (Orgogozo, 1985: 23). Quality circles were first introduced, with the help of consultants and the AFCERQ, in municipalities such as Lyons, Angers, and Amiens, and also spread in regions, departments, and public organizations such as the Caisse des dépôts (Chevallier, 1988: 133). By March 1985, the number of quality circles implemented in local governments had become sufficiently large for the first conference to be organized on 'Les cercles de qualité dans l'Administration' (Orgogozo, 1985: 23). The conference was sponsored by the AFCERQ and attended by consultants, local and

---

[5] For instance, CEGOS pubished *Pratique des cercles de qualité* in 1982 and the director of Eurequip published *Mobiliser l'intelligence dans l'entreprise* in 1982, and *L'entreprise du 3ème type* in 1984. For the complete list of TQM books published by French consultancies, see Chevalier (1991: 17).

central government officials, and even by the Socialist minister responsible for administrative reform.

In the mid-1980s, after having been elected on a strongly statist or *dirigiste* platform, the Socialist government became more open to private sector experiences (Hall, 1990a). After the resignation of Prime Minister Mauroy and the resignation of the four Communist ministers from the governing coalition, the government undertook in 1984 a 'Great U-turn' in the management of the economy and adopted a policy of economic austerity to damp inflation and reduce the deficit—the size of which had increased significantly as a result of the nationalization programme introduced in 1981 (Durupty, 1988). This shift in policy signalled the beginning of a major transformation from a state-directed economy to a more market-oriented one.

A reflection of this shift was the growing interest of the government in TQM ideas. In 1985, following the conference on quality circles in government, the civil service minister promised that his officials would study the applicability of TQM ideas for the central administration (reported in Chevallier, 1988: 134). Subsequently, in January 1986, the AFCERQ created within its organizational structure a 'Civil Service Group' designed to study the transposition of TQM ideas from the local to the central administration. The translation of these ideas into policies was greatly facilitated when in April 1986, following the election of the right-wing coalition of Jacques Chirac, the government appointed, as its senior policy advisers on bureaucratic reform, the two consultants who led the AFCERQ.

The policy on quality and innovation

The Right came to power in 1986 committed to reversing the nationalization policy of the Socialist government. The Gaullist-led coalition developed a neo-liberal programme inspired by what was happening in Britain and the United States. Government spending was to be cut; 20,000 civil service positions were to be eliminated in two years and a study commissioned by the finance minister called for the abolition of some thirty administrative bodies (Claisse, 1989). Privatization was high on the public agenda and the civil service became the target of many criticisms, for its costs, archaic culture, and working methods (Bodiguel and Rouban, 1991).

Under the Chirac government, administrative reform policy was primarily a strategy for enhancing the quality and productivity of services delivered to the public (Orgogozo, 1987). One month after its election, the government commissioned studies from two leading private sector management consultants on innovation and quality in the public service (Orgogozo and Sérieyx, 1989). One study, on quality, was directed by Gilbert Raveleau and the other, on innovation, by Hervé Sérieyx. Both were senior partners of the management consulting firm Eurequip and founding members of the AFCERQ. One management consultant (Raveleau) was appointed as adviser on quality to the minister of economy, finance, and privatization, Édouard Balladur. The other (Sérieyx) served as adviser on innovation to the minister for administrative reform, Hervé de Charette, an outspoken critic of the ÉNA who once attacked it as a 'symbol of the ever-growing state' (quoted in Claisse, 1989: 167).

On the advice of the two consultants, the policy introduced by the government in 1987 was primarily based on employee participation in the operational definition of administrative duties, intradepartmental communication, and improved relations with users of public services (Barouch and Chavas, 1993: 38–9). The new policy was influenced by TQM and theories of participative management. It was intended to facilitate: (a) the introduction of 'administrative statements' clearly specifying tasks and objectives, and defined by each departmental head; (b) the development of 'quality' indicators to improve understanding of user satisfaction; (c) the setting up of quality circles to enable information flow between the different statement participants; and finally (d) the linkage between individual performance and ancillary monetary awards through the introduction of an employee incentive plan stemming from 'performance contracts' (Rouban, 1989: 455).

According to the minister for administrative reform, the implementation of the quality policy 'traduit une volonté d'adaptation à la culture administrative du savoir-faire du privé' (reported in Rouban, 1989: 450). And, while the government showed signs of receptivity to managerialist ideas, consulting firms began more actively to try to recruit ÉNA graduates and senior civil servants to join their ranks. For instance, since the late 1980s, large consulting firms like Arthur Andersen, CEGOS, Bossard, Ernst & Young, and others have regularly placed recruitment advertisements in the *Revue des anciens de l'ÉNA* (Abiker, 1996: 21). There is anecdotal evidence showing that consulting firms have had some success in recruiting former members of the administrative élite (*La Gazette*, 1993). Part of the reason for this has to do with the more market-oriented approach to policy making that the government began to pursue in the 1980s. The disengagement of the state from the economy has transformed the institutional space that traditionally sustained the practice of *pantouflage*. Privatization has opened up new opportunities in the private sector while closing many in the public sector.

In much the same way, budget cutbacks and fiscal austerity are also part of the reason why the civil servant is said to have been 'dethroned' (Bodiguel and Rouban 1991). Factors that traditionally made the civil service attractive —job security and upward mobility—have been undermined by government austerity measures that from 1983 reduced the size of the civil service through attrition and the elimination of budgetary lines (Schmidt, 1996: 294). As a result of these measures, senior civil servants experienced, throughout the 1980s, a real reduction in their purchasing power (Rouban, 1996) and the flight of the *grands corps* to the private sector intensified (Clark, 1998: 102). And all of this was happening at a time when the French management consulting industry was witnessing—with the help of state policy—unprecedented growth, thus making it a more attractive destination for those wishing to leave state service. But so far, there has been no wholesale exodus from government to the private sector. No doubt the significance of state service in and of itself has diminished. It no longer means what it once did. But the 'political and economic changes that have transformed society have in no way lessened the attractiveness of state service' (Suleiman, 1995: 169).

The quality initiative and its aftermath

Largely implemented by departments themselves, the innovation and quality policy was loosely supervised by two new organizations: the Observatoire de l'innovation et la qualité located in the Cabinet office, and the Comité interministérielle sur la qualité made up of 20 ministries operating under the aegis of the minister of finance (Rouban, 1989: 460). The Observatoire was responsible for the diffusion of information pertaining to the introduction of new management methods in government, the private sector, and in other countries (Barouch and Chavas, 1993: 40). The Observatoire consisted of senior officials and representatives of the AFCERQ, which at that time was chaired by one of the management consultants (Raveleau) advising the government on its quality and innovation policy.[6]

On the surface, the innovation and quality policy has had far-reaching effects, with the development of several hundred quality circles throughout the French administrative system. It was estimated that 3,000 quality circles were in existence in the central administration by 1988 (Pochard 1995: 49). Budget appropriations for the development and implementation of the innovation and quality initiative rose from 10 million francs in 1987 to 13.6 million in 1988. A portion of that money was spent on management consultants whose expertise was increasingly sought by the civil service to appraise the functioning of the quality policy in departments (Rouban, 1989: 457).

The Right lost the legislative elections of 1988, one year after having launched its TQM policy. This, some argued, gave the quality approach the negative image of 'an initiative with no durability' (Trosa, 1995b: 267). The new Socialist ruling majority elected in 1989 did not continue the policy and the Observatoire de l'innovation et la qualité no longer appears in the organizational chart of the Cabinet office (*Services publics*, 1995: 32–3). Indeed, the members of the AFCERQ abolished their own association in 1989, thereby indicating a diminution of French interest in TQM ideas (Chevalier, 1991: 17).

---

[6] Following the creation of the Observatoire, it was suggested that the penetration of TQM ideas into the French administration was facilitated by 'la nomination des dirigeants de l'AFCERQ au coeur de l'appareil d'État' and that the government discourse on quality 'n'est en fait que la reproduction, à l'identique, du discours tenu depuis plusieurs années par l'AFCERQ, promue au rang de laboratoire d'idées' (Chevallier, 1988: 134).

The quality approach, and especially the introduction of quality circles, is said to have been a relative 'failure' because 'quality circles were often modelled on those of the private sector' and were not sufficiently adapted to the public sector (Trosa, 1995*b*: 268). In the private sector, the quality approach assumes that organizations are able to evaluate customer satisfaction through the market. Quality circles ended up being too inward looking because they did not have the means to seek the opinions and expectations of their users. Quality circles ended up reproducing the methods of the private sector without sufficiently adapting them to the public sector.

The Renewal policy introduced by the Rocard government in 1989 tried to remedy this by giving greater recognition to the public dimension of government administration and by blending statist with managerialist ideas. The Renewal initiative was a key element of the Left's response to the neo-liberal critique of the state. It gave political endorsement to a body of new managerialist ideas that were already in good currency within the senior ranks of the Socialist government as a result of the activities of a political club known as the Association Services Publics (Chaty, 1997: 21). The Association brings together senior officials from the administrative *grands corps* and like-minded academics in support of a policy that seeks to reform the civil service through 'more systematic programme evaluation, greater transparency of public action and the importation of private sector norms and techniques' (Clark, 1998: 105). In the prime minister's private *cabinet*, Sylvie François, ÉNA graduate, founding member of the Association, and Socialist supporter, was in charge of the Renewal initiative (Chaty, 1997: 26–7).

Another channel through which managerialist ideas came to the attention of Socialist politicians and policy makers in the late 1980s, is the *cumul des mandats*, a practice where most leading national politicians are also leading local politicians (Dion, 1986). The *cumul* has deep historical roots, though its widespread practice is a twentieth-century phenomenon (Grémion, 1976). For instance, almost half of the deputies in the four National Assemblies of 1978, 1981, 1986, and 1988 have been mayors (Knapp, 1991). The *cumul* implies that many politicians sitting in the National Assembly—in their duties as local elected officials—are likely to have been in contact with the managerialist approaches that consultants have been actively promoting in local governments as a result of the 1982 decentralization policy. Such at least was the case of Prime Minister Rocard who, in his position as mayor of Conflans St-Honorine, undertook a number of reform projects that were conducted by management consultants from the private sector (Chaty, 1997: 30).

The use of external consulting services by the central administration initiated with the quality policy was not immediately affected by the change of government in 1989—even if public servants began to raise questions about the usefulness of this trend.[7] In fact, the available evidence suggests that it

---

[7] See Boissard and Lemaitre (1989).

increased considerably.[8] As one French colleague noted, 'Avec le Renouveau du Service Public en 1989, les cabinets conseil se sont vu ouvrir le vaste marché du secteur public' (Chaty, 1997: 226). Soon after the introduction of the Renewal policy, Bossard—which claims to be the largest provider of consulting services to local governments—began to put together a team of 15 to 20 people responsible for developing contacts with central government ministries (Crawford, 1991: 11).

According to Syntec Management, the trade association of consulting firms in France, consultants warmly welcomed the Renewal policy. 'Les cabinets de conseil en management ont reçu avec satisfaction l'ensemble du discours lié à la modernisation du secteur public' (Syntec Management, 1996: 57). A study released by Syntec Management shows that in 1995, nearly 600 million francs of the revenues of the some 50 firms which were members of the association came from local and central governments. As Figure 5.2 indicates, local and central government represented in 1995 almost 16 per cent of the total income of Syntec member firms.

But this same study also reveals that after a period of 'strong increase' beginning in the late 1980s, there has been in the last few years a 'slow down', even a 'regression', in the central government's use of external consulting services (Syntec Management, 1996: 15). In the late 1980s, 'un marché nouveau s'annonçait . . . [mais] c'est plutôt la déception qui domine aujourd'hui' (Syntec Management, 1996: 57). Syntec wonders whether this reduction implies 'une remise en cause des consultants' (Syntec Management, 1996: 49).

The creation of internal management consulting services

What happened to consultants in central government following the Renewal policy? Why did bureaucratic reformers decide to develop their own internal management consulting capacities? In 1990, the government created the Groupe de modernisation des consultants internes dans l'Administration, an *ad hoc* commission designed to advise the government on how to establish its internal management consulting services (DGAFP, 1991). Consisting of a majority of civil servants, the group issued its final report in January 1991. Clearly statist in orientation and style, the report recommended the establishment of a training programme for internal consultants designed to 'développer le sens du Service Public, favoriser l'intégration des valeurs et l'appropriation des objectifs institutionnels assignés à la Fonction Publique'

---

[8] Unlike those of Britain and Canada, the French government does not have centralized information on the money spent by government departments on the use of external management consulting services. But according to Isabelle Orgogozo, a senior official in the Direction générale de l'Administration et de la Fonction publique, 'les consultants externes ont été très actifs dans les premières années de la politique du Renouveau' but the government 'n'a pas de données d'ensemble permettant d'indiquer les budgets que cela a pu représenter'. Written communication from Ms Orgogozo to the author, 14 September 1994.

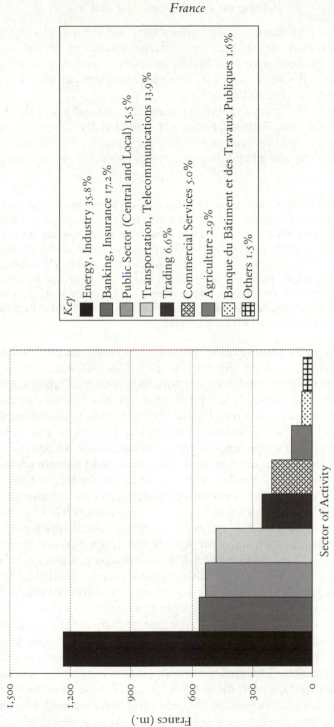

Key

■ Energy, Industry 35.8%

▨ Banking, Insurance 17.2%

▨ Public Sector (Central and Local) 15.5%

▨ Transporation, Telecommunications 13.9%

■ Trading 6.6%

▨ Commercial Services 5.0%

▨ Agriculture 2.9%

▨ Banque du Bâtiment et des Travaux Publiques 1.6%

▨ Others 1.5%

Sector of Activity

FIGURE 5.2. Total management consulting revenues of Syntec member firms, by sector of activity

Source: Syntec Management, *L'année 1995 des adhérents* (study conducted by GMV Conseil), p. 15 (Paris, 1995).

(DGAFP, 1991: Appendix 3). The group concluded that it was preferable for the government to have its own internal consulting service because 'les solutions proposées par les consultants internes sont en général mieux acceptées que celles des consultants externes marquées par une culture de l'entreprise privée' (DGAFP, 1991: 3).

According to the group, experience since the mid-1980s and during the first year of the 1989 Renewal policy showed that the advice of outside consultants was sometimes resisted by civil servants. As one member of the group argued, the administration's experience with the use of consultants showed that

l'appel à des consultants externes présente quelquefois des inconvénients, dans la mesure où les gens venus de l'extérieur connaissent mal le fonctionnement de la maison. Le fonctionnement de l'administration est très particulier. Et chaque administration a même un fonctionnement particulier. Par ailleurs, cela entraîne un obstacle financier (ça coûte cher), parce qu'on met plus longtemps pour pénétrer dans la maison, et un obstacle psychologique, parce qu'on est plus difficilement admis par les gens de la maison. L'oeil extérieur est toujours un peu rejeté. C'est la raison pour laquelle nous avons constitué un groupe de consultants internes qui essaient de remédier à ces défauts. (B. Gauthier, reported in MFPRA, 1993: 134)

It was thus partly because consultants were 'rejected' that the decision to establish internal consulting services was made (Bec, Granier, and Singery, 1993). But rejected by whom? A study issued in 1993 by the Direction générale de l'Administration et de la Fonction publique (DGAFP) shows that the *corps des Inspecteurs* was the most reluctant to welcome management consultants in government. As is well known, the corps system is one that generates great rivalry as each corps seeks to retain its monopoly of expertise in its 'reserved' sector, to conquer new policy domains, and to obtain prestigious postings for its members (Kessler, 1986). According to the DGAFP study, the government's growing use of external consulting services created 'rivalries' and 'tensions' between consultants and the inspectors (DGAFP, 1993: 3). The inspectors suspected that the use of external consultants would limit their role to financial audit and control work and thus would not allow them to promote their skills in the broader field of management and organization (DGAFP, 1993: 18). This is why, when the government decided to develop its own management consulting services, the new position of internal consultant was incorporated into the inspection function.

Whether this will facilitate the acceptance of managerialist ideas by the French bureaucracy in the future is an open question. But if generalizations can be drawn from the British and Canadian cases, in these two instances we saw that the creation of internal consulting services in the 1960s left legacies that subsequently facilitated the entry of managerialist ideas into policy. Internal consultants often worked in partnership with business consultants. By doing so, private sector consultants acquired experience of work in government and built networks of expertise with the state which, through the years, provided them with opportunities to advocate managerialist ideas in centres of national power.

Ideas are more likely to influence policy when they are advocated by those who have some expertise in the matter at hand. But the acquisition of expertise is powerfully shaped by time (or history) and institutions. As a Bossard consultant said soon after the introduction of the Renewal policy in 1989, 'All the ministries are potential markets. But it takes time—you need the expertise, you need to know the milieu and to have good references' (reported in Crawford, 1991: 11).

Conclusion

Because of the legacies of statism left by the creation of the ÉNA, and because of the concentration of administrative expertise in the hands of the *grands corps*, French administrative institutions have not been open to advice from outside consultants, thereby affecting the speed with which managerialist ideas influenced policy. In Britain and Canada there is no institution comparable to the ÉNA.[9] In this institutional vacuum, private sector consulting organizations became for decision makers a key source of management expertise and, consequently, managerialist ideas made faster inroads into policy in these two states. By comparison, managerialist ideas penetrated only slowly in France because the expertise and instruments required for policy making in the area of management reform have been centralized within the state in a number of key agencies. This limited the points of contact between these agencies and consultants and ensured that the initiatives for policy always came from within the state.

This situation broadly describes the statist approach to bureaucratic reform that prevailed in France until the 1982 decentralization. The 1982 decentralization undermined statism. With decentralization, the civil service at the local level was no longer under the formal responsibility of the centre. Local officials were given greater flexibility in the rules governing recruitment, greater financial resources, and the powers to reorganize their bureaucracies. This allowed local government to increasingly bring in external consultants as a source of policy advice on management reform.

As a result of decentralization, policy making in the area of bureaucratic reform became less impermeable than before. The monopoly of expertise that central government officials had traditionally exercised in the area of management was eroded by decentralization. Decentralization multiplied

---

[9] Of course, as discussed in Chapter 3, in Britain there is the Civil Service College, which was created in 1970. However, it never became the élite training school that the ÉNA is in France.

the points of contact between central government officials responsible for bureaucratic reform and other 'societal' actors involved in management reform at the local level. This was seen, for instance, with the conference on 'Les cercles de qualité dans l'Administration' organized in 1985 by the AFCERQ, which brought together consultants and local and central government officials.

Following this conference, management consultants and the AFCERQ became actively involved in attempting to transpose TQM ideas from the local to the central level of government. Of course, this process of transposition was facilitated by the election of the right-wing coalition in 1986. However, to argue that managerialist ideas (in the form of TQM policy innovations) became influential after 1986 because of the election of a New Right government is to forget that central government's interest in TQM began under the Socialists.

The emergence of managerialism in France in the mid-1980s has much to do with the 1982 decentralization, which opened the doors of local government to management consultants. Local government became the main access point or channel through which consultants and managerialist ideas started, in the mid-1980s, to penetrate the institutions of central government. However, although decentralization may well have opened a route that initially facilitated the entry of consultants into the French state, it became much more difficult to travel on that route when consultants passed the local government 'station' and tried to continue their way into central government. As one French consultant indicated in discussing the entry of members of his profession into the French state, 'l'ouverture au conseil s'est faite progressivement des marges (collectivités locales) vers le coeur (administrations centrales) . . . D'autre part, plus on se rapproche du coeur, moins la culture d'entreprise du consultant est pertinente' (Bruston, 1993: 178). In the central administration, the ideas sponsored by consultants were not received as well as they had previously been in local government. The statist approach to bureaucratic reform may well have been undermined by the 1982 decentralization, but it has not yet disappeared, as both the TQM experience and the construction of internal management consulting capacities indicate. Decentralization has certainly allowed managerialist ideas to emerge and to become more visible in the French administrative landscape, but these ideas have not yet influenced policy as much as they did in Britain and, to a lesser extent, Canada.

6

Conclusion: Consultants, the state, and the politics of managerialism

This study has analysed the interrelations between management consultants and the state to provide an answer to the puzzling question of why, in the face of similar fiscal and global economic challenges, governments embraced managerialist ideas differently in the course of reforming their bureaucracies in the 1980s and early 1990s. Linking the 'new' public management of the 1980s to the 'old' public management and rationalism that characterized public administration reform in the 1960s, I have tried to show that the reception given by states to managerialist ideas depended on the organizational development of management consultancy and on whether the legacies left by past policies of bureaucratic reform facilitated (or impeded) the access of consultants to decision-making centres.

Existing explanations of the rise and influence of managerialism generally focus on three models: (a) the political or ideological model which stresses the emergence of the New Right and the election of market-oriented governments; (b) the structural and technological approach emphasizing the process of economic globalization and the rise of the information society; and (c) a more recent and largely unexamined line of argument that stresses the interests of profit-maximizing management consultants from the business sector as the determinant of managerialist policies.

The New Right approach links the emergence of managerialism in public administration to the election of neo-conservative and anti-statist governments since the late 1970s. This explanation assumes that managerialist ideas are by definition right-wing ideas, but ignores the fact that some of these ideas, such as the accountable management unit in the case of the Next Steps in Britain for instance, were initially introduced under a left-wing government. The same can be said about the French case, where it was a Socialist minister of administrative reform who first became interested in the ideas and techniques that led to the Total Quality Management policy adopted by Chirac's right-wing coalition in 1987. The New Right model also assumes that the political interests of right-wing governments almost always coincide with managerialist ideas. However, the Canadian case has clearly shown that the state's prior experience with bureaucratic reform policies, and the way managerialist ideas have been packaged since the 1970s by the Auditor General with ideas that seek to restructure the balance of power between the executive and the legislature, led the Mulroney government to view managerialism as inimical to its political interests. As a result, government support for the managerialist ideas that were part of the PS 2000 initiative has been weak. The interests of the Mulroney government *vis-à-vis* managerialism could not simply be 'read off' its ideological position as a New Right party. Instead, it has been important to examine how these interests were defined in relation to the legacies of past bureaucratic reform policies.

In the globalization approach, the determinants of managerialism are to be found in the fiscal crisis, in the process of global economic restructuring, and in the rapid development of information technology. In this interpretation, the story of managerialism starts in the late 1970s and early 1980s. It is a story that emphasizes constraints rather than choice and one where the key actors in the drama are structures rather than social or political agents. As the preceding chapters have shown, however, a number of the ideas informing managerialist policies adopted in the late 1980s go back at least to the 1960s when concepts such as the fiscal crisis and globalization were largely unknown. These ideas were originally imported from the private sector as a way to rationalize and strengthen, rather than weaken, state intervention. Globalization and the fiscal crisis in the 1980s did not give birth to new managerialist ideas, but changed the meaning and the political justification for the use of what often were already existing policy ideas.

The third approach essentially argues that the interests of management consultants from the private sector drive the diffusion of managerialist ideas. While in this approach changes come from the actions of real human beings and not simply from 'invisible' ideological and structural forces, the consultant-centred view of managerialism tends to overestimate the rationality of consultants and their capacity to have their preferences translated into policy. It is assumed that consultants are everywhere a powerful group and that 'consultocracy' is the logical consequence of their growing presence as advisers in the bureaucratic reform policy process.

Although they are all quite convincing, none of these three models seems entirely appropriate for explaining variations in the acceptance of managerialist ideas and policies across nations. They are all, to various extents, ahistorical and they neglect the importance of institutional factors and the state in the determination of policy outcomes. They are either too 'macro' or too 'micro' and explain too much or too little. In an effort to test the claims of the consultant-centred approach—while adding to it a more complete model of the policy-making process as a whole—this study has aimed to develop a more middle-range approach that looks at the interactions between consultants and the state to explain variations in the acceptance of managerialist ideas and policies. Of course, in focusing on the role of management consultants in the bureaucratic reform policy process, this study has not given equal analytical weight to all the variables that could explain the influence of managerialism. Rather, its aim has been more modest and the intent has been to shed some light on a topic—the role of management consultants in public administration—that has never been looked at in studies of managerialism and bureaucratic change. The remainder of this chapter examines the general findings of this book. The relevance for democracy of issues raised by the role of management consultants from the private sector in the public policy process is discussed by way of conclusion.

Establishing the authority of management consultancy

Clearly, if management consultancy does not exist or is relatively undeveloped in a national setting, there is little chance that consultants can be involved in the process of administrative modernization and diffuse within the state management ideas based on private sector experience. Put differently, if a given state does not have access to the knowledge base and expertise that political leaders think they need to implement given line of policies, they are not likely to pursue them. This is why the first task of this research has been to study the history and organization of management consultancy in Britain, Canada, and France.

Of the three cases examined, management consulting, both as an industry and as a profession, is much less developed in France than in Britain and Canada. France has a smaller management consulting market and a more recently organized consulting industry and profession. Since the entry of the large international accounting firms in the 1960s, management consulting has become a major industry in Britain and Canada where it has developed as the extension of the institutional relationship that accountants have established with their audit clients. In Britain and Canada, the accounting professions are self-regulating bodies, largely autonomous from state intervention, which allow their members to provide management consulting services to their audit clients. For a number of reasons that have to do with historical patterns of industrial and corporate development, in France the accounting profession is smaller and less important than in Britain and Canada. The French accounting profession is directly controlled and regulated by the state. Unlike their British and Canadian counterparts, French accountants cannot perform management consulting work for their audit clients.

One of the most important findings of this study is that the historical and institutional link with accountancy is a key variable for explaining the growth of management consulting. In Britain and Canada, accountants have had important involvement since the early 1960s in the organizational and professional development of management consulting, and these two countries are also the ones where the management consulting industry is most developed. The link between accounting and management consulting in Britain and Canada helped to strengthen the professional reputation and attenuate the 'credibility problem' of management consultancy (Roberts, 1996a:

77). The association of accounting with management consulting in these two countries in the 1960s improved the image of consulting, thereby helping to establish it as a more respectable and serious occupation or business. The dominance of the world management consulting market by the Big Five international accounting firms provides ample evidence of the fact that the historical and institutional association with accounting acted as a locomotive in the development and growth of management consulting.

In Britain and Canada, accountants became active in the organization and professionalization of management consulting in the 1960s. Although in Britain engineers created the first business association of consultants, it was the accountants who took the lead in the professionalization of consultancy with the creation of the Institute of Management Consultants (IMC) in 1962. It was also during that period that the British and Canadian states both started to make relatively important use of management consulting knowledge by launching, with the Fulton and Glassco commissions, bureaucratic reform initiatives that sought to modernize management practices as a way to rationalize the intervention of the state in society.

Similar timing in terms of the relationship between the organizational development of management consultancy and the participation of consultants in the process of bureaucratic reform also characterizes France. However, the difference between France, on the one hand, and Britain and Canada, on the other, is that the growth and professionalization of management consulting in France took place much later, during the 1980s under the leadership of the Department of Industry. French management consultants only started to participate in the process of bureaucratic restructuring in the mid-1980s, following the decentralization reforms. What the French situation shows is that when there is no link with accounting, the consulting industry tends to be weaker and the possibilities for management consultants to help shape bureaucratic reform policy with their private sector experience more limited. But as the French case also indicates, the state can compensate for the absence of a link with accountancy by playing a leadership role in the development of management consulting. The state can assist the development of management consultancy by encouraging businesses to use consulting services and by taking the initiative for professionalizing this field of activity, as the French state did in creating the Office Professionnel de Qualification des Conseils en Management (OPQCM) in the 1980s.

The political construction of management consulting expertise

Although the role of the state has been much more direct in France, in Britain and Canada the state also contributed to the development of management consulting by using the services of consultants who, as a result, acquired experience in public administration, built networks of expertise with the state, and expanded their market into public sector consulting. It was the state and the political goals of government leaders seeking to make government more 'business like' that enabled consultants to make claims to expertise in the field of public sector management. And consequently, during the 1980s most large firms created 'government consulting divisions' within their organization (Jarrett, 1998).

More recently, global consultancies have even started to create new foundations and research bodies designed specifically for improving efficiency in government. For instance, in Canada KPMG established the KPMG Centre for Government whose goal is, according to publicity material, to 'help elected representatives and senior public servants find successful, business-oriented solutions to today's pressing public sector needs'. The Centre publishes various studies on managerial innovations in the public sector and has put together a network—known as the 'Alternative Network'—made up of academics, consultants, and senior bureaucrats, which publishes a monthly newsletter to facilitate 'the transfer of ideas' and the 'exchange of information' on public sector reform. As one can read on the website of the KPMG Centre for Government:

Our recommendations are drawn from long experience helping our clients meet new needs. We also draw on the best ideas from academia and former public servants. We can assist you in achieving true innovation. Our confidence derives from a large number of successful assignments, and having senior specialist partners across the country exclusively devoted to serving public sector organizations and Crown corporations.

Upon its creation in 1995, the KPMG Centre was headed by Ian Clark, a former senior public servant who used to be secretary to the Treasury Board, the central agency that has jurisdiction over public management reform in Ottawa. Although there is no empirical study on this issue, anecdotal evidence from the previous chapters show that, in staffing their government divisions, consulting firms have been recruiting individuals familiar with public sector management. As one Canadian colleague recently noted, 'former bureaucrats and others with public sector expertise have been hired by these firms to develop a rapport with civil servants and to sell the firms' many and varied services' (Bakvis, 1997: 109).

A number of reports or studies in countries like Australia, Canada, and Britain, have documented the so-called revolving-door syndrome whereby civil servants leave government to join or establish management consulting firms. In Britain, Hood found that 'there was no attempt to deprivilege senior civil servants by tightening the rules restricting "revolving-door" appointments of civil servants in the private sector' (Hood, 1999: 111). In Australia, the Joint Parliamentary Committee of Public Accounts noted in a study on the engagement of external consultants by government departments in 1990 that in most countries there is nothing to 'prevent a public service employee from resigning a position only to return as a consultant to do precisely the same tasks at a significantly higher fee' (Australia, 1990: vii).

In the face of downsizing and cutbacks, the prospects for advancement in the civil service have diminished (Bodiguel and Rouban, 1991; Peters, 1991). In this context, management consulting firms have become more attractive for those in the senior bureaucracy who no longer see the rewards of a career in the public service. No government can compete with the salaries offered by large consulting firms. In addition, the fact that the market for management consulting services in the public sector has become more important in the last 15 years means that consultancies are making more conscious efforts than before to recruit either former civil servants or those who are graduating from schools (the ÉNA in France or the JFK School of Government in the United States for instance) where they have received public administration training.

But the hiring of former bureaucrats by management consulting firms raises a very interesting question about the involvement of consultants in public administration reform. In general, the rationale is that governments use the services of consultants because they help to transfer business management practices and ideas from the private to the public sector. The logic is one of learning: consultants help governments to learn from best practices in business management (Henkel, 1991a: ch. 4). But if the consultants who participate in the bureaucratic reform process are former civil servants, to what extent are they likely to have extensive practical experience of private sector management? How can they help to transfer business management know-how to government if they have spent an important part of their career in the public sector?

One of the key conclusions of this book is that political factors—and not technical expertise alone—are an important part of the reason that management consultants are brought into government to reform public administration practices. In this sense, governments not only rely on consultants to help them strengthen their *management* capacities, as consultants and other advocates of managerialism claim. As students of public administration and policy know well, there is no politics-administration dichotomy. Consultants also strengthen the *political* capacities of those who are responsible for leading the reform process by helping to overcome bureaucratic resistance and mobilizing support for the policy ideas that they promote and that decision makers seek to implement.

But to do this, to play this political role, management consultancy has to be a relatively respectable or credible field of activity. What has been called 'arm's-length policy-making via consultants' advice' is more likely to be successful when the expertise of consultants is more or less widely recognized (Martin, 1998: 11). In his book on the role of consultants in Australian government, Martin writes that it was 'the widely acknowledged expertise of consultants' that explains why they were so 'successful in getting their recommendations adopted by government' (1998: 1). Research has indeed shown that when the claim to expertise made by a knowledge-bearing group is regarded dimly, the prospects for the adoption of its policy proposals is also dim (Roberts, 1996a: 10). This is in part why managerialist ideas have emerged later and been much less influential in France than in Britain and Canada, where management consultancy is more developed and where the expertise of consultants is more widely acknowledged because of the historical and institutional link to accountancy.

The legacies of past bureaucratic reform policies

But the strengths or weaknesses of the management consulting industry, as well as its social recognition or prestige, do not, by themselves, determine the fate of managerialism. The cases of Britain and Canada clearly show that although they both have a well-developed management consulting industry and profession, managerialist ideas have not been equally influential in the two countries. Differences in the reception given to managerialist ideas have also been caused by the state's prior experience with bureaucratic reform. In examining these past reforms, this book has primarily looked at whether they left legacies that facilitated the penetration of consultants into the state and their access to decision-making centres. In the three cases, the openings created by past legacies included: the 1966 Fulton Committee in Britain; the 1960 Glassco Commission in Canada; and the 1982 decentralization in France.

Fulton, Glassco, and the entry of consultants into the state

The 1960 Glassco Royal Commission in Canada and the creation of a Management Consultancy Group attached to the Fulton Committee in Britain in 1966 were two instances where the 'expertise' of private sector management consultants in the bureaucratic reform policy domain was given official or public recognition by the state. Through their participation in the 1960s on Glassco and on Fulton's Management Consultancy Group, management consultants in Canada and Britain contributed to framing what they thought to be significant managerial 'problems' and the necessary solutions. One of the main problems identified by Fulton and Glassco had to do with what they saw as the archaic character of state management processes. In Britain, Fulton contended that the Whitehall bureaucracy was still following a nineteenth-century philosophy of public administration while in Canada, Glassco dismissed as out of date and 'complicated' the government management system which, it argued, had virtually been 'unchanged in the past thirty years' (Canada, 1962a: 91). The two commissions recommended that management methods in government had to be modernized with management ideas and techniques imported from the private sector. In order to modernize administrative practices, both Fulton and Glassco suggested the creation of new internal management consulting services which were to be primarily located in the Civil Service Department (CSD) and in the Treasury Board Secretariat (TBS). The legacies left by the Fulton and Glassco reforms powerfully influenced the way subsequent bureaucratic reform policies unfolded. First, they granted new central agencies such as the TBS in Canada and the CSD in Britain jurisdiction over bureaucratic reform. Secondly, they also gave consultants a professional and institutional hold on bureaucratic reform policy issues. This happened because both Fulton and Glassco recommended that the TBS and the CSD be staffed, at least in part, with management consultants drawn from the private sector.

In the Canadian case, the new TBS and the construction of internal management consulting capacities were closely related to the development of the Planning, Programming, and Budgeting System (PPBS), the implementation of which required the use of new management techniques that were in part to be provided by consultants. In Britain, the creation of the CSD in 1968 was not linked to PPBS. The British version of PPBS was implemented later than in Canada, in 1970, when the Heath government launched its Programme Analysis and Review (PAR) proceeds. As has been noted, Britain did not embrace PPBS as strongly as Canada did (Plumptre, 1988: 251).

In Canada, as we saw in Chapter 4, the presentation to Parliament of expenditures in the programme budget form created an opportunity for the Office of the Auditor General (OAG) to justify an expansion of its mandate in order to adapt is functions to the new PPBS approach. This happened at a moment where the government was, politically, in a minority situation and when James J. Macdonell, a management consultant from Price Waterhouse, co-founder and past president of the Canadian Association of Management Consultants (CAMC), was appointed to the position of Auditor General of Canada. The appointment of Macdonell greatly facilitated the entry of consultants in the federal state. Auditor General Macdonell expanded the power of his office through the adoption of the value-for-money clause in the Auditor General Act 1977. He also significantly contributed to the development of management consulting. During Macdonell's tenure, more than 500 private sector consultants were reported to have acquired, through their work in the OAG, first-hand knowledge of public administration. Some of these consultants subsequently became directors of government consulting (or services) divisions in a number of large management consulting firms in Ottawa.

In contrast to Britain, the Canadian Auditor General is not a civil servant appointed from the permanent bureaucracy, but a professional accountant appointed from the private sector. This practice is believed to enhance the political independence of the Auditor General from the bureaucracy and the government. And being more independent, the OAG in Canada is also much more vocal than its British counterpart in matters related to government management. In Britain, research shows that 'the National Audit Office documents tend to avoid any direct or general approbation of managerialism' (Pollitt and Summa, 1997*a*: 334). This is in sharp contrast with the Canadian Auditor who, in 1988, was advocating in his report to Parliament 'the need for public servants to develop a greater spirit of entrepreneurship. I believe that an entrepreneurial public service would be good for Canada' (Auditor General of Canada, 1988: 1).

In Canada, the fact that the Auditor General is an 'outsider' also means that when the government decides to appoint a new auditor, its choice is to some extent structured by the organization of the market for accounting services, dominated by the Big Five. Since the 1960s, almost all auditors have come from the Big Five. In addition, given that in Canada the accounting profession dominates the management consulting market and that accounting firms do not maintain an institutional separation between their accounting and consulting activities, this means that the auditor appointed by the government may have either an accountancy or a consultancy background. Thus, the Canadian practice of appointing the Auditor General from the private sector, and the structure of the market for accounting and consulting services, creates possibilities for consultants to gain access to decision-making centres in the OAG.

As a body that is located outside the permanent executive, the OAG has institutional arrangements governing recruitment and budgetary procedures that differ from those that apply to the civil service. Much of the expert advice on which the OAG relies does not come from an echelon of permanent civil servants but from professional service contracts or from the Executive Interchange Program, which links the OAG to a large number of accounting and management consulting firms. The OAG is thus much more permeable or open to advice from outside experts than is the permanent bureaucracy. This is why managerialism took hold more rapidly in the OAG where the use of outside consultants is an institutionalized practice. However, once managerialist ideas had been introduced in the OAG, the same institutional feature that facilitated their entry (separation from the executive), also affected the degree to which they would become an entrenched component of government policy.

Contrasting patterns of institutionalization

For Canadian management consultants, being institutionally linked to the OAG is like a double-edged sword. On the one hand, consultants have greatly benefited from their institutionalization in the OAG, with revenues derived from contract work in the Audit Office growing from $Can.5,000 to $Can.7 million between 1971 and 1981. On the other hand, the strategic opportunities for consultants to help shape government policy are limited because the managerialist solutions that they advocate are packaged by the OAG with ideas intended to redesign accountability relationships that are not politically popular with the government. As a body attached to the legislature, the OAG is also linked to political actors (MPs, the opposition, legislative committees, for instance) who have an interest in changing the balance of power between the executive and the legislature as a way of enhancing their role in the scrutiny of government business. Since the 1976 Lambert report, the OAG has been advocating ideas that seek to separate the political responsibility of ministers from the administrative responsibility of their senior officials by making the latter directly accountable to the House of Commons. However, such ideas have generally been strongly opposed by the government because they would reduce the powers of ministers who would see whole areas of public administration being subtracted from their responsibility. The managerialist ideas that consultants sponsored through the OAG are thus packaged with ideas designed to empower the legislature but which do not mobilize strong government support.

By comparison, in Britain management consultants were originally institutionalized in the CSD in 1968. Soon after the creation of the CSD, which was to be the main internal management consulting service in British central government, consulting revenues from government business were reported to be 'pretty low' (Wilding, 1976: 69). As mentioned in Chapter 3, part of the reason for this is the way the British state during the 1970s was building its own management consulting capacities. Thus, unlike their Canadian counterparts, British consultants did not originally benefit much from their link with the CSD. This situation changed rapidly, however, when the access point of consultants to the British state was brought closer to the political control of the prime minister as a result of the creation of Thatcher's Efficiency Unit and the abolition of the CSD in 1981. Once linked to the centre of the executive machinery, consultants had more direct access to decision-making positions. Their ideas entered the process of administrative reform and became an important component of government policy.

Thus, although the construction of institutional links with the OAG may initially have appeared to be a positive development for Canadian management consultants, in the long term this association has limited their capacity to shape policy. By contrast, British developments opened up, for management consultants, new opportunities that were not possible under previous institutional arrangements. The reorganization of the institutions that have jurisdiction over bureaucratic reform policy issues in Britain in the early 1980s facilitated the formation of what may be called a 'managerialist policy coalition' between consultants and the Thatcher government. The formation of such an alliance might have been more difficult before 1981 when the CSD was still in existence. The CSD, which had been since Fulton the main access point of consultants to the British state, was not very popular with the Thatcher government (Fry, 1984). The CSD was seen as inimical to the interests of the Thatcher government because it was associated with the interventionist ideology of Labour in the 1960s. Moreover, we saw in Chapter 3 that those who gained control of most decision-making positions in the CSD were not outsiders from the private sector, as was originally intended by Fulton, but 'generalist' senior civil servants. As a result, senior officials in the CSD often defended civil service management practices, arguing that public administration was very different from business management (Savoie, 1994: 201). For private sector management consultants, the CSD was, therefore, as much an adversary as an ally, in so far as many of its senior officials were not strong supporters of managerialist ideas. Although the CSD provided one access point to the British state, this access was not as interesting or useful as consultants probably expected, for at least two reasons. First, it limited their influence on bureaucratic reform policy. And secondly, the revenues of consulting firms from government work did not increase significantly in the 1970s following the creation of the CSD.

In Britain, although the strongest political impulse for the managerialization of the state came from the Thatcher government, it would be a mistake to assume that these changes could be satisfactorily attributed solely to the charismatic and determined leadership of Mrs Thatcher. This was, of course, an important influence, but it seems unlikely that change would have gone as far as it did if Thatcher's programme for reforming the state had not been enriched by the presence of allies such as management consultants who contributed important ideas about how to adapt business management practices to the public sector.

Between local governments and internal consultants at the centre

In terms of the access point though which management consultants have entered the state, the cases of France and Canada share some similarities. In both states management consultants have been primarily institutionalized in organizations (local government and the OAG) that are outside the control and direction of the political executive. As a result, their access to decision-making centres in government and the possibilities for their ideas to strongly influence policy have been more limited.

In France, managerialist ideas were kept off the policy agenda until the mid-1980s because of both the centralized and impermeable character of bureaucratic reform policy making and the weak development of consulting. But the 1982 decentralization reforms opened the doors of local government to private sector consultants. With decentralization, the services of consultants were increasingly sought by local officials to help them put in place the systems and techniques needed to manage their new administrative functions. During the 1980s, consultants began to sponsor Total Quality

Management (TQM) ideas which were first translated into policy at the local level, and then later spread in the central government following the appointment of Chirac as prime minister in 1986. However, Chapter 5 showed that TQM ideas were not as well accepted in the central government as in local administration. Local government does not share the statist tradition of the central administration. It is more open to outside advice and it thus provides a much more hospitable setting for innovative management policy proposals than central government. But because of the failure of the TQM policy experience, the central government decided in 1990 to have its own internal management consulting capacities rather than rely on external consultants whose ideas are often resisted by civil servants. If the lessons drawn from the British case are of any use (i.e. the reduction of consulting revenues from government business after the creation of the CSD), the creation of such internal services should narrow, at least in the short term, the opening through which French consultants entered central government in the mid-1980s following the decentralization reforms. For now, French management consultants are somewhat 'cornered', between local government and internal consulting services at the centre. As a result, managerialism will probably continue to penetrate French (central) administrative institutions only slowly.

'Accountingization' and the content of consultants' advice

One intriguing feature of the French case, when compared to Britain and Canada, is that while French consultants were busy sponsoring TQM ideas in the public sector in the 1980s, their British and Canadian counterparts were involved in contributing to what Chistopher Hood has called the 'accountingization' of public sector management (Hood, 1994: 138–9). Why did managerialism in France take the form of TQM ideas whereas, at almost the same time, it was expressed in terms of a strong focus on accounting procedures in Britain and Canada? How can we try to interpret this difference? The answer can only be hypothetical because the goal of this book was to explain differences in the reception given by states to managerialist ideas in general—and not to explain differences in the content of the advice provided by consultants or differences between the various models of management promoted by consultants and used by governments in an attempt to become more 'businesslike'.

Managerialism is a broad term and it tends to neglect the differences that exist between models of business management. There are many ways by which governments can become more businesslike: they can do this by employing different management models and ideas. At any one time, there are always various management theories and concepts competing in the market to attract the support of managers. Consulting firms offer diverse management models and fashions to differentiate themselves in the market

(Micklethwait and Wooldridge, 1996). But in general, the models that tend to dominate the market are those produced by the big firms that have the resources, the capacities, and the global networks to spread the managerialist gospel around the world. As discussed in Chapter 2, this was the case, for instance, of McKinsey and *In Search of Excellence*.

Peters and Waterman's book is clearly rooted in human relations theories of management. It does not seem to be related to the kind of 'accounting-ization' approach that Hood sees as the most prominent feature of British administrative reform. As much as in Britain (if not more so) there has also been in Canada a tremendous emphasis on new accounting procedures, with managerialist innovations implemented in the 1970s such as value for money, programme evaluation, and so forth. Is it possible that the process that Hood describes may be, in some way, related to the fact that accounting firms in countries like Britain and Canada have historically dominated the management consulting market? Can the knowledge base of the firms that dominate the consulting market (accounting knowledge in Britain and Canada) have an impact on the policies that states implement based on the advice that they buy from private sector consultants? In other words, to what extent are the management policies that the state adopts as a result of advice provided by consultants shaped by the nature of the professional expertise that dominates the consulting market? These are questions for future research that are well beyond the scope of this book.

Consultocracy and democracy

There at least four issues raised by the role of management consultants in government that are relevant to democracy and that I would like to address by way of conclusion. Whether management consultants from the private sector are becoming part of 'shadow government' and taking policy-making powers away from democratic institutions, as was argued some time ago in the United States, is an open question (Guttman and Willner, 1976). But it is one the importance of which is not likely to vanish soon. Management consultancy is still a growth industry and the state is still an important source of revenue. In the United States, the Kennedy Research Group estimates that the world market for management consulting services will be around $US113 billion for 2000. Likewise, a survey issued in 1999 by the European Federation of Management Consultancy Associations found that more than 13 per cent of the total fee revenue of management consulting firms in Europe comes from government. According to the survey, this proportion will increase in the future as a result of deeper continental economic integration (FEACO, 1999*b*).

The first issue relevant to democracy is that of 'consultocracy'. Are consultants increasingly usurping the power of elected officials by bringing into their sphere of expertise matters that they define as managerial but that are, in fact, essentially political? Most of the time, they probably do not. However well developed and powerful their internal organizational resources, the degree of influence that management consultants exercise on the way the state is managed is largely determined by the political process. As our cases have shown, this sometimes imposes severe limits on the capacity of management consultants to shape policy.

But this cautious assessment does not mean that management consultants have no impact on the democratic process. A second issue relevant for democracy is that the state's increasing reliance on consultants in the provision of management policy advice negatively affects the openness and transparency of public debates. In Britain, where the term 'consultocracy' was first coined, it has been argued that management consultants have become the 'key profession for advising and assisting [the government] . . . Where once royal commissions were appointed to review problems requiring attention, today it is more likely that Coopers and Lybrand will be asked to file a report' (*Political Quarterly*, 1993: 269). Government research that might once have been carried out by public bodies, the argument goes on, will today be done by management consultants who belong to a very secretive industry. Unlike other sectors that have become increasingly more open as a result of strong public pressures, the bureaucratic reform policy domain is still a closed sector dominated by senior officials and consultants. This closed character may create problems for democracy because of the difficulties involved in trying to distinguish managerial from political issues. This means that bureaucrats and consultants can negotiate and settle political issues with one another, without choices being drawn to the attention of politicians or the electorate.

The third issue concerns the distinctive character of consultants as policy 'experts' and their neutrality or independence in the provision of management advice to state officials. Studies that have examined the role and influence of specialists in the diffusion of policy ideas have generally looked at two types of policy expert: the think-tank and the academic analyst. The kinds of experts on which this study has focused, however, are different from other policy specialists because of the nature of the organization for which they work. Unlike the policy experts who work in non-profit research institutes and in the academic sector, consultants work for profit-based organizations. As noted in Chapter 2, the 'expert' status of management consultants is often questioned. Consultancy is seen as a business as much as a profession and the sector is generally divided (except in Canada) between business and professional associations.

Not only do the knowledge and ideas that consultants produce have a problem-solving function; they also are 'products' designed to generate revenues. As a result, consultants' neutrality in the provision of policy advice is sometimes more contested than that of the academic or the think-tank policy expert (Pal, 1992: 224). 'The management consultants who have profited extensively from being brought in to assist New Public Management (NPM) reforms', writes Christopher Pollitt, are 'anything but neutral witnesses' (1995*b*: 204).

But in government circles, questioning the neutrality of management consultants in the provision of policy advice does not yet seem to be a common practice. In the three countries studied in this book, government documents pertaining to the engagement of external consultants, all—with no exception—indicate that policy makers use consultants because of their independence and neutrality. For instance, in Britain, the 1994 study on consultants conducted by the Efficiency Unit claims that 'consultants are employed principally because of the specialist expertise, broader perspective and independence of view that they bring to issues' (p. 3). The rationale is that, unlike permanent career bureaucrats, consultants are 'outsiders': they are seen as having an independent status from government and thus, are supposed to be more objective than public servants who are 'insiders' and presumed to be less neutral because they have their own entrenched interest to defend and promote. According to this logic, policy makers use consultants because they 'are perceived by the wider community as disinterested and objective experts, less "politicial" than governments and hence more legitimate' (Martin, 1998: 11).

But the question of whether consultants from the private sector represent a more 'disinterested' source of advice than government employees needs to be critically examined, simply because independence and neutrality are important pillars of the modern democratic state. As Max Weber told us long ago, independence and objectivity in the discharge of public duties are guaranteed by tenure (Gerth and Mills, 1946: 202). In the nineteenth century, national bureaucracies were often staffed by people who were appointed for partisan reasons (Silberman, 1993). As a result, the technical skills of the civil service were low, as were the salaries. This meant that most people working in the public service had to complement their income by working for other employers—a situation that increased the potential for conflict of interests. In the late nineteenth and early twentieth centuries, reformers saw the creation of a permanent career bureaucracy as a way to strengthen the power of democratically elected politicians because those advising the rulers at the top would no longer be afraid of losing their job; they would no longer seek to please their political superiors by always agreeing with their policy proposals, even when these made no sense at all. Permanence meant that bureaucrats could speak without fear, frankly, openly, and honestly, and thus give to the democratic rulers the best policy advice possible. In other words, permanence meant that bureaucrats could be 'disinterested'.

But now, thanks to Public Choice ideas, Weber's argument has been turned on its head: permanence and job security have allowed bureaucrats to develop interests of their own and this is why they would be less independent and neutral than consultants from the private sector. But the desire to make a client happy so that he or she keeps using the service of the firm in the future may not always go hand in hand with the provision of the most objective and honest piece of advice. Repeat business is becoming an important trend in management consultancy, as firms try to build and maintain clients' loyalty in an increasingly competitive market (Rassam, 1998). The evidence available from countries like Britain shows that government departments often select (through single tendering process) the services of the same management consulting firms with which they had favourable experiences in the past (Efficiency Unit, 1994: 71).

But if a consulting firm often works with the same department, what does that mean for the status of consultant as 'outsider'? The employment of the same consultants implies that the line between external, impartial adviser and someone from within becomes blurred. As one study found, this trend is becoming so important that 'a greater number of consultants are finding themselves as semi-permanent members of their clients' senior management teams' (Clark, 1995: 9). Essentially, the practice of repeat business challenges beliefs about the externality of consultants and the objectivity that this organizational location is supposed to produce.

This, of course, raises the important problem of 'speaking truth to power' (Wildavsky, 1979). As already mentioned, Weber thought that security of tenure would make it possible for bureaucrats to give blunt advice to politicians, as opposed to someone with no job security, who may not be as frank and critical for fear of losing his/her job. This is not to suggest that, because of the competitive pressures of the market, it is structurally impossible for management consultants to provide frank advice to policy makers in government. A good consultant is likely to be one who is able to earn the respect of clients by identifying the pros and cons of any given situation. The point is that the objectivity argument used to justify the growing involvement of private sector consultants in government is ideological. It is not more empirically founded than the one about the supposedly biased character of the advice that permanent bureaucrats provide to policy makers.

The fourth and final issue relevant for democracy is accountability. In Chapter 3 we saw that, in 1993, the British Cabinet ordered a study examining the practices concerning the government's use of external consulting services. The study identified a number of problems in the government's relationship with management consultants. For instance, a press leak of an unpublished document sent to permanent secretaries, setting out the emerging findings of the study on consultants, contained warnings 'of the dangers of conflict of interests and instances where firms might win work with the aim of getting inside knowledge to take over other work' (Hencke, 1994). The study was made public, its conclusions debated in the media and the House of Commons, and a number of measures intended to improve the government's use of consultants were implemented. It has been possible for the government to take some corrective action because in Britain, management consulting interests have primarily been institutionalized in the Cabinet Office, a body under the control of ministers who are publicly accountable to the House of Commons. In Canada, however, consultants are primarily linked to the OAG, a body for which the concept of ministerial responsibility does not apply and for which there exists no clear mechanism of democratic accountability. In contrast to the situation in Britain, in Canada the possibilities for reviewing and perhaps correcting, any perceived problems that may arise from the OAG's close links with management consulting interests, are more limited. For this reason it would be difficult for parliamentarians to learn whether, for example, there was any benefit to the Big Five firms as a result of the fact that these firms were in the majority on the Auditor General's Panel of Senior Advisers. For instance, might this help them to influence the OAG's programme of work in order to increase the likelihood of their obtaining more consulting work from the government? Thus, differences in the way consulting interests have been institutionalized in Britain and Canada have an important impact not only on the influence of managerialism, but also on the operation of accountability mechanisms and, ultimately, on the quality of democratic life in the two countries.

Bibliography

ABBOTT, P. (1993). 'Vigorous Times in the Public Sector', *Management Consultancy*, June: 27–8.

—— (1994). 'Government Work Fulfils Expectations', *Management Consultancy*, April: 31–4.

ABIKER, D. (1996). *Les consultants dans les collectivités locales*. Paris: Travaux de recherches Panthéon-Assas Paris II.

ABRAHAMSON, E. (1986). 'Organizational Fashion: One Explanation for the Evolution of Technological, Structural and Strategic Myths'. Paper presented at the annual meeting of the Academy of Management, Chicago.

—— (1991). 'Managerial Fads and Fashions: The Diffusion and Rejection of Innovations', *Academy of Management Review*, 16/3: 586–612.

Accountancy Age (1995). 'Consultants Strike Back at Clarke Over Attack on Costs', 1 June.

ADLER, D. A. (1970). *British Investment in American Railways 1834–1898*. Charlottesville: University Press of Virginia.

AICPA: American Institute of Certified Public Accountants (1964). *Professional Accounting in 25 Countries*. AICPA Committee on International Relations.

—— (1977). *The Commission on Auditors' Responsibilities: Report of Tentative Conclusions*. New York.

ALLEN, D. G., and McDERMOTT, K. (1993). *Accounting for Success: A History of Price Waterhouse in America 1890–1990*. Boston: Harvard Business School Press.

ALLISON, G. (1982). 'Public and Private Management', in F. S. Lane (ed.), *Current Issues in Public Administration*. New York: St. Martin's Press.

ALVAREZ, L. J. (1996). 'The International Popularization of Entrepreneurial Ideas', in S. R. Clegg and G. Palmer (eds.), *The Politics of Management Knowledge*. London: Sage, 80–98.

—— (ed.) (1998). *The Diffusion and Consumption of Business Knowledge*. London: Macmillan.

ANDERSON, R. J. (1984). *The External Audit* (2nd edn.). Toronto: Copp Clark Pitman Ltd.

ANDRIEU, C., LE VAN, L., and PROST, A. (eds.) (1987). *Les nationalisations de la Libération*. Paris: Presses de la Fondation des Sciences politiques.

ARCHER, J. N. (1968). 'Management Consultants in Government', *O&M Bulletin*, 23/1: 23–33.

—— (1971). 'A New Look for CSD Management Services', *O&M Bulletin*, 26/1: 4–13.

—— (1972). 'Business Methods in Government', *O&M Bulletin*, 27/1: 5–15.

ARMSTRONG, J. A. (1973). *The European Administrative Elite*. Princeton: Princeton University Press.

ARMSTRONG, P. (1987). 'The Rise of Accounting Controls in British Capitalist Enterprises', *Accounting, Organization and Society*, 414–36.

ARMSTRONG, W. (1970). 'The Civil Service Department and its Tasks', *O&M Bulletin*, 25/2: 63–83.

ARNOLD, P. E. (1988). 'Reorganization and Regime in the United States and Britain', *Public Administration Review*, 48: 726–34.

ARNOTT, D. (1983). 'Whitehall's MOD management', *Management Today*, February: 70–6.

Arthur Young (1990). *The Next Steps: A Review of the Agency Concept*. London.

ASHFORD, D. (1977). 'The Wonderful World of French Administration', *Administrative Science Quarterly*, 22: 140–50.

—— (1982). *Policy and Politics in France*. Philadelphia: Temple University Press.

ATKINSON, M., and COLEMAN, W. D. (1989). *The State, Business and Industrial Change in Canada*. Toronto: Toronto University Press.

ATKINSON, R., and LUPTON, C. (1990). 'Towards an Enterprise Culture? Industrial and Training Policy Under the Conservatives', in S. P. Savage (ed.), *Public Policy Under Thatcher*. London: Macmillan, 45–59.

AUCOIN, P. (1985). *Party Government and Regional Representation*. Toronto: University of Toronto Press.

—— (1986). 'Organizational Change in the Machinery of Canadian Government: From Rational Management to Brokerage Politics', *Canadian Journal of Political Science*, 19/Spring: 3–27.

—— (1988a). 'Contraction, Managerialism and Decentralization in Canadian Government', *Governance*, 1/2: 144–61.

—— (1988b). 'The Mulroney Government, 1984–1988: Priorities, Positional Policy and Power', in A. B. Gollner and D. Salée (eds.), *Canada Under Mulroney*. Montreal: Véhicule Press, 335–56.

—— (1990). 'Administrative Reform in Public Management: Paradigms, Principles, Paradoxes and Pendulums', *Governance*, 3/2: 115–37.

—— (1995). *The New Public Management: Canada in Comparative Perspective*. Montreal: The Institute for Research on Public Policy.

—— and BAKVIS, H. (1986). *The Centralization-Decentralization Conundrum: Organization and Management in the Canadian Government*. Halifax: Institute for Research on Public Policy.

Auditor General of Canada. (1974). *Report of the Auditor General of Canada to the House of Commons*. Ottawa: Supply and Services Canada.

—— (1975). *Report of the Auditor General of Canada to the House of Commons*. Ottawa: Supply and Services Canada.

—— (1976). *Report of the Auditor General of Canada to the House of Commons*. Ottawa: Supply and Services Canada.

—— (1977). *Report of the Auditor General of Canada to the House of Commons*. Ottawa: Supply and Services Canada.

—— (1978a). *Comprehensive Auditing: Planning for Century II. Centennial Conference Proceedings*. Ottawa.

—— (1978b). *100th Annual Report of the Auditor General of Canada to the House of Commons*. Ottawa: Supply and Services Canada.

—— (1979). *Report of the Auditor General of Canada to the House of Commons*. Ottawa: Supply and Services Canada.

—— (1980). *Report of the Auditor General of Canada to the House of Commons*. Ottawa: Supply and Services Canada.

—— (1985). *Report of the Auditor General of Canada to the House of Commons*. Ottawa: Supply and Services Canada.

Auditor General of Canada. (1987). *Report of the Auditor General of Canada to the House of Commons*. Ottawa: Supply and Services Canada.

—— (1988). *Report of the Auditor General of Canada to the House of Commons*. Ottawa: Supply and Services Canada.

—— (1991). *Report of the Auditor General of Canada to the House of Commons*. Ottawa: Supply and Services Canada.

—— (1993). *Report of the Auditor General of Canada to the House of Commons*. Ottawa: Supply and Services Canada.

Australia (1990). Joint Committee of Public Accounts. Report No. 302 of the Commonwealth Parliament, *Engagement of External Consultants by Commonwealth Departments*. Canberra: Australian Government Publishing Service.

BAGGOTT, R. (1995). *Pressure Groups Today*. Manchester: Manchester University Press.

BAILEY, D. T. (1984). 'European Accounting History', in H. P. Holzer (ed.), *International Accounting*. New York: Harper & Row, 17–43.

—— (1990). 'Accounting: Tool of Business or Tool of Society?', in D. J. Cooper and T. M. Hopper (eds.), *Critical Accounts*. London: Macmillan, 193–215.

BAILEY, M. T., and MAYER, R. T. (1992). *Public Management in an Interconnected World*. New York: Greenwood Press.

BAKVIS, H. (1997). 'Advising the Executive: Think Tanks, Consultants, Political Staff and Kitchen Cabinets', in P. Weller, H. Bakvis, and R. A. W. Rhodes (eds.), *The Hollow Crown*. London: Macmillan, 84–125.

BALOGH, T. (1959). *The Establishment*. London: Blond.

BANTA, M. (1993). *Taylored Lives: Narrative Productions in the Age of Taylor, Veblen, and Ford*. Chicago: University of Chicago Press.

BARCUS, W. W., and WILKINSON, J. W. (eds.) (1986). *Handbook of Management Consulting Services*. New York: McGraw-Hill.

BARNES, J., and COCKETT, R. (1994). 'The Making of Party Policy', in A. Seldon and S. Ball (eds.), *Conservative Century: The Conservative Party Since 1900*. Oxford: Oxford University Press, 347–82.

BAROUCH, G., and CHAVAS, H. (1993). *Où va la modernisation? Dix années de modernisation de l'administration d'État en France*. Paris: L'Harmattan.

BARRINGTON, K. (1989). 'France: Revolution is in the Air', *The Accountant*, 5822/February: 18–22.

BARSOUX, J. L., and LAWRENCE, P. (1990). *Management in France*. London: Cassell.

BARZELAY, M. (1992). *Breaking Through Bureaucracy: A New Vision for Managing in Government*. Berkeley: University of California Press.

BASINI, B. (1994). 'Dossier: Le Consulting', *Le Nouvel Économiste*, 927/7 January: 71–5.

BASTON, L., and SELDON, A. (1996). 'Number 10 Under Edward Heath', in S. Ball and A. Seldon (eds.), *The Heath Government, 1970–74*. London: Longman, 47–74.

BEALE, D. (1994). *Driven by Nissan? A Critical Guide to the New Management Techniques*. London: Lawrence & Wishart.

BEC, J., GRANIER, F., and SINGERY, J. (1993). *Le consultant et le changement dans la Fonction publique*. Paris: L'Harmattan.

BEER, S. (1966). *Decision and Control: The Meaning of Operational Research and Management Cybernetics*. New York: John Wiley & Sons.

BEER, S. H. (1982). *Modern British Politics: A Study of Parties and Pressure Groups* (3rd edn.). London: Faber.

BELLAMY, C., and TAYLOR, J. A. (1998). *Governing in the Information Age.* Buckingham: Open University Press.

BELLON, M. (1983). 'La réforme administrative: Une utopie réaliste?', *La revue administrative,* 215: 505–8.

BELLOUBET-FRIER, N., and TIMSIT, G. (1993). 'Administration Transfigured: A New Administrative Paradigm?', *International Review of Administrative Sciences,* 59: 531–68.

BENEVISTE, G. (1977). *The Politics of Expertise* (2nd edn.). San Francisco: Boyd and Fraser.

BENNETT, C. (1991). 'Review Article: What is Policy Convergence and What Causes it?', *British Journal of Political Science,* 21: 215–33.

BERLINSKI, D. (1976). *On System Analysis.* Cambridge, MA: MIT Press.

BERNARD, P. (1983). *L'État et la décentralisation.* Paris: Documentation française.

BIRNBAUM, P. (1977). *Les Sommets de l'État.* Paris: Seuil.

—— (1978). *La classe dirigeante française.* Paris: Presses Universitaires de France.

—— (ed.) (1985). *Les élites socialistes au pouvoir.* Paris: Presses Universitaires de France.

BLACKABY, F. T. (1978). *British Economic Policy, 1960–74.* New York: Cambridge University Press.

BLACKBURN, G. A. (1969). 'A Bilingual and Bicultural Public Service', *Canadian Public Administration,* Spring, 12.

BLAIS, A., and DION, S. (eds.) (1991). *The Budget Maximizing Bureaucrat: Appraisals and Evidence,* Pittsburgh: University of Pittsburgh Press.

—— BLAKE, D. E., and DION, S. (1997). *Governments, Parties and Public Sector Employees.* Pittsburgh: University of Pittsburgh Press.

BLAKE, J., and AMAT, O. (1993). *European Accounting.* London: Pitman Publishing.

BLAU, P. M., and MEYER, M. W. (1987). *Bureaucracy in Modern Society* (3rd edn.). New York: Random House.

BLUMBERG, D. F. (1994). 'Marketing Consulting Services Using Public Relations Strategies', *Journal of Management Consulting,* 8/1: 42–8.

BLUMER, H. G. (1969). 'Fashion: From Class Differentiation to Collective Selection', *Sociological Quarterly,* 10: 275–91.

BLYMKE, O. (1995). 'Government Agency and Consultancy', in H. Von Weltzein Hoivik and A. Follesdal (eds.), *Ethics and Consultancy: European Perspectives.* Dordrecht: Kluwer, 128–35.

BODIGUEL, J. L. (1978). *Les anciens élèves de l'ÉNA.* Paris: Presses de la Fondation Nationale des Sciences Politiques.

—— (1992). 'Les centres de responsabilité ou l'imputabilité à la française', *Management,* 3: 4.

—— and ROUBAN, L. (1991). *Le fonctionnaire détrôné? L'État au risque de la modernisation.* Paris: Presses de la Fondation Nationale des Sciences Politiques.

BOISSARD, D., and LEMAITRE, D. (1989). 'Faut-il faire confiance aux consultants?', *Liaisons sociales* 39 (May): 48–50.

BOLTANSKI, L. (1987). *The Making of a Class: Cadres in French Society.* Cambridge: Cambridge University Press.

—— (1990). 'Visions of American Management in Postwar France', in S. Zukin and P. DiMaggio (eds.), *Structures of Capital.* Cambridge: Cambridge University Press.

Borins, S. (1988). 'Public Choice: Yes Minister Made It Popular But Does Winning the Nobel Prize Make it True?', *Canadian Public Administration*, 31: 12–26.

Boston, J. (1991). 'The Theoretical Underpinnings of Public Sector Restructuring in New Zealand', in J. Boston (ed.), *Reshaping the State: New Zealand Bureaucratic Revolution*. Auckland: Oxford University Press, 1–26.

—— (1994). 'Purchasing Policy Advice: The Limits to Contracting-Out', *Governance*, 7/1, January: 1–30.

—— Martin, J., Pallott, J., and Walsh, P. (eds.) (1996). *Public Management: The New Zealand Model*. Auckland: Oxford University Press.

Bothwell, R., Drummond, I., and English, J. (1981). *Canada Since 1945*. Toronto: Toronto University Press.

Bourdieu, P. (1989). *Noblesses d'Etat*. Paris: Editions de Minuit.

Braybrooke, D., and Lindblom, C. (1963). *A Strategy of Decision*. London: Free Press.

Bréaud, P. (1970). 'La rationalisation des choix budgétaires', *International Review of Administrative Sciences*, 36/4: 317–19.

—— and Gergorin, J. L. (1973). 'An Appraisal of Program Budgeting in France', in D. Novik (ed.), *Current Practice in Program Budgeting (PPBS)*. New York: Care and Russak, 111–18.

Brint, S. (1994). *In an Age of Experts: The Changing Role of Professionals in Politics and Public Life*. Princeton: Princeton University Press.

Briston, R. (1979). 'The UK Accounting Profession: The Move Towards Monopoly Power', *The Accountants Magazine*, November.

Brittan, S. (1970). *Steering the Economy: The Role of the Treasury*. London: Penguin Books.

Brodie, J., and Jenson, J. (1988). *Crisis, Challenge and Change: Party and Class in Canada Revisited*. Ottawa: Carleton University Press.

Brown, R. (1905). *A History of Accounting and Accountants*. Edinburgh: T. C. & E. C. Jack.

Bruce-Gardyne, J. (1974). *Whatever Happened to the Quiet Revolution?* London: Charles Knight & Co. Ltd.

Bruston, A. (1993). 'Table ronde: Le rôle des consultants dans la modernisation de la gestion publique', *Politiques et Management Public*, 11/1: 175–86.

Burdeau, F. (1989). *Histoire de l'Administration française du 18ᵉ au 20ᵉ siècle*. Paris: Monchrestien.

Burke, S. (1995). 'World Survey 1995', *Management Consultant International*, June: 10–15.

Burt, T. (1998). 'Management Consultancy: A Special Report', *Accountancy*, August: 94–100.

Busch, A. (1997). *Outsiders and Openness in the Presidential Nominating System*. Pittsburg: Pittsburg University Press.

Butler, D., and Pinto-Duschinsky, M. (1971). *The British General Election of 1970*. London: Macmillan and St. Martin's Press.

Butler, R. (1990). 'New Challenges or Familiar Prescriptions?', *The Radcliffe-Maud Memorial Lecture*. London: PA Consulting Group.

—— (1994). 'Reinventing British Government', *Public Administration*, 72/Summer: 263–70.

Cabinet Office (1998). *Service First: the New Charter Programme*. Office of the Public Service, June.

Cabinet Office, MPO (1983). *Civil Service Management Development in the 1980s*. London.

Cahiers français (1992). 'L'état de la décentralisation', 256/May–June. Paris: La documentation française.

CAIDEN, G. E. (1991). *Administrative Reform Comes of Age*. Berlin: Walter de Gruyter.

CAMPANELLA, M. L. (1993). 'The Effects of Globalization and Turbulence on Policy-Making Process', *Government and Opposition*, 28/2: 190–205.

CAMPBELL, C. (1983). *Governments Under Stress: Political Executives and Key Bureaucrats in Washington, London and Ottawa*. Toronto: University of Toronto Press.

—— and SZABLOWSKI, G. J. (1979). *The Super-Bureaucrats: Structure and Behaviour in Central Agencies*. Toronto: The Macmillan Company of Canada.

—— and WILSON, G. K. (1995). *The End of Whitehall: Death of a Paradigm?* Oxford: Blackwell.

—— and WYSZOMIRSKI, M. J. (eds.) (1991). *Executive Leadership in Anglo-American Systems*. Pittsburgh: University of Pittsburgh Press.

CAMPBELL, J. (1993). *Edward Heath: A Biography*. London: Jonathan Cape.

CAMPBELL, L. G. (1985). *International Auditing: A Comparative Survey of Professional Requirements in Australia, Canada, France, West Germany, Japan, The Netherlands, the UK and the USA*. London: Macmillan.

Canada (1962a). *The Royal Commission on Government Organization. Volume 1: Management of the Public Service*. Ottawa: The Queen's Printer. [The Glassco Report.]

—— (1962b). *The Royal Commission on Government Organization. Volume 5: The Organization of the Government of Canada*. Ottawa: The Queen's Printer. [The Glassco Report.]

—— (1975). *Report of the Independent Review Committee on the Office of the Auditor General of Canada*. Ottawa: Information Canada. [The Wilson Report.]

—— (1979). *Royal Commission on Financial Management and Accountability. Final Report*. Ottawa: Ministry of Supply and Services. [The Lambert Report.]

—— (1985). *New Management Initiatives: Initial Results from the Ministerial Task Force on Program Review*. Ottawa: Department of Finance, May.

—— (1986). *Task Force on Program Review. Introduction to the Process of Program Review*. Ottawa: Supply and Services Canada.

—— (1990). *Public Service 2000. The Renewal of the Public Service of Canada*. Ottawa: Supply and Services.

—— (1992). *Public Service 2000. A Report on Progress*. Ottawa: Supply and Services.

CCAF (1985). *Comprehensive Auditing in Canada: The Provincial Legislative Audit Perspective*. Ottawa: CCAF.

Canadian Study of Parliament Group (1992). *Year 7: A Review of the McGrath Report on the Reform of the House of Commons*. Proceedings, Ottawa, 2 December.

CAREW, A. (1987). *Labour Under the Marshall Plan*. Detroit: Wayne State University Press.

CAREY, J. (1969). *The Rise of the Accountancy Profession from Technical to Professional, 1896–1936*. New York: AICPA.

CARR, D. K., and LITTMAN, I. D. (1991). *Excellence in Government*. Washington: Coopers & Lybrand.

CARRINGTON, A. (1984). 'Accounting in Industrialized Commonwealth Countries: Canada, Australia, New Zealand and South Africa', in H. P. Holzer (ed.), *International Accounting*. New York: Harper & Row, 273–93.

CARTER, N. (1988). 'Performance Indicators: "Backseat Driving" or "Hands Off" Control?', *Policy and Politics*, 17/2: 131–8.

—— KLEIN, R., and DAY, P. (1992). *How Organizations Measure Success: The Use of Performance Indicators in Government*. London: Routledge.

CASTLES, F. G. (1993). *Family of Nations*. Dartmouth: Aldershot.

CHAMPY, J., and HAMMER, M. (1993). *Re-Engineering the Corporation*. London: Nicholas Brealey.

CHAN, J. L., and JONES, R. H. (1988). *Governmental Accounting and Auditing: International Comparisons*. London: Routledge.

CHANDLER, A. D. (1977). *The Visible Hand: The Managerial Revolution in American Business*. Cambridge, MA: The Belknap Press of Harvard University Press.

CHANNON, D. F. (1973). *The Strategy and Structure of British Enterprise*. Boston: Harvard Business School.

CHAPMAN, R. A. (1983). 'The Rise and Fall of the CSD', *Policy and Politics*, 11/1: 41–61.

—— (ed.) (1973). *The Role of Commissions in Policy-Making*. London: George Allen & Unwin.

CHATY, L. (1997). *L'Administration face au management*. Paris: L'Harmattan.

CHEADLE, N. (1994). 'The History and Growth of the Profession', in Institute of Management Consultants, *The Ivanhoe Career Guide to Management Consultants 1995*. London: Cambridge Market Intelligence Ltd., 7–11.

CHEVALIER, F. (1991). *Cercles de qualité et changement organisationnel*. Paris: Economica.

CHEVALLIER, J. (1988). 'Le discours de la qualité administrative', *Revue française d'Administration publique*, 46/April–June: 121–43.

—— (1996). 'Public Administration in Statist France', *Public Administration Review*, 56/1: 67–74.

—— and LOSCHAK, D. (1982). 'Rationalité juridique et rationalité managériale dans l'Administration francaise', *Revue française d'Administration publique*, 24/October–December: 53–92.

CHEVILLY, P. (1994). 'Andersen, Bossard et Peat Marwick en tête du marché français du conseil', *Les Échos*, 17 June.

CHIROT, F. (1993). 'Les élus se font conseiller', *Le Monde*, 11 October, 17.

CHRISTOPH, J. B. (1984). 'Rubbing Up or Running Down: Dilemmas of Civil Service Reform in Britain', in D. T. Studlar and J. L. Waltman (eds.), *Dilemmas of Change in British Politics*. Jackson: University Press of Mississippi, 48–68.

Citizen's Charter (1991). *Raising the Standards*. Presented to Parliament by the Prime Minister by Command of Her Majesty, July.

—— (1992). *The Citizen's Charter First Report: 1992*. Presented to Parliament by the Prime Minister and the Chancellor of the Duchy of Lancaster by Command of Her Majesty, November 1992. London: HMSO.

Civil Service Commission: CSC (1947). *Annual Report of the Civil Service Commission*. Ottawa: Queen's Printer.

Civil Service Department (1970a). *CSD News*, 1/4, March.

—— (1970b). *First Report of the Civil Service Department 1969*. London: HMSO.

—— (1972). *CSD News*, 3/2, February.

—— (1974). *Third Report of the Civil Service Department 1971–73*. London: HMSO.

CLAISSE, A. (1989). 'Question of Rolling Back the State in France', *Governance*, 2/2: 152–71.

CLARK, D. (1984*a*). 'The Citizen and the Administration in France—the Conseil d'État versus Ombudsman Debate Revisited', *Public Administration*, 62/Summer: 161–79.

—— (1984*b*). 'The Ombudsman in Britain and France: A Comparative Evaluation', *Western European Politics*, 7/3: 64–85.

—— (1998). 'The Modernization of the French Civil Service', *Public Administration*, 76/Spring: 97–115.

CLARK, I. D. (1991–2). 'Special Operating Agencies: The Challenges of Innovation', *Optimum*, 22/2: 13–19.

CLARK, T. (1995). *Managing Consultants: Consultancy as the Management of Impressions*. Buckingham: Open University Press.

CLARKE, J., and NEWMAN, J. (1997). *The Managerial State*. London: Sage.

CLEGG, S. R., and PALMER, G. (1996). *The Politics of Management Knowledge*. London: Sage.

CLEVELAND, H. (1987). 'The Twilight of Hierarchy: Speculations on the Global Information Society', *International Journal of Technology Management*, 2/1: 45–60.

CLIFF, T. (1988). *The Labour Party: A Marxist History*. London: Bookmarks.

Cmnd 4506 (1970). *The Reorganisation of Central Government*. London: HMSO.

Cmnd 8616 (1982). *Efficiency and Effectiveness in the Civil Service: Government Observations on the 3rd Report of the Treasury and Civil Service Committee HC 236*. London: HMSO.

COHEN, S. S. (1977). *Modern Capitalist Planning: The French Model*. Berkeley: University of California Press.

COLEMAN, W. D. (1994). 'Policy Convergence in Banking: a Comparative Study', *Political Studies*, XLII: 274–92.

—— and SKOGSTAD, G. (1990). *Policy Communities and Public Policy in Canada: A Structural Approach*. Mississauga: Copp Clark Pitman Ltd.

COLLARD, E. A. (1980). *First in North America, One Hundred Years in the Life of the Ordre des Comptables Agréés du Québec*. Montreal: Ordre des Comptables Agréés du Québec.

COLLIGNON, E., and WISSLER, M. (1988). *Qualité et compétitivité des entreprises*. Paris: Economica.

COLLIS, D. J. (1994). 'The Management Consulting Industry', in W. C. Chan (ed.), *Management Consulting 1994*. Harvard Business School Career Guide. Boston: Harvard Business School Press, 1–5.

Commissariat général du Plan (1991). *Outils, pratiques, institutions pour évaluer les politiques publiques*. Paris: La documentation française.

Comptroller General (1981). *Program Evaluation Newsletter*, 1: November.

—— (1983). *Program Evaluation Newsletter*, 7: September.

Conservative Central Office (1970). *A New Style of Government*. London.

CONSIDINE, M. (1990). 'Managerialism Strikes Out', *Australian Journal of Public Administration*, 49/2, June: 166–78.

COOPER, D., PUXTY, T., LOWE, T., and WILLMOTT, H. (1990). 'The Accounting Profession, Corporatism and the State', in W. F. Chua, T. Lowe, and T. Puxton (eds.), *Critical Perspectives in Management Control*. London: Macmillan, 245–70.

COOPER, P. J. (1995). 'Accountability and Administrative Reform: Toward Convergence and Beyond', in B. G. Peters and D. J. Savoie (eds.), *Governance in a Changing Environment*. Montreal and Kingston: McGill-Queen's University Press, 173–202.

CORNEILLE, J. (1994). 'Pros and Cons of Public Duties', *Management Consultancy*, March: 27.

CRAWFORD, J. (1991). 'French Consultancies Continue to Prosper', *Management Consultant International*, May: 11–15.

CSD. See Civil Service Department.

CROZIER, M. (1973). *The Stalled Society*. New York: Viking Press.

—— (1988). *Comment reformer l'Etat? Trois pays, trois stratégies: Suède, Japon, Etats-Unis. Rapport au ministre de la Fonction publique et des Réformes administratives*. Paris: La documentation française.

CUTLER, T., and PAYNE, B. (1994). *Managing the Welfare State: The Politics of Public Sector Management*. London: Berg.

DAVIDSON, F. (1972). *Management Consultants*. London: Nelson.

DAVIDSON, R., and LOWE, R. (1981). 'Bureaucracy and Innovation in British Welfare Policy', in W. J. Mommsen (ed.), *The Emergence of the Welfare State in Britain and Germany*. London: Croom Helm, 264–77.

DAWSON, R. M. (1929). *The Civil Service of Canada*. London: Oxford University Press.

DERLIEN, H. U. (1990). 'Genesis and Structure of Evaluation Efforts in Comparative Perspective', in C. Rist (ed.), *Program Evaluation and the Management of Government*. New Brunswick: Transaction Publishers, 147–76.

—— (1992). 'Observations on the State of Comparative Administration Research in Europe—Rather Comparable than Comparative', *Governance*, 5/3: 279–311.

DESCHEEMAEKER, C. (1992). *La Cour des comptes. Notes et études documentaires*. Paris: La documentation française.

DESPATIS, J., and TUNNEY, T. (1987). *Public Accounting and Management Consulting Industries. Report on Exploratory Research*. Ottawa: Statistics Canada.

DGAFP: Direction Générale de L'Administration et de la Fonction Publique (1991). *Consultants internes dans L'Administration. Groupe de modernisation consultants internes dans l'Administration*. January. Paris.

—— (1993). *Complémentarités des fonctions d'inspection et de conseil dans la modernisation des services publics*. November. Paris.

DION, S. (1986). *La politisation des mairies*. Paris: Économica.

DJELIC, M. L. (1998). *Exporting the American Model*. Oxford: Oxford University Press.

DOBELL, R., and STEENKAMP, P. (1993). 'Preface to the Symposium on Public Management in a Borderless Economy', *International Review of Administrative Sciences*, 59: 569–77.

DOERN, G. B. (1971). 'The Budgetary Process and the Policy Role of the Federal Bureaucracy', in G. B. Doern and P. Aucoin (eds.), *The Structures of Policy-Making in Canada*. Toronto: Macmillan of Canada, 79–112.

—— (1993). 'Efficiency-Democracy Bargains in the Reinvention of Federal Government Organization', in S. D. Philips (ed.), *How Ottawa Spends 1993–94: A More Democratic Canada . . . ?* Ottawa: Carleton University Press, 203–30.

DONOUGHUE, B. (1986). *Prime Minister*. Oxford: Basil Blackwell.

DREWRY, G., and BUTCHER, T. (1991). *The Civil Service Today* (2nd edn.). Oxford: Basil Blackwell.

DREYFUS, F. (1990). 'The Controls of Government', in P. Hall, J. Hayward, and H. Machin (eds.), *Developments in French Politics*. London: George Allen & Unwin, 133–51.

DUCROS, J. C. (1976). 'The Influence of RCB on Parliament's Role in Budgetary Affairs', in D. Coombes (ed.), *The Power of the Purse: The Role of European Parliaments in Budgetary Decisions*. London: George Allen & Unwin, 148–162.

DUNLEAVY, P. (1991). *Democracy, Bureaucracy and Public Choice*. London: Harvester Wheatsheaf.

—— and HOOD, C. (1994). 'From Old Public Administration to the New Public Management', *Public Money and Management*, July–September: 9–16.

—— and RHODES, R. A. W. (1990). 'Core Executive Studies in Britain', *Public Administration*, 68/1: 3–28.

DURUPTY, M. (1988). *Les privatisations*. Paris: La documentation française.

DWYER, A., and HARDING, F. (1996). 'Using Ideas to Increase the Marketability of Your Firm', *Journal of Management Consulting*, 9/2: 56–61.

DYAS, G. P., and THANHEISER, H. T. (1976). *The Emerging European Enterprise: Strategy and Structure in French and German Industry*. Boulder: Westview Press.

DYSON, K. J. (1980). *The State Tradition in Western Europe*. New York: Oxford University Press.

Economist, The (1992). 'Accountancy: All Change'. 17 October: 19–21.

—— (1995). 'Manufacturing Best-Sellers: A Scam Over a "Best-Selling" Business Book Shows How Obsessed Management Consultancies Have Become with Producing the Next Big Idea'. 5 August: 57.

—— (1997). 'Management Consulting: Spouse Trouble'. 7 June: 64–5.

EDEY, H. C., and PANITPAKDI, P. (1956). 'British Company Accounting and the Law 1844–1900', in A. C. Littleton and B. S. Yamey (eds.), *Studies in the History of Accounting*. Homewood: Richard D. Irwin Inc., 356.

EFFICIENCY UNIT (1994). *The Government's Use of External Consultants*. London: HMSO. [The Ibbs Report.]

ELSE, P. (1970). *Public Expenditure, Parliament and PPB*. London: George Berridge & Co.

ENTEMAN, W. F. (1993). *Managerialism: The Emergence of a New Ideology*. Wisconsin: University of Wisconsin Press.

ESTRIN, S., and HOLMES, P. (1983). *French Planning in Theory and Practice*. London: George Allen & Unwin.

EZRAHI, Y. (1990). *The Descent of Icarus: Science and the Transformation of Contemporary Democracy*. Cambridge MA: Harvard University Press.

Fabian Society (1964). *The Administrators: The Reform of the Civil Service*. Fabian Tract No. 355. London.

FARNHAM, D., and HORTON, S. (eds.). (1993). *Managing the New Public Service*. London: Macmillan.

FEACO: Fédération Européenne des Conseils en Organisation (1999a). 'The 1998 Report on European Management Consulting Market', *Points of Interest*, 2/Summer.

—— (1999b). *Survey of the European Management Consultancy Market*, 1998. Brussels.

FIALAIRE, J. (1993). 'Les stratégies de mise en oeuvre des centres de responsabilité', *Politiques et management public*, 11/2: 33–49.

FLYNN, A., GRAY, A., JENKINS, W. I., RUTHERFORD, B., and PLOWDEN, W. (1988). 'Accountable Management in British Government: Some Reflections on the Official Record', *Financial Accountability and Management*, 4/3, Autumn: 169–89.

FLYNN, G. (ed.) (1995). *Remaking the Hexagon: The New France in the New Europe*. Boulder: Westview Press.

FOLEY, M. (1993). *The Rise of the British Presidency*. Manchester: Manchester University Press.

Foreign & Commonwealth Office (1992). *Raising the Standard: Britain's Citizen's Charter and Public Service Reforms*. London: HMSO.

FORRESTER, D. A. R. (1985). 'Aspects of French Accounting History', *Working Paper of the Academy of Accounting Historians*, 64: 56–81.

FORTIN, Y. (1988). 'Reflections on Public Administration in France, 1986–87', *Governance*, 1/1: 101–10.

FOSTER, C. D., and PLOWDEN, F. J. (1996). *The State Under Stress*. Buckingham: Open University Press.

FRANKS, C. E. S. (1987). *The Parliament of Canada*. Toronto: Toronto University Press.

—— (1997). 'Not Anonymous: Ministerial Responsibility and British Accounting Officers', *Canadian Public Administration*, 4/4: 626–52.

FRY, G. (1984). 'The Development of the Thatcher Government's Grand Strategy for the Civil Service', *Public Administration*, 62/4: 322–35.

FRY, G. K. (1993). *Reforming the Civil Service: The Fulton Committee on the Home Civil Service of 1966–1968*. Edinburgh: Edinburgh University Press.

FULTON, LORD (1968a). *The Civil Service. Volume 1. Report of the Committee 1966–68*. Cmnd. 3638. London: HMSO.

—— (1968b). *The Civil Service. Volume 2. Report of a Management Consultancy Group*. Cmnd. 3638. London: HMSO.

—— (1968c). *The Civil Service. Volume 4. Factual, Statistical and Exploratory Papers*. Cmnd. 3638. London: HMSO.

FURNER, M. O., and SUPPLE, B. (1990). *The State and Economic Knowledge*. Cambridge: Cambridge University Press.

GAGNON, A. G., and TANGUAY, A. B. (1989). *Canadian Parties in Transition*. Scarborough: Nelson Canada.

GAMBLE, A. (1988). *The Free Economy and the Strong State*. London: Macmillan.

GARRETT, J. (1972). *The Management of Government*. London: Pelican Books.

—— (1980). *Managing the Civil Service*. London: Heinemann.

—— (1986). 'Developing State Audit in Britain', *Public Administration*, 64.

GASTOU, G., and THÉVENET, M. (1990). 'La relation conseil-entreprise et son évolution', *Problèmes économiques*, 2/159, January: 24–8.

GEISON, G. L. (1984). *Professions and the French State 1700–1900*. Philadelphia: University of Philadelphia Press.

GERTH, H. H., and MILLS, C. W. (1946). *From Max Weber: Essays in Sociology*. New York: Oxford University Press.

GLADDEN, E. N. (1972). *Central Government Administration*. London: Staples Press.

GLASSCO COMMISSION REPORT. See Canada (1962a, 1962b).

GOLDSTEIN, J. (1989). 'The Impact of Ideas on Trade Policy: The Origins of U.S. Agricultural and Manufacturing Policies', *International Organization*, 43/Winter: 31–71.

—— (1993). *Ideas, Interests, and American Trade Policy*. Ithaca: Cornell University Press.

GOLEMBIEWSKI, R. T. (ed.) (1993). *Handbook of Organizational Consultation*. New York: Marcel Dekker.

GOLLNER, A. B., and SALÉE, D. (eds.) (1988). *Canada Under Mulroney*. Montreal: Véhicule Press.

GOOD, D. (1993). 'Reinventing Government: Innovating to Serve Canadians Better', paper presented to the Canadian Center for Management Development's Annual University Seminar, 19 February.

GOPALAN, S. (1986). 'Bouquets and Brickbats for Accountant Consultancies', *The Accountant*, 3 March, 194/5774, 10–11.

GOUREVITCH, P. (1989). 'Keynesian Politics: The Political Sources of Economic Policy Choices', in P. A. Hall (ed.), *The Political Power of Economic Ideas*. Princeton, NJ: Princeton University Press, 87–106.

Government of Canada (1969). *Planning Programming Budgeting Guide*. Ottawa: President of the Treasury Board.

Government Statistical Service (1998). *Civil Service Statistics 1998*. London: HMSO.

GOW, J. I. (1994). *Learning from Others: Administrative Innovations Among Canadian Governments*. Ottawa: Canadian Center for Management Development.

GRANATSTEIN, J. L. (1982). *The Ottawa Men*. Toronto: Oxford University Press.

GRANT, W. (1987). *Business Interests, Organizational Development and Private Interest Government*. Berlin: Walter de Gruyter.

GRAY, A., and JENKINS, B. (1993). 'Markets, Managers and the Public Service: The Changing of a Culture', in P. Taylor-Gooby and R. Lawson (eds.), *Markets and Managers. New Issues in the Delivery of Welfare*. Buckingham: Open University Press, 9–23.

GRAY, A., and JENKINS, W. I. (1985). *Administrative Politics in British Government*. Sussex: Wheatsheaf Books.

GRAY, A., JENKINS, B., FLYNN, A., and RUTHERFORD, B. (1991). 'The Management of Change in Whitehall: The Experience of the FMI', *Public Administration*, 69/1: 41–59.

GREBENIK, E. (1972). 'The Civil Service College: The First Year', *Public Administration*, 50/Summer: 127–38.

GREEN, D. (1980). 'The Budget and the Plan', in P. G. Cerny and M. A. Schain (eds.), *French Politics and Public Policy*. London: Frances Pinter, 101–25.

GREENWOOD, J., and WILSON, D. (1989). *Public Administration in Britain Today* (2nd edn.). London: Unwin Hyman.

GREER, P. (1994). *Transforming Central Government: The Next Steps Initiative*. Buckingham: Open University Press.

GRÉMION, C. (1979). 'De Gaulle et la réforme administrative', in G. Pilleul (ed.), *'L'Entourage' et de Gaulle*. Paris: Plon, 200–9.

—— (1982). 'Le mileu décisionnel central', in F. de Baecque and J. L. Quermonne (eds.), *Administration et politique sous la Cinquième République*. Paris: Presses de la Fondation Nationale des Sciences Politiques, 205–25.

GRÉMION, P. (1976). *Le pouvoir périphérique*. Paris: Seuil.

GUESLIN, A. (1992). *L'Etat, l'économie et la société française, XIXe–XXe siècle*. Paris: Hachette.

GUILLÉN, M. F. (1994). *Models of Management*. Chicago: University of Chicago Press.

GUTTMAN, D., and WILLNER, B. (1976). *The Shadow Government: The Government's Multi-Billion Dollar Giveaway of its Decision-Making Powers to Private Management Consultants, 'Experts', and Think Tanks*. New York: Pantheon Books.

HABER, S. (1964). *Efficiency and Uplift: Scientific Management in the Progressive Era*. Chicago: University of Chicago Press.

HALL, P. A. (1983). 'Policy Innovation and the Structure of the State: The Politics-Administration Nexus in France and Britain', *Annals*, 466/March: 43–59.

—— (1986). *Governing the Economy. The Politics of State Intervention in Britain and France*. New York: Oxford University Press.

—— (ed.) (1989). *The Political Power of Economic Ideas. Keynesianism Across Nations*. Princeton: Princeton University Press.

—— (1990a). 'Policy Paradigms, Experts and the State', in S. Brooks and A. G. Gagnon (eds.), *Social Scientists, Policy and the State*. New York: Praeger, 53–78.

—— (1990b). 'The State and the Market', in P. A. Hall, J. Hayward, and H. Machin (eds.), *Developments in French Politics*. London: Macmillan, 171–87.

HALLIGAN, J. (1995). 'Policy Advice and the Public Service', in B. G. Peters and D. J. Savoie (eds.), *Governance in a Changing Environment*. Montreal and Kingston: McGill-Queen's University Press, 138–72.

—— (1996). 'The Diffusion of Civil Service Reform', in H. A. G. M. Bekke, J. L. Perry, and T. A. J. Toonen (eds.), *Civil Service Systems in Comparative Perspective*. Indianapolis: Indiana University Press, 288–317.

HALLORAN, P., and HOLLINGWORTH, M. (1994). *A Bit on the Side: Politicians and Who Pays Them? An Insider's Guide*. London: Simon & Schuster.

HANLON, G. (1994). *The Commercialisation of Accountancy*. London: Macmillan.

HARTLE, D. G. (1979). 'The Lambert Report', *Canadian Public Policy*, 3/Summer: 366–82.

HARTLE, T. W. (1985). 'Sisyphus Re-Visited: Running the Government Like a Business', *Public Administration Review*, 45/2: 341–51.

HAYWARD, J. (1973). *The One and Indivisible French Republic*. London: Weidenfeld & Nicolson.

—— (1986). *The State and the Market Economy: Industrial Patriotism and Economic Intervention in France*. Brighton: Wheatsheaf Books.

HAYZELDEN, J. E. (1972). 'An Insider's View of Management Consultancy', *O&M Bulletin*, 27/1: 21–6.

HC [House of Commons] 588, 1986–87. *The Financial Management Initiative. Report by Comptroller & Auditor General, National Audit Office*. London: HMSO.

HEADY, B. (1974). *British Cabinet Ministers*. London: Unwin.

HECLO, H. and WILDAVSKY, A. (1981). *The Private Government of Public Money*. London: Macmillan.

HEINTZMAN, R. (1993). 'A Word from the CCMD', in D. J. Savoie (ed.), *Globalization and Governance*. Ottawa: Canadian Center for Management Development.

HENCKE, D. (1994). '£65 is wasted on Whitehall Consultants', *Manchester Guardian Weekly*, 14 August: 10.

HENKEL, M. (1991a). *Government, Evaluation and Change*. London: Jessica Kingsley.

—— (1991b). 'The New Evaluative State', *Public Administration*, 69/Spring: 121–36.

HENNESSY, P. (1986). *Cabinet*. Oxford: Basil Blackwell.

—— (1989). *Whitehall*. London: Secker & Warburg.

HENRY, O. (1994). 'Le conseil, un espace professionnel autonome?', *Entreprises et Histoire*, 7: 37–58.

HESELTINE, M. (1987). *Where There's a Will*. London: Hutchinson.

HIGDON, H. (1969). *The Business Healers*. New York: Random House.

HINRICHS, H. H., and TAYLOR, G. M. (eds.) (1969). *Program Budgeting and Cost Benefit Analysis*. Pacific Palisades: Goodyear Publishing Co.

HIRSCH, P. M. (1972). 'Processing Fads and Fashion: An Organizational Analysis of Cultural Industry Systems', *American Journal of Sociology*, 77: 639–59.

HM Treasury (1990). *Seeking help from Management Consultants*. Accountancy Advice Division of HM Treasury. London.

—— (1991). *Competing for Quality*. Presented to Parliament by the Chancellor of the Exchequer by Command of Her Majesty, November, Cm 1730. London: HMSO.

HODGETTS, J. E. (1973). *The Canadian Public Service: A Physiology of Government, 1867–1970*. Toronto: University of Toronto Press.

—— McCLOSKEY, W., WHITAKER, R., and WILSON, V. S. (1972). *The Biography of an Institution: The Civil Service Commission of Canada, 1908–1967*. Montreal: McGill-Queen's University Press.

HOLMES, M. (1992). 'Public Sector Management Reform: Convergence or Divergence?', *Governance*, 5/4: 472–83.

HOOD, C. (1990). 'De-Sir Humphreyfying the Westminster Model of Bureaucracy: A New Style of Governance?', *Governance*, 3/2: 205–14.

—— (1991). 'A Public Management for All Seasons?', *Public Administration*, 69/Spring: 3–19.

—— (1994). *Explaining Economic Policy Reversals*. Buckingham: Open University Press.

—— (1995). 'Contemporary Public Management: A New Global Paradigm?', *Public Administration*, 76/Spring: 97–115.

—— (1996). 'Exploring Variations in Public Management Reform of the 1980s', in H. A. G. M. Bekke, J. L. Perry, and T. A. J. Toonen (eds.), *Civil Service Systems in Comparative Perspective*. Indianapolis: Indiana University Press, 268–87.

—— (1999). 'Deprivileging the UK Civil Service in the 1980s: Dreams or Reality?', in J. Pierre (ed.), *Bureaucracy in the Modern State*. Cheltenham: Edward Elgar, 118–39.

—— DUNSIRE, A., and THOMSON, L. (1988). 'Rolling Back the State: Thatcherism, Fraserism and Bureaucracy', *Governance*, 3/2: 205–14.

—— JACKSON, M. (1991). *Administrative Argument*. Aldershot: Dartmouth.

HOOK, K. (1994). 'The Institute and the Profession', in 'The Institute of Management Consultants', *The Ivanhoe Career Guide to Management Consultants 1995*. London: Cambridge Market Intelligence Ltd., 22–25.

HORN, M. (1995). *The Political Economy of Public Administration*. Cambridge: Cambridge University Press.

HOSKING, P. (1987). 'Consultants Take Giant Stride in Popularity', *The Independent*, 23 April.

HOUSE, E. R. (1993). *Professional Evaluation: Social Impact and Political Consequences*. Newbury Park: Sage Publication.

House of Commons [Canada] (1976). *House of Commons Debates*. Ottawa. 22 November.

—— (1982). *Minutes of Proceedings and Evidence of the Special Committee on Standing Orders and Procedure*, Issue No. 5, 13 July: 59. Ottawa.

—— (1985). *Report of the Special Committee on Reform of the House of Commons: Third Report*. Ottawa: Queen's Printer, June.

—— (1992a). *Minutes of Proceedings and Evidence of the Standing Committee on Public Accounts*, Issue No. 26, 12 May: 10. Ottawa.

—— (1992b). *Minutes of Proceedings and Evidence of the Standing Committee on Public Accounts*, Issue No. 27, 14 May: 5. Ottawa.

House of Commons [UK] (1986). *Thirty-Ninth Report from the Committee of Public Accounts. The Rayner Scrutiny Programme.* Session 1985–86. House of Commons Parliamentary Paper No. 365. London.

—— (1993). *Treasury and Civil Service Committee. The Role of the Civil Service. Minutes of Evidence.* 27 April: 53. London.

House of Commons Debates [UK] (1966). *Debates 5s cols. 209–10.* London.

Huet, P. (1970). 'The Rationalization of Budget Choices in France', *Public Administration,* 48: 273–89.

—— and Bravo, J. (1973). *L'expérience française de rationalisation des choix budgétaires.* Paris: Presses Universitaires de France.

Hughes, A. (1993). 'Big Business, Small Business and the "Enterprise Culture"', in J. Michie (ed.), *The Economic Legacy, 1979–1992.* London: Harcourt, Brace Jovanovich, 296–311.

Hughes, O. (1994). *Public Management & Administration: An Introduction.* London: Macmillan.

Hunt, N. C. (1964). *Whitehall and Beyond.* London: BBC.

Hussein, M. E., and Ketz, J. (1980). 'Ruling Elites of the FASB: A Study of the Big Eight', *Journal of Accounting, Auditing and Finance,* 354–67.

Ibbs Report. See Efficiency Unit.

ICMCC: Institute of Certified Management Consultants of Canada (1995). *Consulting Industry Survey.* Toronto, September.

Immergut, E. M. (1992). *Health Politics: Interests and Institutions in Western Europe.* Cambridge: Cambridge University Press.

Industry Canada (1997). *Key Points About the Management Consulting Industry.* Retrieved from the Internet: http//info.ic.gc.ca/ic-data. See 'Strategis' Program.

Institute of Management Consultants (1994). *The Ivanhoe Career Guide to Management Consultants 1995.* London: Cambridge Market Intelligence.

Institute of Public Administration (1970). *Consultants in Public Administration.* Seminar Proceedings, Toronto Regional Group.

ISÉOR: Institut de Socio-Économie des Entreprises et des Organisations (1993). *Évolution de l'export-comptable: Le conseil en management.* Paris: Economica.

ISTC: Industry, Science and Technology Canada (1991a). *Management Consultants: Industry Profile.* Ottawa.

—— (1991b). *Public Accounting.* Ottawa.

James, M. (1994). 'Heavyweights in a League of Their Own', *Management Consultancy,* April: 36–8.

Jarrett, G. M. (1998). 'Consultancy in the Public Sector', in P. Sadler (ed.), *Management Consultancy: A Handbook for Best Practices.* London: Kogan Page, 369–83.

Jeans, M. (1993). 'Management Consultancy: Past, Present and Future', *Consult,* November: 16–18.

Jenkins, K., Caines, K., and Jackson, A. (1988). *Improving Management in Government: The Next Steps.* Efficiency Unit. London: HMSO.

Jenkins, P. (1987). *Mrs. Thatcher's Revolution: The Ending of the Socialist Era.* Cambridge MA: Harvard University Press.

Jenkins, W., and Gray, A. (1990). 'Policy Evaluation in British Government: From Idealism to Realism?', in R. C. Rist (ed.), *Program Evaluation and the Management of Government.* New Brunswick: Transaction Publishers, 53–70.

JENSON, J. (1986). 'Gender and Reproduction, or Babies and the State', *Studies in Political Economy*, 20 Summer: 9–46.

—— (1991*a*). 'All the World's a Stage: Ideas, Space and Time in Canadian Political Economy', *Studies in Political Economy*, 36/Fall: 43–72.

—— (1991*b*). 'The French Left: A Tale of Three Beginnings', in J. F. Hollifield and G. Ross (eds.), *Searching for the New France*. New York: Routledge, 85–112.

—— (1994). 'Commissioning Ideas: Representation and Royal Commissions', in S. D. Philips (ed.), *How Ottawa Spends 1994–95*. Ottawa: Carleton University Press, 39–70.

JESSOP, B. (1993). 'Towards a Schumpeterian Workfare State? Preliminary Remarks on Post-Fordist Political Economy', *Studies in Political Economy*, 40/Spring: 7–40.

JOHNMAN, L. (1993). 'The Conservative Party in Opposition, 1964–1970', in R. Coopey, S. Fielding, and N. Tiratsoo (eds.), *The Wilson Governments 1964–1970*. London: Pinter Publishers, 184–206.

JOHNSON, A. W. (1963). 'Efficiency in Business and Government', *Canadian Public Administration*, 6: 145–260.

—— (1992). *Reflections on Administrative Reform in the Government of Canada, 1962–1991*. Ottawa: Office of the Auditor General of Canada.

JONES, B., and KEATING, M. (1985). *Labour and the British State*. Oxford: Clarendon Press.

JONES, C. O. (1994). *The Presidency in a Separated System*. Washington: The Brookings Institution.

JONES, E. (1981). *Accountancy and the British Economy 1840–1980*. London: B. T. Batsford.

JONES, G. W. (1987). 'The United Kingdom', in W. Plowden (ed.), *Advising the Rulers*. London: Basil Blackwell, 36–65.

—— (1991). 'Presidentialization in a Parliamentary System?', in S. J. Campbell and M. J. Wyszomirski (eds.), *Executive Leadership in Anglo-American Systems*. Pittsburgh: University of Pittsburgh Press, 111–38.

JONES, R. (1970). 'Towards a Businesslike Government', *The Times*, 3 August: 19.

JUDGE, D. (1993). *The Parliamentary State*. London: Sage.

JURAN, J., and GRYNA, F. M. (1988). *Juran's Quality Control Handbook* (4th edn.). New York: McGraw-Hill.

KAMENSKY, J. (1996). 'The Role of the "Reinventing Government" Movement', *Public Administration Review*, 56/3: 247–55.

KATZENSTEIN, P. (ed.) (1978). *Between Power and Plenty*. Cambridge: Cambridge University Press.

KAVANAGH, D. (1987*a*). 'The Heath Government, 1970–1974', in P. Hennessy and A. Seldon (eds.), *Ruling Performance: British Governments from Attlee to Thatcher*. Oxford: Basil Blackwell, 216–40.

—— (1987*b*). *Thatcherism and British Politics*. Oxford: Oxford University Press.

KELLNER, H., and HEUBERGER, F. W. (1992). *Hidden Technocrats*. New Brunswick: Transaction.

KELLNER, P., and CROWTHER-HUNT, L. (1980). *The Civil Servants: An Inquiry into Britain's Ruling Class*. London: Macdonald.

Kennedy Research Group (1999). *The Global Management Consulting Marketplace: Key Data, Forecast, and Trends*. Fitzwilliam: Kennedy Research Group.

KEPOS, P. (ed.) (1994). *International Directory of Company Histories*. Volume 9. Detroit: St. James Press.

KERNAGHAN, K. (1992). 'Empowerment and Public Administration: Revolutionary Advance or Passing Fancy?', *Canadian Public Administration*, 33/2: 194–214.

—— Siegel, D. (1991). *Public Administration in Canada*. Toronto: Methuen.

KESSLER, M. C. (1986). *Les grands corps de l'État*. Paris: Presses de la Fondation Nationale des Sciences Politiques.

KESSLER, P., and TIXIT, F. (1973). *Les budgets de programmes*. Paris: Berger-Levrault.

KETTL, D. F. (1997). 'The Global Revolution in Public Management: Driving Themes, Missing Links', *Journal of Policy Analysis and Management*, 16/3: 446–62.

KICKERT, W. J. M. (1997). *Public Management and Administrative Reform in Western Europe*. Cheltenham: Edward Elgar.

KILEEN, R. (1994). 'France endures another sluggish year', *Management Consultant International*, April.

KINARD, J. C. (1986). 'The Management Consulting Profession and Advisory Services', in S. W. Barcus and J. W. Wilkinson (eds.), *Handbook of Management Consulting Services*. New York: McGraw-Hill, 17–35.

KING, A. (1975) 'Overload: Problems of Governing in the 1970s', *Political Studies*, 22/2–3: 284–96.

—— (ed.) (1985). *The British Prime Minister* (2nd edn.). Raleigh: Duke University Press.

KING, D. S. (1987). *The New Right*. London: Macmillan.

KINGDON, J. W. (1994). 'Agendas, Ideas and Policy Changes', in L. C. Dodd and C. Jillson (eds.), *New Perspectives on American Politics*. Washington: CQ Press, 215–29.

KIPPING, M. (1996). 'The U.S. Influence on the Evolution of Management Consultancies in Britain, France and Germany since 1945', *Business and Economic History*, 25/1.

—— (1997). 'Consultancies, Institutions and the Diffusion of Taylorism in Britain, Germany and France, 1920s to 1950s', *Business History*, 39/4: 67–83.

KIRKPATRICK, I., WHIPP, R., and DAVIES, A. (1996). 'New Public Management and Professions', in I. Glover and M. Hughes (eds.), *The Professional-Managerial Class*. Aldershot: Avebury, 195–216.

KLEIN, H. (1977). *Other People's Business: A Primer on Management Consultants*. New York: Mason/Charter Publishers Inc.

KNAPP, A. (1991). 'The Cumul des mandats, Local Power and Political Parties in France', *West European Politics*, 14/1: 18–40.

KNOKE, D., PAPPI, F. U., BROADBENT, J., and TSUJINAKA, Y. (1996). *Comparing Policy Networks*. Cambridge: Cambridge University Press.

KNOTT, J., and MILLER, G. J. (1987). *Reforming Bureaucracy: The Politics of Institutional Choice*. Englewood Cliffs: Prentice-Hall.

KRAMER, F. A. (1983). 'Public Management in the 1980s and Beyond', *Annals, AAPSS*, 466/March: 91–102.

KUBR, M. (1986). *Management Consulting: A Guide to the Profession* (2nd edn.). Geneva: International Labor Office.

—— (1993). *How to Select and Use Consultants*. Geneva: International Labor Office.

KUISEL, R. (1981). *Capitalism and the State in Modern France*. New York: Cambridge University Press.

—— (1993). *Seducing the French: The Dilemma of Americanization*. Berkeley: University of California Press.

KYMLICKA, B. B., and MATTHEWS, J. V. (1988). *The Reagan Revolution?* Chicago: Dorsey Press.

Labour Party (1964). *Labour Party Manifesto, 1964.* London.

Labour Research Department (1988). *Management Consultants: Who They Are and How to Deal With Them.* London: LRD.

LACAM, J.-P. (1994). 'Haute fonction publique et politique', *Regards sur l'Actualité,* 204/Sept.–Oct.: 25–44.

LAFFERTY, M. (1975). *Accounting in Europe.* London: Woodhead-Faulkner Ltd.

La Gazette. (1993). Quand le consultant passe de l'interne à l'externe', 18 January: 33.

LAMARQUE, G. (1996). 'Le rôle des agences de conseil', *Pouvoirs,* 79: 121–33.

Lambert Report. See Canada (1979).

LAN, Z., and ROSENBLOOM, D. H. (1992). 'Editorial', *Public Administration Review,* 52/6.

LANZA, A. (1968). *Les projects de réforme administrative en France de 1919 à nos jours.* Paris: Presses Universitaires de France.

LARSON, M. S. (1984). 'The Production of Expertise and the Constitution of Expert Power', in T. L. Haskell (ed.), *The Authority of Experts.* Bloomington: Indiana University Press, 28–83.

LASSERRE, B., LENOIR, N., and STIRN, B. (1987). *La transparence administrative.* Paris: Presses Universitaires de France.

LAUBER, V. (1983). *The Political Economy of France.* New York: Praeger.

LAUMANN, E. O., and KNOKE, D. (1987). *The Organizational State.* Madison: University of Wisconsin Press.

LAVER, M. J., and BUDGE, I. (1992). *Party Policy and Government Coalitions.* London: Macmillan.

LAYCOCK, D. (1990). *Populism and Democratic Thought in the Canadian Prairies, 1910 to 1945.* Toronto: University of Toronto Press.

LEACH, C. W. (1976). *Coopers & Lybrand in Canada.* Toronto: Coopers & Lybrand Canada.

LEE, G. A. (1984). 'Accounting in the United Kingdom', in H. P. Holzer (ed.), *International Accounting.* New York: Harper & Row, 253–71.

LEGENDRE, P. (1968). *Histoire de l'Administration de 1750 à nos jours.* Paris: Presses Universitaires de France.

LERUEZ, J. (1975). *Economic Planning and Politics in Britain.* London: Martin Robertson.

LESTER, T. (1970). 'Businessmen in Government', *Management Today,* January: 49–51.

LEVITAS, R. (ed.) (1986). *The Ideology of the New Right.* Cambridge: Policy Press.

LÉVY-LAMBERT, H., and GUILLAUME, H. (1971). *La Rationalisation des Choix Budgétaires.* Paris: Presses Universitaires de France.

LIKIERMAN, A. (1988). *Public Expenditure: Who Really Controls it and How?* London: Penguin Books.

LINDBLOM, C. E. (1977). *Politics and Markets.* New York: Basic Books.

LINDSAY, T. F., and HARRINGTON, M. (1979). *The Conservative Party, 1918–1979.* London: Macmillan.

LITTLETON, A. C. (1966). *Accounting Evolution to 1900.* New York: Russell & Russell.

LOCKE, R. (1996). *The Collapse of the American Management Mystique.* Oxford: Oxford University Press.

LORWIN, V. R. (1954). *The French Labor Movement.* Cambridge, MA: Harvard University Press.

Love, A. J. (ed.) (1991). *Evaluation Methods Sourcebook*. Toronto: Canadian Evaluation Society.

McDonald, O. (1992). *The Future of Whitehall*. London: Weidenfeld & Nicolson.

MacInnes, J. (1987). *Thatcherism at Work: Industrial Relations and Economic Change*. Buckingham: Open University Press.

McKenna, C. D. (1995). 'The Origins of Modern Management Consulting', *Business and Economic History*, 24/1: 51–8.

—— (1996). 'Agents of Adhocracy: Management Consultants and the Reorganization of the Executive Branch, 1947–1949', *Business and Economic History*, 25/1: 101–11.

Mackenzie, G. C. (1987). *The In and Outers: Presidential Appointees and Transient Government in Washington*. Baltimore: Johns Hopkins Press.

McKibbin, R. (1974). *The Evolution of the Labour Party*. Oxford: Oxford University Press.

Mackintosh, W. A. (1964). *The Economic Background of Dominion-Provincial Relations*. Appendix III of the Royal Commission Report on Dominion-Provincial Relations. Toronto: McClelland and Stewart.

McLeod, T. H. (1963). 'The Glassco Commission Report', *Canadian Public Administration*, 6: 386–406.

McQueen, C. (1992). 'Program Evaluation in the Canadian Federal Government', in J. Hudson, J. Mayne, and R. Thomlinson (eds.), *Action-Oriented Evaluation in Organizations: Canadian Practices*. Toronto: Wall & Emerson, 28–47.

McRoberts, K. (1988). *Quebec: Social Change and Political Crisis* (3rd edn.). Toronto: McClelland & Stewart.

Mallory, J. R. (1979). 'Parliament: Every Reform Creates a New Problem', *Journal of Canadian Studies*, 14/2: 26–34.

Mansbridge, S. H. (1979). 'The Lambert Report: Recommendations to Departments', *Canadian Public Administration*, 22/4: 530–41.

March, J. G., and Olsen, J. P. (1984). 'The New Institutionalism: Organizational Factors in Political Life', *American Political Science Review*, 78/3: 734–49.

—— —— (1989). *Rediscovering Institutions*. New York: Free Press.

Margolis, H. (1973). *Technical Advices on Policy Issues*. Newbury Park: Sage.

Marin, B., and Mayntz, R. (eds.) (1991). *Policy Networks: Empirical Evidence and Theoretical Considerations*. Boulder: Westview Press.

Marshall, G. (1989). *Ministerial Responsibility*. Oxford: Oxford University Press.

Martin, J. F. (1998). *Reorienting a Nation: Consultants and Australian Public Policy*. Aldershot: Ashgate.

Mascarenhas, R. C. (1993). 'Building an Enterprise Culture in the Public Sector: Reform of the Public Sector in Australia, Britain, and New Zealand', *Public Administration Review*, 53/4: 319–27.

Massey, A. (1993). *Managing the Public Sector. A Comparative Analysis of the United Kingdom and the United States*. Aldershot: Edward Elgar.

Massot, J. (1979). *Le chef du gouvernement en France*. Paris: La documentation française.

Matthews, R. S., and Maxwell, R. J. (1974). 'Working in Partnership with Management Consultants', *Management Services in Government*, 29/1: 27–39.

Mayne, J., and Hudson, J. (1992). 'Program Evaluation: An Overview', in J. Hudson, J. Mayne, and R. Thomlinson (eds.), *Action Oriented Evaluation in Organizations: Canadian Practices*. Toronto: Wall & Emerson, 1–21.

MAYSTON, D. (1985). 'Non-Profit Performance Indicators in the Public Sector', *Financial Account & Management*, 1/1.

MAZEY, S. (1990). 'Power Outside Paris', in P. Hall, J. Hayward, and H. Machin (eds.), *Developments in French Politics*. London: Macmillan, 152–70.

MCA: Management Consultancies Association (1987). *President's Statement and Annual Report*. London.

—— (1989). *President's Statement and Annual Report*. London.

—— (1994). *President's Statement and Annual Report*. London.

—— (1995). *President's Statement and Annual Report*. London.

—— (1996). *President's Statement and Annual Report*. London.

—— (1998). *President's Statement and Annual Report*. London.

MELLETT, E. B. (1988). *From Stopwatch to Strategy: A History of the First Twenty-Five Years of the Canadian Association of Management Consultants*. Toronto: CAMC.

MÉNY, Y. (1987). 'A la jonction du politique et de l'administratif: les hauts fonctionnaires', *Pouvoir*, 40: 5–24.

MEREDITH, H., and MARTIN, J. (1970). 'Management Consultants in the Public Sector', *Canadian Public Administration*, 13/4: 383–95.

METCALFE, L. (1993). 'Convinction Politics and Dynamic Conservatism: Mrs. Thatcher's Managerial Revolution', *International Political Science Review*, 14 /4: 351–72.

—— RICHARDS, S. (1987). *Improving Public Management*. London: Sage.

—— —— (1990). *Improving Public Management* (2nd edn.). London: Sage.

MFPMA: Ministère de la Fonction publique et de la modernisation de l'Administration (1991a). *La Fonction Publique de l'Etat 1991*. Paris: La documentation française.

—— (1991b). *Renouveau du Service public. Séminaire gouvernemental*. 11 April.

—— (1992). *Le dialogue social, enjeu de la modernisation de l'Administration*. Les Cahiers du renouveau. Journée d'étude interrégionale, Beaune, 14 January.

MFPRA: Ministère de la Fonction publique et de la réforme administrative (1990). *Sélection des textes officiels. Renouveau du service public. Les rencontre 1990*. Paris: Imprimerie des journaux officiels.

—— (1992). *La charte des services publics*. Paris: La documentation française.

—— (1993). *Les Actes du Forum Innovations du service public*. Paris: La documentation française.

MICKLETHWAIT, J., and WOOLDRIDGE, A. (1996). *The Witch Doctors: Making Sense of the Management Gurus*. New York: Random House.

MIDDLEMAS, K. (1990). *Power, Competition and the State*, Vol. 2: *Threats to the Postwar Settlement in Britain, 1961–74*. London: Macmillan.

MILLWARD, D. (1990). 'Alarm at Rising Whitehall Cost of Consultants', *Daily Telegraph*, 26 February: 4.

MILWARD, H. B. (1994). 'Nonprofit Contracting and the Hollow State', *Public Administration Review*, 54/1: 73–7.

MINTZBERG, H. (1973). *The Nature of Managerial Work*. New York: Harper & Row.

MOLITERNO, S. F. (1992). *The Accounting Profession in France* (2nd edn.). New York: American Institute of Certified Public Accountants.

Moody's Investors Service and United Nations Centre on Transnational Corporations (1990). *Directory of the World's Largest Service Companies*. Series I, December. New York: UN.

MOORE, G. L. (1984). *The Politics of Management Consulting*. New York: Praeger.

MORGAN, K. (1984). *Labour in Power*. Oxford: Oxford University Press.

MORGAN, K. O. (1997). *Callaghan: A Life*. Oxford: Oxford University Press.

MOST, K. S. (1984). 'Accounting in France', in H. P. Holzer (ed.), *International Accounting*. New York: Harper & Row, 292–314.

NAO: National Audit Office (1989). *Selection and Use of Management Consultants*. London: HMSO.

—— (1991). *Performance Measurement in the Civil Service*. House of Commons Paper No. 399, 3 May.

—— (1996). *State Audit in the European Union*. London.

NAUGHTON, M. (1988). 'The Chaos Consultants Cause', *Morning Star*, London, 20 September.

NETHERCOTE, J. R. (1989). 'The Rhetorical Tactics of Managerialism', *Australian Journal of Public Administration*, 48/4, December: 363–7.

NEWMAN, P. C. (1963). *Renegade in Power: The Diefenbaker Years*. Toronto: McClelland and Stewart.

Next Steps (1993). *Briefing Note*. 5 August.

NISKANEN, W. (1971). *Bureaucracy and Representative Government*. Chicago: Aldine and Atherton.

—— (1973). *Bureaucracy: Servant or Master?* London: Institute of Economic Affair.

NOBES, C. (1991). 'Financial Reporting in France and Spain', *Management Accounting*, 69/9: 26–7.

NORDLINGER, E. (1981). *On the Autonomy of the Democratic State*. Cambridge, MA: Harvard University Press.

NORMANTON, E. L. (1966). *The Accountability and Audit of Governments*. Manchester: Manchester University Press.

NORTON, P. (1978). *Conservative Dissidents: Dissent Within the Conservative Parliamentary Party 1970–1974*. London: Temple Smith.

—— (ed.) (1990). *Legislatures*. Oxford: Oxford University Press.

OCG: Office of the Comptroller General (1991). *Treasury Board Program Evaluation Policy*. Ottawa.

—— (1992). *Your Guide to Measuring Client Satisfaction*. Ottawa: Minister of Supply and Services.

OECD (1980). *Accounting Practices in OECD Member Countries*. Paris: OECD.

—— (1990a). *Public Management Developments. Survey 1990*. Paris: OECD.

—— (1990b). 'Financing Public Expenditures through User Charges', *Occasional Papers on Public Management*. Paris: OECD.

—— (1992). *Public Management: OECD Country Profiles*. Paris: OECD.

—— (1993). *Public Management Developments. Survey 1993*. Paris: OECD.

—— (1995a). *Best Practices for Small and Medium-Sized Enterprises*. Paris: OECD.

—— (1995b). *Governance in Transition*. Paris: OECD.

O&M Bulletin (1966). 'The Use of Management Consultants', 21/4: 173–84.

O'MALLEY, S. F. (1990). 'Price Waterhouse: 100 Years of Service in the United States', Address Delivered to the Newcomen Society of the USA, New York, 1 November.

ORGOGOZO, I. (1985). 'Des cercles de qualité dans l'Administration: pourquoi pas?', *Regards sur l'actualité*, 116/December: 23–32.

—— (1987). *Les paradoxes de la qualité*. Paris: Éditions d'organisation.

—— SÉRIEYX, H. (1989). *Changer le changement: on peu abolir les bureaucraties*. Paris: Éditions du Seuil.

ORLOFF, A. S. (1993). *The Politics of Pensions: A Comparative Analysis of Britain, Canada and the United States*. Madison: University of Wisconsin Press.

OSBALDESTON, G. (1989). *Keeping Deputy Ministers Accountable*. Toronto: McGraw-Hill Ryerson.

OSBORNE, D., and GAEBLER, T. (1992). *Reinventing Government: How the Entrepreneurial Spirit is Transforming the Public Sector*. New York: Plume.

OSBORNE, T. (1983). *A Grande École for the Grands Corps: The Recruitment and Training of the French Administrative Elite in the 19th Century*. New York: Columbia University Press.

OWEN, B. G. (1990). 'France', in J. E. Kingdom (ed.), *The Civil Service in Liberal Democracies*. London: Routledge, 64–89.

PAL, L. A. (1992). *Public Policy Analysis: An Introduction*. Scarborough: Nelson Canada.

—— (1994). 'From Society to State: Evolving Approaches to the Study of Politics', in J. P. Bickerton and A. G. Ggnon (eds.), *Canadian Politics 2*. Peterborough: Broadview Press.

PAQUIER, A., and TOWHILL, B. (1991). 'Municipal Accounts in France', *Public Finance and Accountancy*, January: 12–13.

PARRIS, H. (1969). *Constitutional Bureaucracy*. London: Allen & Unwin.

PATTENAUDE, R. L. (1979). 'Consultants in the Public Sector', *Public Administration Review*. Symposium on Consultants in the Public Sector, 3/May–June: 203–5.

PAXTON, R. (1972). *Vichy France: Old Guard and New Order*. New York: Columbia University Press.

PE Consulting (1985). *Fifty Years of Professional Enterprise: The Story of PE*. London.

Peat Marwick (1986). *Current Issues in Public Sector Management*. London.

PÊCHEUR, B. (1992). 'France: un processus continu relayé par un projet politique', *Revue française d'administration publique*, 61/Jan.–Mar.: 71–4.

PEET, J. (1988). 'The New Witch-Doctors: A Survey of Management Consultancy', *The Economist*, 13 February, 2–18.

PERRET, B. (1994). 'Le contexte français de l'évaluation: approache comparative', *Canadian Journal of Program Evaluation*, 9/2: 93–114.

PETERS, B. G. (1991). 'Morale in the Public Service: A Comparative Inquiry', *International Review of Administrative Sciences*, 57: 421–40.

—— (1997). 'North American Perspective on Administrative Modernization in Europe', in W. J. M. Kickert (ed.), *Public Management and Administrative Reform in Western Europe*. Cheltenham: Edward Elgar, 251–66.

—— and PIERRE, J. (1998). 'Governance without Government? Rethinking Public Administration', *Journal of Public Administration Research and Theory*, 8/2: 223–43.

—— and SAVOIE, D. J. (1998). *Taking Stock: Assessing Public Sector Reforms*. Montreal and Kingston: McGill-Queen's University Press.

PETERS, T., and WATERMAN, R. (1982). *In Search of Excellence: Lessons from America's Best-Run Companies*. New York: Harper & Row.

PFISTER, T. (1988). *La République des fonctionnaires*. Paris: Fayard.

PIERSON, P. (1994). *Dismantling the Welfare State?* Cambridge: Cambridge University Press.

PINET, M. (ed.) (1993). *Histoire de la Fonction publique en France*. Vol. III: *Les XIXe et Xxe siècles*. Paris: Nouvelle Librarie de France.

PLOWDEN, E. (1961). *Control of Public Expenditure HM Treasury*. Cmnd. 1432. London: HMSO. [The Plowden Report.]

PLOWDEN, F. (1995). 'The Appropriate Use of Management Consultants in Government'. Coopers & Lybrand, London. Paper prepared for the meeting of the Public Service seminar at the London School of Economics, November 3.

PLOWDEN, W. (1991). 'Providing Countervailing Analysis and Advice in a Career-Dominated Bureaucratic System: The British Experience, 1916–1988', in C. Campbell and M. J. Wyszomirski (eds.), *Executive Leadership in Anglo-American Systems*. Pittsburgh: University of Pittsburgh Press, 219–48.

PLUMPTRE, T. W. (1988). *Beyond the Bottom Line: Management in Government*. Montreal: The Institute for Research on Public Policy.

POCHARD, M. (1995). 'Current and Future Developments in Service Quality Initiatives: The Situation in France', in OECD (ed.), *Responsive Government Service Quality Initiatives*. Paris: OECD, 49–57.

Political Quarterly (1993). 'Commentary: Auditing the Accountants', 269–71.

POLLITT, C. (1974). 'The Central Policy Review Staff 1970–1974', *Public Administration*, 52/4: 375–92.

—— (1984). *Manipulating the Machine Changing the Patterns of Ministerial Departments, 1960–83*. London: George Allen & Unwin.

—— (1986a). 'Beyond the Managerial Model: The Case for Broadening Performance Assessment in Government and Public Services', *Financial Accountability & Management*, 2/3, Autumn: 155–70.

—— (1986b). 'Performance Measurement in the Public Services: Some Political Implications', *Parliamentary Affairs*, 39/3: 315–29.

—— (1988). 'Bringing Consumers Into Performance Measurement: Concepts, Consequences and Constraints', *Policy and Politics*, 16/2: 77–87.

—— (1990). *Managerialism in the Public Services: The Anglo-American Experience*. Oxford: Basil Blackwell.

—— (1993). 'Occasional Excursions: A Brief History of Policy Evaluation in the UK', *Parliamentary Affairs*, 46/3: 353–62.

—— (1995a). 'Justification by Works or By Faith? Evaluating the New Public Management', *Evaluation*, 1/20: 133–54.

—— (1995b). 'Management Techniques for the Public Sector: Pulpit and Practice', in B. G. Peters and D. J. Savoie (eds.), *Governance in a Changing Environment*. Montreal and Kingston: McGill-Queen's University Press, 203–38.

—— (1996). 'Antistatist Reforms and New Administrative Directions: Public Administration in the U.K.', *Public Administration Review*, 56/1: 81–7.

POLLITT, C., and SUMMA, H. (1997a). 'Reflexive Watchdog? How Supreme Audit Institutions Account for Themselves', *Public Administration*, 75: 313–36.

—— —— (1997b). 'Trajectories of Reform: Management Change in Four Countries', *Public Money & Management*, 17/1: 7–18.

PONTING, C. (1989). *Breach of Promise: Labour in Power 1964–1970*. London: Hamish Hamilton.

POSTIF, T. (1997). 'Public Sector Reform in France', in J.-E. Lane (ed.), *Public Sector Reform*. London: Sage, 209–24.

PREMFORS, R. (1998). 'Reshaping the Democratic State: Swedish Experiences in a Comparative Perspective', *Public Administration*, 76/Spring: 141–59.

Program Evaluation Branch (1981). *Guide on the Program Evaluation Function*. Ottawa.

Progressive Conservative Party of Canada (1984). *Towards Productive Management— The PC Approach*. Background Note No. 2. Ottawa.

PROSS, P. A. (1992). *Group Politics and Public Policy* (2nd edn). Toronto: Oxford University Press.

PUXTY, A. (1990). 'The Accountancy Profession in the Class Structure', in D. J. Cooper and T. M. Hopper (eds.), *Critical Accounts*. London: Macmillan, 332–65.

QUERMONNE, J.-L. (1991). *L'appareil administratif de l'Etat*. Paris: Seuil.

—— ROUBAN, L. (1986). 'French Public Administration and Policy Evaluation: The Quest for Accountability', *Public Administration Review*, September–October: 397–405.

RADCLIFFE, J. (1991). *The Reorganisation of British Central Government*. Aldershot: Dartmouth.

RAGIN, C. C. (1987). *The Comparative Method*. Berkeley: University of California Press.

RAMSDEN, J. (1980). *The Making of Conservative Party Policy: The Conservative Research Department Since 1929*. London.

RASSAM, C. (1998). 'The Management Consulting Industry', in P. Sadler (ed.), *Management Consultancy: A Handbook for Best Practice*. London: Kogan Page.

—— OATES, D. (1991). *Management Consultancy: The Inside Story*. London: Mercury.

RAYNER, D. (1973). 'Making Room for Managers in Whitehall', *Management Services in Government*, 28/2, May: 61–6.

RAYNER, M. H. (1986). 'Using Evaluation in the Federal Government', *Canadian Journal of Program Evaluation*, 1/1, April: 1–10.

Revue française de comptabilité (1989). 'La profession comptable en France et en Europe', 202/June: 34–6.

RHODES, R. A. W. (1994). 'The Hollowing Out of the State: The Changing Nature of the Public Service in Britain', *The Political Quarterly*, 65/2: 138–51.

RICHARD, P. (1988). 'Les finances locales de 1983 à 1987', *Revue française de finances publiques*, 22.

RIDLEY, F., and BLONDEL, J. (1969). *Public Administration in France*. London: Routledge & Kegan Paul.

RIDYARD, D., and DE BOLLE, J. (1992). *Competition in European Accounting: A Study of the EC Audit and Consulting Sectors*. Dublin: Lafferty Publications.

RIPA: Royal Institute of Public Administration (1987). *Top Jobs in Whitehall: Appointments and Promotions in the Senior Civil Service*. London.

ROBERTS, A. (1996a). *So-Called Experts: How American Consultants Remade the Canadian Civil Service 1918–1921*. Toronto: Institute of Public Administration of Canada.

—— (1996b). 'Worrying about Misconduct: The Control Lobby and the PS 2000 Reforms', *Canadian Public Administration*, 39/4, Winter: 489–523.

ROBERTS, S., and POLLITT, C. (1994). 'Audit or Evaluation? A National Audit Office VFM Study', *Public Administration*, 72: 527–49.

ROBERTSON, G. (1992). *Globalization: Social Theory and Global Culture*. London: Sage.

ROBERTSON, J. H. (1971). *Reform of the British Central Government*. London: Chatto & Windus.

ROBINSON, R. B. (1984). 'Building Professionalism in Canada', *Journal of Management Consulting*, 1/4: 15–18.

ROGERS, H. (1978). 'Management Control in the Public Service', *Optimum*, 9/3: 17–25.

—— (1979). 'Program Evaluation and its Role in Management of the Federal Public Service'. Notes for an Address to the Management Consulting Institute Workshop on Program Evaluation, 10 April.

—— (1980). 'The Impact of IMPAC', *Optimum*, 11/1: 40–51.

ROSANVALLON, P. (1990). *L'Etat en France de 1789 à nos jours*. Paris: Seuil.

ROSELL, S. A. (1992). *Governing in an Information Society*. Montreal: Institute for Research on Public Policy.

ROSS, G. (1982). *Workers and Communists in France*. Berkeley: University of California Press.

ROUBAN, L. (1989). 'The Civil Service and the Policy of Administrative Modernization in France', *International Review of Administrative Sciences*, 55: 445–65.

—— (1993a). 'L'évaluation, nouvel avatar de la rationalisation administrative?', *Revue française d'Administration publique*, 66/April–June: 197–208.

—— (1993b). 'France in Search of a New Administrative Order', *International Political Science Review*, 14/4: 403–18.

—— (1996). *La fonction publique*. Paris: La Découverte.

—— (1997). 'The Administrative Modernisation Policy in France', in W. J. Kickert (ed.), *Public Management and Administration Reform in Western Europe*. Cheltenham: Edward Elgard, 141–56.

RUESCHEMEYER, D., and SKOCPOL, T. (1996). *States, Social Knowledge, and the Origins of Modern Social Policies*. Princeton: Princeton University Press.

RUSSELL, A. W. (1984). 'The Financial Management Unit of the Cabinet Office (MPO) and the Treasury', *Management in Government*, 2: 146–52.

SAINT-MARTIN, D., and SUTHERLAND, S. L. (1995). 'Conflits d'intérêts dans la bureaucratie fédérale: Qui surveille le surveillant?', *Le Devoir*, 27 June: A7.

SALVALL, H. (1988). 'Les enjeux de l'Opération "Développement du professionalisme des consultants"', in ISÉOR (ed.), *Qualité intégrale dans les entreprises et professionalisme des consultants*. Paris: Economica, 267–70.

—— (1992). 'Développement du professionalisme des consultants', in ISÉOR (ed.), *Qualité du conseil et mutation du secteur public*. Paris: Economica, v–x.

SAUVIAT, H. C. (1991). *Conditions d'émergence et caractéristiques du développement d'un marché de l'expertise et du conseil en France*. Paris: IRES, Working Document No. 9101.

SAVOIE, D. J. (1990). *The Politics of Public Spending in Canada*. Toronto: Toronto University Press.

—— (1992). 'Public Service Reforms: Looking to History and Other Countries', *Optimum*, 23/2: 6–11.

—— (1993). *Globalization and Governance*. Ottawa: Canadian Centre for Management Development.

—— (1994). *Thatcher, Reagan, Mulroney: In Search of a New Bureaucracy*. Toronto: Toronto University Press.

SCHEID, J. C., and WALTON, P. (1988). 'Decade of Change for French Accounting', *The Accountant's Magazine*, January: 24–6.

SCHIESL, M. J. (1977). *The Politics of Efficiency: Municipal Administration and Reform in America: 1880–1920*. Berkeley: University of California Press.

SCHMIDT, V. A. (1987). 'Decentralization: A Revolutionary Reform?', in P. McCarthy (ed.), *The French Socialists in Power 1981–1986*. Westport: Greenwood.

—— (1991). *Democratizing France: The Political and Administrative History of Decentralization*. Cambridge: Cambridge University Press.

—— (1996). *From State to Market? The Transformation of French Business and Government*. Cambridge: Cambridge University Press.

SCHMITTER, P. C., and STREEK, W. (1981). *The Organization of Business Interests*. Discussion Paper IIM/LMP 81-13. Berlin.

SCOTT, W. G. (1992). *Chester I. Barnard and the Guardians of the Managerial State*. Lawrence: University Press of Kansas.

SEGSWORTH, R. V. (1990). 'Policy and Program Evaluation in the Government of Canada', in R. C. Rist (ed.), *Program Evaluation and the Management of Government*. New Brunswick: Transaction Publishers, 21–36.

SEIDLE, F. L. (1995). *Rethinking the Delivery of Public Services to Citizens*. Montreal: Institute for Research on Public Policy.

SELDON, A. (1994). 'Conservative Century', in A. Seldon and S. Ball (eds.), *Conservative Century: The Conservative Party Since 1900*. Oxford: Oxford University Press, 17–68.

—— (1996). 'The Heath Government in History', in S. Ball and A. Seldon (eds.), *The Heath Government*. London: Longman, 1–20.

SÉRIEYX, H. (1993). *Le Big Bang des organisation*. Paris: Calmann-Lévy.

SERVAN-SCHREIBER, J. J. (1968). *The American Challenge*. New York: Atheneum.

Services publics (1995). Numéro spécial: Cinquante ans d'histoire de la Fonction publique. Le mensuel de l'Administration et de la Fonction publique.

SHARP, D. E. (1967). 'The British Civil Service: Changes Under Discussion', *Canadian Public Administration*, 10: 282–97.

SHAYS, E. M. (1985). 'Growing International Consulting Body', *Journal of Management Consulting*, 2/3: 52–3.

SHONFIELD, A. (1965). *Modern Capitalism: The Changing Balance of Public and Private Power*. Oxford: Oxford University Press.

SILBERMAN, B. S. (1993). *Cages of Reason: The Rise of the Rational State in France, Japan, the United States and Great Britain*. Chicago: University of Chicago Press.

SIMPSON, J. (1988). *Spoils of Power: The Politics of Patronage*. Toronto: Collins.

SINCLAIR, A. (1989). 'Public Sector Culture: Managerialism or Multiculturalism?', *Australian Journal of Public Administration*, 4: 382–97.

SINCLAIR, S. (1979). *Cordial but not Cosy: A History of the Auditor General*. Toronto: McClelland and Stewart.

SKOCPOL, T. (1979). *States and Social Revolutions: A Comparative Analysis of France, Russia, and China*. Cambridge: Cambridge University Press.

—— (1992). *Protecting Soldiers and Mothers. The Political Origins of Social Policy in the United States*. Cambridge: The Belknap Press of Harvard University Press.

—— SOMERS, M. (1994). 'The Uses of Comparative History in Macrosocial Inquiry', in T. Skocpol, *Social Revolutions in the Modern World*. Cambridge: Cambridge University Press, 72–95.

SKOWRONEK, S. (1982). *Building a New American State*. Cambridge: Cambridge University Press.

SMITH, D. E. (1981). *The Regional Decline of a National Party: Liberals on the Prairies*. Toronto: University of Toronto Press.

SMITH, J. A. (1991). *The Idea Brokers: Think Tanks and the Rise of the New Policy Elite*. New York: The Free Press.

SMITH, T. (1972). *Anti-Politics: Consensus, Reform and Protest in Britain*. London: Charles Knight.

—— (1994). 'Post-Modern Politics and the Case for Constitutional Renewal', *Political Quarterly*, 65/2: 128–38.

—— YOUNG, A. (1996). *The Fixers: Crisis Management in British Politics*. Aldershot: Dartmouth.

STACEY, N. A. A. H. (1954). *English Accountancy: A Study in Social and Economic History, 1800–1954*. London: Gee.

STANDISH, P. (1990). 'Financial Reporting in France', in C. Nobes and R. Parker (eds.), *Comparative International Accounting*. New York: Prentice Hall.

STEINMO, S. (1993). *Taxation and Democracy: Swedish, British and American Approaches to Financing the Welfare State*. New Haven: Yale University Press.

STERN, P., and TUTOY, P. (1995). *Le métier de consultant*. Paris: Les Éditions d'Organisation.

STEVENS, A. (1978). 'Politicization and Cohesion in the French Administration', *West European Politics*, 1: 68–80.

—— (1992). *The Government and Politics of France*. London: Macmillan.

STEVENS, M. (1991). *The Big Six: The Selling Out of America's Top Accounting Firms*. New York: Simon & Schuster.

STEWART, G. T. (1986). *The Origins of Canadian Politics*. Vancouver: University of British Columbia Press.

STONE, B. (1995). 'Administrative Accountability in Westminster Democracies: Towards a New Conceptual Framework', *Governance*, 8/4: 505–26.

STUDER, S., and WALTERS, B. (1994). 'The Structure of the Management Consultancy Market', in Institute of Management Consultants, *The Ivanhoe Career Guide to Management Consultants 1995*. London: Cambridge Market Intelligence Ltd.: 11–15.

SULEIMAN, E. N. (1974). *Politics, Power and Bureaucracy in France: The Administrative Elite*. Princeton: Princeton University Press.

—— (1978). *Elites in French Society*. Princeton: Princeton University Press.

—— (1987). *Private Power and Centralization in France: The Notaires and the State*. Princeton: Princeton University Press.

—— (1990). 'The Politics of Privatization in Britain and France', in E. N. Suleiman and J. Waterbury (eds.), *The Political Economy of Public Sector Reform and Privatization*. Boulder: Westview Press, 113–36.

—— (1995). 'Change and Stability in French Elites', in G. Flynn (ed.), *Remaking the Hexagon: The New France in the New Europe*. Boulder: Westview Press, 161–80.

—— WATERBURY, J. (1990). 'Introduction: Analyzing Privatization in Industrial and Developing Countries', in E. N. Suleiman and J. Waterbury (eds.), *The Political Economy of Public Sector Reform and Privatization*. Boulder: Westview Press, 1–21.

SUTHERLAND, S. L. (1980). 'On the Audit Trail of the Auditor General: Parliament's Servant, 1973–1980', *Canadian Public Administration*, 23/4: 617–44.

—— (1981). 'The Office of the Auditor General: Watching and Watchdog', in G. B. Doern (ed.), *How Ottawa Spends your Tax Dollars*. Toronto: James Lorimer & Co., 184–231.

—— (1991). 'Responsible Government and Ministerial Responsibility: Every Reform is its Own Problem', *Canadian Journal of Political Science*, 24/1: 91–120.

—— (1993). 'Independent Review and Political Accountability: Should Democracy be on Autopilot?', *Optimum*, 24/2: 23–40.

—— DOERN, G. B. (1985). *Bureaucracy in Canada: Control and Reform*, Vol. 43: *Royal Commission on the Economic Union and Development Prospects for Canada*. Toronto: University of Toronto Press.

SWANN, D. (1998). *The Retreat of the State: Deregulation and Privatization in the UK and the US*. New York and London: Harvester Wheatsheaf.

SWIMMER, G. (1992). 'Staff Relations Under the Conservative Government', in F. Abele (ed.), *How Ottawa Spends 1992–93: The Politics of Competitiveness*. Ottawa: Carleton University Press.

—— HICKS, M., and MILNE, T. (1994). 'Public Service 2000: Dead or Alive?', in S. D. Philips (ed.), *How Ottawa Spends 1994–95: Making Change*. Ottawa: Carleton University Press, 165–204.

Syntec Management (1994). *Syntec Management Official Directory, 1994–95*. Paris: Chambre Syndicale des Sociétés de Conseils.

—— (1996). *Revue de presse de Syntec Management*. Paris.

TARROW, S. (1989). 'Struggle, Politics and Reform'. Cornell University, Western Societies Paper No. 21.

TAYLOR, J. A., and WILLIAMS, H. (1991). 'Public Administration and the Information Polity', *Public Administration*, 69/Summer: 171–90.

TAYLOR, J. R., and VAN EVERY, E. J. (1993). *The Vulnerable Fortress: Bureaucratic Organization and Management in an Information Age*. Toronto: University of Toronto Press.

TAYLOR, R. (1996). 'Heath Government and Industrial Relations', in S. Ball and A. Seldon (eds.), *The Heath Government*. London: Longman, 161–90.

TAYLOR, S. R. (1983). 'Using Management Consultants in Government', *Management in Government*, 38/3: 158–67.

TAYLOR-GOOBY, P., and LAWSON, R. (eds.) (1993). *Markets and Managers. New Issues in the Delivery of Welfare*. Buckingham: Open University Press.

TELLIER, P. M. (1990). 'Public Service 2000: The Renewal of the Public Service', *Canadian Public Administration*, 33/2: 123–32.

TBS: Treasury Board Secretariat (1996). *Service Standards in Departments and Agencies*. Ottawa.

THEAKSTON, K. (1992). *The Labour Party and Whitehall*. London: Routledge.

—— (1996). 'The Heath Government, Whitehall and the Civil Service', in S. Ball and A. Seldon (eds.), *The Heath Government*. London: Longman, 75–106.

—— FRY, G. (1994). 'The Party and the Civil Service', in A. Seldon and S. Ball (eds.), *Conservative Century: The Conservative Party Since 1900*. Oxford: Oxford University Press, 383–402.

THELEN, K., STEINMO, S. (1992). 'Historical Institutionalism in Comparative Politics', in S. Steinmo, K. Thelen, and F. Longstreth (eds.), *Structuring Politics: Historical Institutionalism in Comparative Perspective*. Cambridge: Cambridge University Press, 1–32.

THOENIG, J. C. (1988). 'La modernisation de la fonction publique dans les Etats membres de la Communauté européenne', *Revue politiques et management public*, 6/2: 69–80.

THORNBURN, H. G. (1991). *Party Politics in Canada* (6th edn.). Scarborough: Prentice-Hall.

TILLY, C. (1984). *Big Structures, Large Processes, Huge Comparisons.* New York: Russell Sage Foundation.

Times Higher Education Supplement (1986). 28 March: 3.

TIRATSOO, N., and TOMLINSON, J. (1993). *Industrial Efficiency and State Intervention: Labour 1939–51.* London: Routledge.

—— —— (1998). *The Conservatives and Industrial Efficiency, 1951–64: Thirteen Wasted Years?* London: Routledge.

TISDALL, P. (1982). *Agents of Change: The Development and Practice of Management Consultancy.* London: Heinemann.

TONNERRE, L. (1991). 'Les centres de responsabilité', *Revue française d'administration publique*, 57/Jan.–Mar.: 143–52.

TOOZE, R. (1992). 'Conceptualizing the Global Economy', in A. G. McGrew and P. G. Lewis *et al.* (eds.), *Global Politics: Globalization and the Nation-State.* Cambridge: Polity Press, 233–49.

TORSTENDAHL, R., and BURRAGE, M. (1990). *The Formation of Professions: Knowledge, State and Strategy.* London: Sage Publications.

TOWNSEND, R. (1971). *Up the Organization.* Greenwich: Fawcett Publications, Inc.

TREACY, M., and WIERSEMA, F. D. (1993). *The Discipline of Market Leaders.* Reading, Mass.: Addison-Wesley.

Treasury Board [Canada] (1974). *Operational Performance Measurement.* January.

Treasury Board of Canada (1992). *A Manager's Guide to Operating Budgets.* Ottawa: Supply and Services.

Treasury Board Secretariat (1994). *Contracting for services: an overview.* Ottawa, 11 April.

TROSA, S. (1995a). *Moderniser l'Administration: Comment font les autres?* Paris: Les éditions d'organisation.

—— (1995b). 'Quality Strategies in Three Countries: France, the U.K., and Australia', in OECD (ed.), *Responsive Government: Service Quality Initiatives.* Paris: OECD, 265–95.

TUNNOCH, G. V. (1964). 'The Glassco Commission Report: Did It Cost More Than It Was Worth?', *Canadian Public Administration*, 7: 389–97.

ULLMO, Y. (1974). *La planification française.* Paris: Dunod.

United Nations (1993). *Management Consulting: A Survey of the Industry and its Largest Firms.* United Nations Conference on Trade and Development, Programme on Transnational Corporations. New York.

VAN GUSTEREN, G. (1976). *The Quest for Control: A Critique of the Rational-Central Rule Approach in Public Affairs.* London: John Wiley & Sons.

VON BEYME, K. (1983). 'Governments, Parliaments and the Structure of Power in Political parties', in H. Daalder and P. Mair (eds.), *Western European Party Systems: Continuity and Changes.* London: Sage, 341–67.

WALSH, K. (1995). *Public Services and Market Mechanisms: Competition, Contracting and the New Public Management.* Basingstoke: Macmillan.

WEIR, M. (1989). 'Ideas and Politics: The Acceptance of Keynesianism in Britain and the United States', in P. A. Hall (ed.), *The Political Power of Economic Ideas: Keynesianism Across Nations*. Princeton: Princeton University Press, 53–86.

—— (1992). *Politics and Jobs*. Princeton: Princeton University Press.

—— SKOCPOL, T. (1985). 'State Structures and the Possibilities for "Keynesian" Responses to the Great Depression in Sweden, Britain, and the United States', in P. Evans, D. Rueschemeyer, and T. Skocpol (eds.), *Bringing the State Back In*. Cambridge: Cambridge University Press.

WELCHMAN, T. (1983). 'French Rules Inhibit Growth of Large, U.K.-Style Firms', *Accountancy*, 94/1081: 64–5.

WHITAKER, R. (1977). *The Government Party*. Toronto: University of Toronto Press.

WHITE, W. L., and STRICK, J. C. (1970). *Policy, Politics and the Treasury Board in Canadian Government*. Don Mills: Science Research Associates Limited.

WILDAVSKY, A. (1975). *Budgeting: A Comparative Theory of Budgetary Processes*. Boston: Little Brown.

—— (1979). *Speaking Truth to Power: The Art and Craft of Policy Analysis*. Boston: Little Brown.

—— (1984). *The Politics of the Budgetary Process*. Toronto: Little Brown.

WILDING, R. W. L. (1976). 'The Use of Management Consultants in Government Departments', *Management Services in Government*, 31/2: 60–70.

WILKINSON, J. W. (1986). 'What is Management Consulting?', in S. W. Barcus and J. W. Wilkinson (eds.), *Handbook of Management Consulting Services*. New York: McGraw-Hill, 3–16.

WILKS, S., and WRIGHT, M. (1987). *Comparative Government-Industry Relations*. Oxford: Oxford University Press.

WILLETTS, D. (1987). 'The Role of the Prime Minister's Policy Unit', *Public Administration*, 65/4: 443–54.

WILLMOTT, H. (1986). 'Organizing the Profession: A Theoretical and Historical Examination of the Development of the Major Accountancy Bodies in the U.K.', *Accounting, Organizations and Society*, 11/6: 555–80.

WILSON, D., and WRIGHT, D. (1993). *Next Steps: Inside Perspectives on Civil Service Reform in the United Kingdom*. Ottawa: Consulting and Audit Canada.

Wilson Report. See Canada (1975).

WOOLDRIDGE, A. (1997). 'Trimming the Fat: A Survey of Management Consultancy', *The Economist*, 22 March: 1–22.

WOOTTON, C. W., and WOLK, C. M. (1992). 'The Development of the "Big Eight" Accounting Firms in the United States, 1900 to 1990', *The Accounting Historians Journal*, 19/1: 1–28.

WRIGHT, V. (1990). 'The Administrative Machine: Old Problems and New Dilemmas', in P. Hall, J. Hayward, and H. Machin (eds.), *Developments in French Politics*. London: Macmillan, 114–32.

—— (1994). 'Reshaping the State: The Implications for Public Administration', in W. G. Muller and V. Wright (eds.), *The State in Western Europe: Retreat or Redefinition?* London: Frank Cass. 102–32.

WYMAN, H. E. (1989). 'The Auditing Profession in Europe', *Accountancy*, February: 82–7.

YATES, D. (1982). *Bureaucratic Democracy: The Search for Democracy and Efficiency in American Government*. Cambridge, MA: Harvard University Press.

YEOMANS, D. R. (1975). 'The Canadian Federal PPB System and its Development', *RIA Cost and Management, 49/5*: 23–9.

YOUNG, H., and SLOMAN, A. S. (1982). *No, Minister: An Inquiry into the Civil Service*. London: British Broadcasting Corporation.

ZAHARIADIS, N. (1995). *Markets, States and Public Policy: Privatization in Britain and France*. Ann Arbor: University of Michigan Press.

ZIEGLER, N. (1995). 'Institutions, Elites and Technological Change in France and Germany', *World Politics*, 47/April: 341–72.

—— (1997). *Governing Ideas: Strategies for Innovation in France and Germany*. Ithaca: Cornell University Press.

ZIFCAK, S. (1994). *New Managerialism: Administrative Reform in Whitehall and Canberra*. Buckingham: Open University Press.

Index